I0605498

PRAISE FOR *HOW TO WORSHIP FOR ALL ITS WORTH*

Steven Félix-Jäger offers principles for how to worship with examples from several worship traditions as well as case studies for evaluating worship within those traditions. Not every church worships the same way, and that's okay! Readers will find this book thought provoking, theologically informed, and yet immensely practical. It will set the standard for textbooks on worship and should be required reading for every pastor and worship leader.

—**Dr. Melissa Archer,** Professor of New Testament, Trinity Bible College and Graduate School; author, *"I Was in the Spirit on the Lord's Day": A Pentecostal Engagement with Worship in the Apocalypse*

Steven Félix-Jäger has managed to combine an impressive range of perspectives with his own analysis of different traditions and their practices. His application of biblical, aesthetic, theological, and pastoral lenses to interpret and evaluate worshiping life is fresh and illuminating. Students, pastors, and worship leaders will want to spend time digesting the rich insights contained in this book and return to them again and again. It is highly recommended!

—**Professor Mark J. Cartledge,** Principal, London School of Theology

Steven Félix-Jäger not only provides rich biblical and theological foundations for understanding worship but also equips readers to evaluate worship music, using solid questions and criteria modeled in case studies. I found it incredibly helpful and practical for understanding and leading worship music for all its worth.

—**Jacqueline N. Grey,** Alphacrucis University College, Australia

How to Worship for All Its Worth provides an invaluable new framework for analyzing and celebrating the diverse array of contemporary worship experiences. Steven Félix-Jäger honors the unique sense of calling and community of every congregation and encourages worship leaders to be biblically faithful, aesthetically excellent, and spiritually authentic.

—Douglas Jacobsen, Distinguished Professor of Christian History and Theology Emeritus, Messiah University

There's still widespread confusion about how worship connects to mission and spiritual formation. *How to Worship for All Its Worth* brings clarity. With tools that illuminate why and how communities of faith practice worship and with examples that are informed by real-life practitioners, Steven Félix-Jäger explores how worship practices influence the experience of faith communities and offers lenses through which leaders and worshipers alike can evaluate their liturgical lives and understand the choices and priorities of others. This book is essential reading for anyone seeking to make sense of the complex landscape of Christian worship across the broad Christian landscape of our contemporary world.

—Billy Kangas

Steven Félix-Jäger offers a compelling framework for evaluating congregational worship that is both theologically rigorous and pastorally attuned. With clarity and nuance, he invites leaders to assess worship practices through the lenses of biblical fidelity, aesthetic fit, theological coherence, and pastoral discernment, while honoring the diverse narratives that shape global Christian worship. This is a timely and essential resource for anyone serious about worship formation in context.

—Layla Nahavandi, Founder and Director, The Burning Hearts Movement

Steven Félix-Jäger marshals an impressive and diverse set of academic resources and experiential know-how into a comprehensive tool for strengthening worship-leader education and practice. While no book can magically solve congregational conflicts over worship, the book models a liturgical hospitality rooted in the hope that the church's worship life will flourish across lines of difference.

—**Dr. Adam A. Perez,** Assistant Professor of Worship Studies, Belmont University

Accessible yet robust, diverse and deep, this book is a much needed resource for all worshipers. Steven Félix-Jäger invites pastors, professors, students, and worship leaders to move beyond surface-level responses to worship by discerningly engaging the multifaceted liturgical practices and theological traditions of the global body of Christ.

—**Jeremy Perigo,** Professor of Theology and Worship Arts, Dordt University

Steven Félix-Jäger's book is well conceived and a winning combination. Some worship primers speak only in generalities, while others focus on the nuts and bolts of a worship service. In *How to Worship for All Its Worth*, Félix-Jäger lays out both broad criteria for assessing worship and then juxtaposes them with a range of congregational examples so we can see how worship assessment can and should take place. The result is very useful.

—**Lester Ruth,** Research Professor of Christian Worship, Duke Divinity School

Both shrewd and charitable, Steven Félix-Jäger's book succeeds where other worship books often fail. He seeks first to understand how other traditions, whether Reformed or Pentecostal or otherwise, praise God together in ways that remain both intelligible and meaningful to the tradition, and then, and only then, seeks to be understood. Just as we wouldn't judge jazz a failure because it fails to be classical or folk, so Félix-Jäger argues, rightly, that we should not judge the musical practices of other liturgical traditions a failure simply because they fail to look and sound like ours. With the worship wars still being a scourge to the body of Christ today, Félix-Jäger's book serves to change the rules of engagement by inviting and equipping readers to become agents of God's ministry of reconciliation within the liturgical sphere and thus to find themselves not as fundamentally at war with one another but as fellow citizens in the everlasting praise of the one who sanctifies all of our worship.

—**W. David O. Taylor,** Associate Professor of Theology and Culture, Fuller Theological Seminary; author, *Glimpses of the New Creation* and *A Body of Praise*

This book is a joy to read as Steven Félix-Jäger calls us back to Spirit-filled worship, reminding us that it isn't a performance but a living encounter with the risen Christ. These pages will help you host Christ's presence in a way that transforms lives and communities, and will unite hearts and traditions at the feet of Jesus.

—**Joe Wells,** Director One Hope Project

This gem of a book is practical, pastoral, and wise. Steven Félix-Jäger moves beyond stale debates and easy, one-size-fits-all answers to offer us a more nuanced and theological approach to evaluating congregational worship. Rich in scholarly substance and bursting with ecumenical generosity, this book is a must read for pastors, music leaders, and all who seek to worship in spirit and in truth.

—**Melanie Ross,** Associate Professor of Liturgical Studies, Yale Divinity School and Yale Institute of Sacred Music

How to Worship for All Its Worth

How to Worship for All Its Worth

A Guide for Pastors, Worship Leaders, and Students

Steven Félix-Jäger

ZONDERVAN ACADEMIC

How to Worship for All Its Worth

Published by Zondervan, 3950 Sparks Drive SE, Suite 101, Grand Rapids, MI 49546, USA. Zondervan is a registered trademark of The Zondervan Corporation, L.L.C., a wholly owned subsidiary of HarperCollins Christian Publishing, Inc.

Requests for information should be addressed to customercare@harpercollins.com.

Zondervan titles may be purchased in bulk for educational, business, fundraising, or sales promotional use. For information, please email SpecialMarkets@Zondervan.com.

ISBN 978-0-310-17268-0 (audio)

Library of Congress Cataloging-in-Publication Data

Names: Félix-Jäger, Steven author
Title: How to worship for all its worth : a guide for pastors, worship leaders, and students / Steven Félix-Jäger.
Description: Grand Rapids, Michigan : Zondervan Academic, [2025] | Includes index.
Identifiers: LCCN 2025025129 (print) | LCCN 2025025130 (ebook) | ISBN 9780310172666 paperback | ISBN 9780310172673 ebook
Subjects: LCSH: Worship
Classification: LCC BV10.3 .F45 2025 (print) | LCC BV10.3 (ebook) | DDC 264—dc23/eng/20250808
LC record available at https://lccn.loc.gov/2025025129
LC ebook record available at https://lccn.loc.gov/2025025130

HarperCollins Publishers, Macken House, 39/40 Mayor Street Upper, Dublin 1, D01 C9W8, Ireland (https://www.harpercollins.com)

Cover design: Rob Monacelli
Cover photo: © Salajean / GettyImages
Interior design: Kait Lamphere

Printed in the United States of America

25 26 27 28 29 LBC 5 4 3 2 1

Contents

INTRODUCTION

How Meaning Is Made in Worship

A few years ago, I attended a Christian arts conference. One of the sessions consisted of a panel of Christian artists who were asked to speak about their work. The panel's moderator was a renowned conductor and music director. As the moderator led the discussion, he frequently griped about the state of musical and artistic education in the West. On multiple occasions, he suggested that young people lacked a sophisticated sense of taste and that their attention spans were too short to truly appreciate great art and music. The only conceivable reason he saw for their lack of interest in the music he values was cultural miseducation. Something about his assessment seemed off. I leaned over and asked my friend if she thought the moderator seemed a little out of touch. Is it possible that the young people he encountered held artistic values that merely differed from his? If that was the case, then the young people still held criteria of judgment but used different rubrics. Perhaps they were miseducated or uneducated, or perhaps they simply learned from a different curriculum. This whole scene helped me to see that different art forms require different sets of criteria for evaluation, and one must "learn the language" of the art form in order to responsibly evaluate it. Applying this insight to worship, we can see that ignoring the context of congregational worship music can lead to rash and naïve evaluations of a worship tradition.

The aim of this book is to help readers understand and appreciate some of the many authentic Christian expressions of congregational worship in our world today. As such, this book draws together methods from biblical studies, aesthetics, cultural hermeneutics, practical theology, and ethnography to comprehend what congregational worship means and how we can adequately judge it. The term "judgment" here should not be understood as a bad thing. I am not talking about the sort of judgment that is haphazard or laden with biases and misconceptions. Nor am I talking about "judgmentalism"—the critical attitude of superiority that lacks open-mindedness or empathy toward others. Rather, I refer to **judgment** in the academic sense as *the critical assessment of something to determine its value or significance*. Adopting this sense of the word, we can view the goal of this book as demonstrating how to critically assess congregational worship to determine its value to a worshiping community. Because worship traditions have their own contextual standards of judgment, this book engages various types of judgment utilized when discerning the suitability of a worship expression.

The focus of this book is congregational worship music, but the principles for evaluating worship music that will be discussed could also be applied to other aspects of congregational worship. For instance, evaluating the biblical, aesthetic, theological, and pastoral qualities of a particular song performed in communal worship could also apply to the same congregation's approach to Communion, their practice of baptism, or the role that preaching plays in the life of the congregation. Of course worship is not restricted to congregational music, and in fact these other aspects of worship will be mentioned at times throughout our discussion, but our focus will be congregational worship music.

This introduction explores various ways meaning is made in congregational worship. A couple of definitions should be helpful. This book uses the term **meaning** in the philosophical sense, which refers to *the relationship between signifiers (signs and* *symbols) and what they aim to express.* For example, if I make a thumbs-up gesture to a colleague, that indicates that I think they did a good job on their presentation. Similarly, if I hold up the palm of my hand while someone is backing up a car, that signals to them that they should stop. My gestures are the sign, and they express an intended meaning. The field of **semiotics** considers *how signs are used to make meaning*, and the field of **hermeneutics** looks at *how meaningful human interaction is interpreted*. For a sign to carry meaning, it must first have been ascribed whatever was intended for it to signify. In other words, meaning is not inherent in an object but a person or community confers signification onto it. For example, sports fans in different cities have collectively determined that images or symbols of the team's mascot—a lion, a tiger, or a bear, for instance—indicate support of that team. One of the underlying problems in the academic study of Christian worship is that judgments about congregational worship are often made without proper understandings of how particular communities confer meaning. Since worship music will figure prominently in our discussion, consider the case of a worship song. Does the song mean something different to other worshiping communities than it does to you? One of the fundamental claims of this book is that worship traditions have their own standards of judgment and so must be understood within their own narrative frameworks. To discuss how to worship for all its worth, we must first grasp the various ways worship conveys contextually bound meaning.

Before diving too far into our topic regarding meaning in worship, we must clarify some terms. **Worship** is, at its heart, *the relational act of connecting with the living God through the power and presence of the Holy Spirit*. Elsewhere I have defined the act of worship as "*turning our hearts toward God as a response to God's self-revelation*."[1] In other words, when people "worship God,"

1. Steven Félix-Jäger, *Renewal Worship: A Theology of Pentecostal Doxology* (Downers Grove, IL: InterVarsity, 2022), 5.

they are responding to God, who has first called out to them. When a person "enters worship," they may not have physically gone anywhere, but they have focused their mind and heart on God. Oftentimes the term "worship" is used as a noun to refer to a worship service. Someone might ask, "Are you coming to worship?" meaning "Are you coming to the worship service?" To avoid confusion, I will always refer to this latter sense of worship as "worship service" and will use the term "worship" only in its active sense.

Some people further distinguish between public and private worship.[2] **Public worship** refers to *what believers do when they gather together in a church community as they collectively respond to God*. **Private worship** concerns *what happens between an individual and God as he or she responds to God through private acts of worship like prayer or devotional reading*. Public worship is typically viewed as a communal experience where believers come together to celebrate, pray, and reflect on God's revelation through Scripture, testimony, and exhortation, utilizing a specific structure and order. On the other hand, private worship is personal and individual, and it can be flexible in terms of time and place. Both are interconnected and interrelated since public worshipers experience God both individually and communally when they gather to worship. Furthermore, when believers worship in private, their spiritual growth benefits the whole community. Since this book aims to understand the function and value of congregational worship, especially music, in the shared setting,

2. The Cheshire Pastoral Association, for instance, has released many editions of *Christian Hymns for Public and Private Worship* since 1847, which, even in its title, distinguishes between public and private worship. E. Byron Anderson argues that worship should be regarded as public and personal, rather than private. Calling worship "private" is too individualistic and separate from community, whereas "personal" implies looking at an individual's needs in the community. It is God meeting the individual in the midst of community, rather than God being withheld from the community. See E. Byron Anderson, "Individualism and Community Within Worship Practices," in *Theological Foundations of Worship: Biblical, Systematic, and Practical Perspectives*, ed. Khalia J. Williams and Mark A. Lamport (Grand Rapids: Baker Academic, 2021), 223.

we will primarily look at public worship. Hence, whenever this book refers to "worship," it denotes public worship unless otherwise noted. Now that we've clarified some important terms, let's turn to the topic at hand.

MEANING-MAKING IN WORSHIP

Meanings are not made in a vacuum. Ascribed meanings emerge from deep contexts of preexisting signifiers and interrelated interpretations—contextual frameworks. Taken out of its context, a text or a symbol is a mere design or marker. Consider the Lorem Ipsum texts that web and graphic designers utilize before inserting their client's text-based content. The jumbled Latin was apparently birthed in the fifteenth century by an anonymous typesetter who scrambled Cicero's *De Finibus Bonorum et Malorum*.[3] Today anyone can spawn endless meaningless texts to fill any of their voids by utilizing online Lorem Ipsum generators. The very existence of Lorem Ipsum texts disrupts the idea that words in and of themselves are carriers of meaning. Lorem Ipsum texts are markers of meaning—they indicate that there is supposed to be meaning there—yet they in no way produce any intended meaning. Lorem Ipsum texts demonstrate, therefore, that words are arbitrary unless they are enclosed by a linguistic system. If I say, "Good morning," to my family in the early hours of the day, it will likely be received as a kind greeting. But if I were to use the same greeting at night or in a country that doesn't speak my language, it's likely to cause confusion. As philosopher Ludwig Wittgenstein has taught us, words in themselves are not carriers of meaning, but words carry meaning within their linguistic parameters.[4]

3. "The Story of *Lorem Ipsum*: How Scrambled Text by Cicero Became the Standard for Typesetters Everywhere," Open Culture, March 18, 2015, www.openculture.com/2015/03/the-story-of-lorem-ipsum.html.

4. Ludwig Wittgenstein, *Philosophical Investigations*, 4th ed., trans. G. E. M. Anscombe, P. M. S. Hacker, and Joachin Schulte (Oxford: Blackwell, 2009), 154.

Languages are *entire systems of organized or organizing thought*—the structures from which we interpret and share our experiences. Thus, languages help to comprise the contextual frameworks that carry our meanings. Our utterances become concrete when we allow words to frame our thoughts.

Determining Narrative Frameworks

Throughout this book, I will refer to a community's contextual framework as its guiding narrative. **Narratives** are *stories*, and storytellers are people who make sense of the world through narration.[5] Our experiences unfold in time, and they can thus be recounted. When we recount our experiences, we mark, organize, and clarify what those experiences mean within our guiding narrative.[6] We think of our own experiences temporally as part of a story with a plot, and our particular story fits into the larger chronology of our communal story. In other words, we "story-tell" when we situate our experiences into a larger narrative framework. Philosopher Paul Ricoeur calls this "emplotment"—the act of selecting and arranging events in a way that tells a complete story with a beginning, middle, and end.[7] Through emplotment, our experiences are grafted into narrative unity.[8]

Just as meaning is made in myriad ways, there are also multiple ways of knowing. Along with intellectual knowledge, there are embodied, affective, and symbolic ways of knowing. We come to know things through an affective, narrative knowledge that precedes our propositional knowledge. That is, we might know something because we feel or sense it before we know it cognitively. **Narrative knowledge** is *knowledge that is*

---

5. To see how our personal stories are part of God's larger story, see Jennifer L. Holberg, *Nourishing Narratives: The Power of Story to Shape Our Faith* (Downers Grove, IL: IVP Academic, 2023).

6. Paul Ricoeur, *From Text to Action: Essays in Hermeneutics, II*, trans. Kathleen Blamey and John B. Thompson (Evanston, IL: Northwestern University Press, 2007), 3.

7. Ricoeur, *From Text to Action*, 3.

8. Ricoeur, *From Text to Action*, 5.

rooted in the formational stories we tell, the activities we participate in, and the affections evoked by those stories.[9] Since words carry contextual meanings within formational stories (linguistic systems), we know and communicate meaningful things to one another as we share stories with one another. What is communicated is always contextually bound—one must speak the language of the story to understand what is being expressed. The same is true of worship.

The Language of Music

One of the most significant ways that meaning is conveyed in worship is through music. Music can be seen as a language of sorts, one that holds its own morphology and syntax. Musical meaning is conveyed by the way rhythms and melodies are structured, performed, and received. The formal elements of music—rhythm, pitch, timbre, dynamics, texture, form, melody, harmony—are its grammar and vocabulary, and the way these are all put together constitutes music's semantics. Songs are musical compositions that wed music to poetry, and these two languages form a new multifaceted form of expression. As such, meaning is made in myriad ways through song, not just through a straightforward reading of a song's lyrics.

When we consider congregational worship music, we'll see that a worship song's music and the way it is performed convey meaning to us in many ways. For instance, the somber performance of a Good Friday–themed song tells us that our worship posture should be solemn and reflective. Similarly, the music of a worship song can present us something we already know in a new way. In other words, our *experience* of worship music is amply meaningful to us. In new and varied ways, worship songs can tell us something about God, ourselves, and the church.

9. Steven Félix-Jäger and Yoon Shin, *Renewing Christian Worldview: A Holistic Approach for Spirit-Filled Christians* (Grand Rapids: Baker Academic, 2023), 203.

You might have experienced instances when the music and lyrics of a worship song were conveying different meanings. Perhaps the song's lyrics were about the crucifixion but played in an upbeat celebratory way, or conversely the song expressed triumphant lyrics performed slowly and in a minor key. **Lyrical dissonance** in music is *when the tone of the music contrasts with the theme of the lyrics*. Sometimes songwriters use lyrical dissonance to convey a deeper conceptual meaning (e.g., Foster the People's "Pumped Up Kicks"), but in the examples mentioned above, the dissonance was accidental, which conveys mixed messages to the congregants and can lead to confusion.

Sometimes the musical shifts within a worship song can lead to dissonance and confusion as well. For instance, the song "Gratitude"[10] by Brandon Lake ends with a seemingly unintentional musical dissonance that expresses something musically that is tonally different than what is conveyed in the lyrics. The song begins intimately with a central theme that concerns showing gratitude to God. It's written in a major key and has a slow tempo (52 bpm) with a 6/8 time signature. The song is very settled as the verse, chorus, and bridge all begin with and resolve back to the tonic "1" chord. The bridge gets hyped up with energy but still feels stable because it only slightly modifies the common 1–6–5–4 progression that is employed throughout the whole song. After the bridge, the song ends on a down chorus, but what's interesting is that Lake changes the chord progression in a way that makes the song feel unstable and unsettled. He switches the 5 chord from major to minor and then plays the major 4 before making it minor as well. These particular changes sound musically interesting but work against the message of the song. The lyrics say something peaceful and steady:

10. "Gratitude," words and music by Brandon Lake, Dante Bowe, and Benjamin Hastings © 2019 Bethel Worship Publishing, Brandon Lake Music, Maverick City Publishing, Maverick City Publishing Worldwide, SHOUT! Music Publishing Australia, Bethel Music Publishing (administrated by Capitol CMG Publishing).

And praise You again and again
'Cause all that I have is a hallelujah, hallelujah,

but the progression suggests something unstable.[11]

The listener has spent the whole song expecting a pattern of tension and resolution, but now at the end, the 5min chord introduces something out of the ordinary and unfamiliar so the listener can't telegraph where the progression will end up. Then when the 4 chord transitions into a 4min^6, the song goes beyond a single accidental (a note that is not part of the key signature) and actually shifts modally to Mixolydian b6, a mode of the melodic minor scale. Thus, unexpectantly, the song sounds ethereal and dreamlike. Many composers use the melodic minor scale to illicit feelings of evanescence and unrest, but is this an appropriate musical move for the end of this particular worship song? The problem for "Gratitude" is that worshipers just spent the whole song singing heartfelt and secure words of thanksgiving to God. When this shift happens at the end of such a stable song, the music essentially asks the listener, "Do you really feel this, or was this all a dream?" Thus, the music and the lyrics are unintentionally dissonant. Perhaps this dissonance could have been avoided if greater attention was placed on what the music itself was conveying.

Even the context from which music emerges is ripe with meaning, both historical and sociological. Musicologist Christopher Small coined the term "musicking" to mean taking part "in a musical performance, whether by performing, by listening, by rehearsing or practicing, by providing material for performance (what is called composing), or by dancing."[12] Musicking is an

11. The way this works in music is that the farther you move away from the tonic chord (the 1 chord), the more unresolved the progression is. The 5 chord is the farthest away from the 1, so it wants to pull back to the tonic, or resting position. It's like a spring that is pulled back as far as it can go—the farther it's pulled back, the more tension it has pulling back to a resting position.

12. Christopher Small, *Musicking: The Meanings of Performing and Listening* (Middletown, CT: Wesleyan University Press, 1998), 9.

action that itself constructs meaning through human encounter. Small argues that musicking is not just the act of making music but also constitutes the social interactions and relationships that surround it. He suggests that musicking is a fundamental human activity that is essential to our social and cultural lives. Hence, we can define **musicking** as *the act of engaging music as a social activity, which involves interaction and participation from all those present, not just the performers.*

Musicking doesn't just ask what a song's lyrics mean, but "What does it mean when this performance (of this work) takes place at this time, in this place, with these participants?"[13] Small's definition of musicking, although widely accepted among musicologists, is broad, encompassing not only the performance of music but also the act of listening and the social context in which music is performed. This means that musicking is not limited to a formal concert setting or recordings but extends also to informal settings such as singing in the shower, listening to music while working, or dancing at a party.[14] Musicking considers both the context from which music emerges and how its performance and reception affects its context. Just as words carry meaning only in context, music's full meaning is understood only in context.

Religious Meaning in Music

Congregational worship music has another layer of meaning that is distinct from other forms of music: religious (theological and pastoral) meaning through socioreligious narrative emplotment. Because congregational worship music emerges from a religious context, we can surmise that it also carries religious meaning. **Religious meaning** refers to *the religious significance we place on events, practices, texts, or beliefs.*

In his book *Religious Aesthetics*, Frank Burch Brown discusses

---

13. Small, *Musicking*, 10.
14. Small, *Musicking*, 77.

the ways in which the arts, including congregational worship music, can create religious meaning. First, Brown contends that things have meaning only when they are in relation to someone or something else.[15] He writes, "A meaning that is intended or 'given' must somehow be embodied or encoded in a perceptible form if it is to be received or 'taken'; and it will be 'taken', received, or realized by some person or group only when the elements of the embodiment or code are understood, along with the way the embodied form or code is being used."[16] The meaning of the perceptible form is influenced and even dependent on the social and historical pre-understandings of the receiver. In a liturgical context, pre-understandings are steeped in the biblical narrative that has been recounted and observed by Christians for millennia. This narrative is known through the linguistic expression and symbolic embodiment of the worshiping community.[17] Since these embodiments come as religious rituals, they inevitably carry aesthetic meanings. Rituals are aesthetic forms that are not merely transmitted cognitively but affect the totality of a person. So religious rituals carry aesthetic meanings in ways that are arational and noncognitive.

Brown sees congregational worship and other liturgical arts as carrying religious meaning by the way they holistically move the body, mind, and heart. Aesthetic embodiments evoke the capacities, pleasures, and sensibilities of the perceiver's body.[18] In other words, our own sense of embodiment is heightened when we perceive aesthetically rich, embodied forms. Our aesthetic reflections on perceptible forms help us better appreciate our own finite, creaturely, incorporations. Our mind is enriched as well, because when our body's awareness is heightened, we can interpret our

15. Frank Burch Brown, *Religious Aesthetics: A Theological Study of Making and Meaning* (Princeton, NJ: Princeton University Press, 1989), 101.

16. Brown, *Religious Aesthetics*, 101.

17. Brown, *Religious Aesthetics*, 102.

18. Brown, *Religious Aesthetics*, 103.

experiences more completely.[19] Finally, our heart, or affections, is enriched when art evokes new feelings that have been suppressed or forgotten.[20] In sum, Brown suggests that liturgical arts produce religious meanings as they move bodies, minds, and hearts toward God. As a form of liturgical art, congregational worship music has the ability to form us holistically through its aesthetic embodiment. This formation is holistic and spiritual, steeped in a particular narrative's contextual framework.

Thoughtful aesthetic contemplation can tell us something about an object or experience's broader narrative context, but liturgical art in any form is never made for sheer disinterested contemplation. A vested religious "interest" is always involved. Although aesthetic judgment occurs during the worship service, worship music is not performed purely for aesthetic appreciation. The performance of congregational worship music carries theological meanings and has a pastoral function that is intrinsically tied to the religious community from which it arises. This is what Brown is getting at when he states, "The art of the liturgy (and of other ritual) depends to an exceptional degree on values and meanings shared primarily by a particular group. . . . Its aesthetic features are appreciable chiefly in relation to goals that extend far beyond anything aesthetic in itself."[21] The "group" that shares values and meanings and confers religious meaning onto songs is the worshiping community. Thus, to truly understand what congregational worship means, we must understand the worshiping community it emerges from.

HOW TO ANALYZE COMMUNITIES OF WORSHIP

Worshiping communities can be seen as curators of religious meaning. A curator's task is to keep, manage, and oversee a prized

---

19. Brown, *Religious Aesthetics*, 103.
20. Brown, *Religious Aesthetics*, 104.
21. Brown, *Religious Aesthetics*, 89.

collection of culturally significant artifacts. Curators of art, for instance, gather artworks for display, organizing the works by theme. Situating artworks into narrative contexts, curators confer new meanings onto artworks as they put them in dialogue with other meaningful works. They ascribe value to these artworks by choosing them for inclusion in an exhibition. The curators say to the public, "This work of art is both valuable and meaningful, and worth your attention." When a work enters the public space, it is grafted into a preexisting narrative. Its meaning is conferred through negotiation as it dialogues with and corresponds to other meaningful objects and experiences that surround it. Meaning is thus tied to the communal expression of the object or experience.

Similarly, worshiping communities ascribe worth and meaning to the performance of particular actions. For example, the worshiping community curates meaning by selecting what songs will be performed as acts of worship, when they'll be performed, and in what way they'll be presented. They judge congregational worship songs as they choose what to include and what to exclude from their repertoires. To be included, the new worship song must already fit within the worshiping community's narrative context. Then, as the song is grafted into the narrative context, it expands, broadens, and, at times, refines the community's understanding of itself. It should be noted, however, that the worshiping community does not ascribe *all* meaning onto a worship song. The song that is incorporated into repertoires has already been written, after all. And the new song is often written by members outside of the particular worshiping community. Through various manners of judgment, communities select what songs will be included in their narrative contexts, and then the songs are recontextualized for the worshiping community. Thus, a worship song is ascribed meaning both when it is written and when it is selected and performed. In other words, meaning is made through intention (the artist's vision) and reception (the community's experience of it).

Knowing the General Narrative

Understanding the general narrative of the worshiping community is key to knowing the meaning of the worship. For instance, even if the songs are not written by members of the particular worshiping community, they'll be adopted, adapted, and performed in such a way that resonates with the community and ascribes new meaning to its broader narrative. Therefore, to understand the meaning of congregational worship music, I propose a narrative-hermeneutical approach.

First, we'll come to understand the worshiping community's guiding narrative through a series of analyses. We'll look at the worshiping community's tradition, history, communal impact, and aesthetic impressions.[22] Analyzing a community's tradition and history considers how the community sees itself as part of a larger story. We can look at all the past events that have directly affected and shaped the worshiping community, making it the way it is today. Analyzing a community's social impact considers how the community fits into its surrounding context. We can look at what theological and ecclesial traditions the worshiping community aligns with and how the community engages in and is affected by the surrounding public. We can also look at the aesthetic choices the community makes (i.e., worship style, church architecture, service production, etc.). These aesthetic choices tell us about the community's tastes and values. These analyses will tell us how the community views itself (tradition analysis and historical analysis), and how the public views it (social impact analysis and formal aesthetic analysis).

Second, after the community's guiding narrative is understood, we can assess the biblical, aesthetic, theological, and pastoral fit between a community and its worship. Biblical judgment looks at how a worshiping community reads and

---

22. This is a version of the hermeneutical method I developed for evaluating art in a global pluralistic art-world. See chapter 6 in Steven Félix-Jäger, *Art Theory for a Global Pluralistic Age: The Glocal Artist* (New York: Palgrave Macmillan, 2020).

interprets Scripture in worship. Aesthetic judgment looks at a worship element's fittingness, flow, and experience-making ability. Theological judgment looks at the theological soundness of a worship element while recognizing that authentic expressions between traditions differ and must be understood within their narrative contexts. Finally, pastoral judgment looks at the worship element's capacity for holistic (spiritual and moral) formation and the worship leader's discernment in sensing how and in what way worship can minister to the congregants. For example, does the performance of a congregational song do what it intends to do? Does it draw believers into the presence of God?

These four judgments ultimately work together to assess if God's vision for the kingdom is expressed in the community's worship. David Lemley puts it well: "For leaders of the Christian community, any question of CWM's [contemporary worship music's] suitability for corporate worship is not only, 'Is this text beautiful enough for God?' or, 'Is this text theologically fitted?' or, 'Is this text a product of Christian people with Christ-like motives?' but also should be: 'Does participation in this cultural liturgy rehearse a cruciform identity commensurate with the vision of God's kingdom economy?'"[23]

If the goal is to honor God and be formed by God through worship, we must strive to align with God's kingdom economy—a system based on the idea that God is the ultimate provider and sustainer of all things, and that every possession is a divine gift. Does our worship express God's kingdom principles (i.e., stewardship, generosity, justice, mutuality) as the foundation for a truly abundant and equitable community?

Delineating between these forms of judgment should help us avoid making category errors when determining the merit of

23. David Lemley, *Becoming What We Sing: Formation Through Contemporary Worship Music* (Grand Rapids: Eerdmans, 2021), 7.

congregational worship. I see at least two ways that congregational worship music can be misjudged:

1. *Categories of judgment can be misdirected.* Someone might, for instance, judge a worship song's pastoral function by critiquing its aesthetics, thus utilizing an inappropriate set of criteria for what they intend to judge. For instance, it would be wrong to assume that simple, repeated lines in the bridge of an Evangelical worship song indicate a lack of theological richness. Perhaps the song's liturgical function was to inculcate a new perspective on life's difficulties for the congregant.
2. *Unfitting criteria for judgment can be utilized to inappropriately judge a different tradition's worship practices.* As mentioned, biblical, aesthetic, theological, and pastoral criteria for judgment differ across worshiping communities. Because worship practices are culturally specific, the criteria for evaluating worship practices are set by the worshiping community that performs the practices. The worshiping community thus becomes the arbitrating community that extends its rules of engagement.

To help disentangle these issues, this book seeks to create a framework for evaluating congregational worship on biblical, aesthetic, theological, and pastoral grounds in a way that preserves the localized worship expressions of different traditions.

Critique in a Narrative-Hermeneutical Method

This narrative-hermeneutical method for evaluating congregational worship is a move away from criticism and toward critique. Criticism and critique are related yet distinct concepts. **Criticism** generally refers to *the act of evaluating or judging something, often with the intention of pointing out its faults or shortcomings.* Criticism can actually be negative or positive but is typically associated with negative evaluations. Criticism tends to focus on the work or product itself rather than the process or context in which it was created. **Critique**, on the other hand, refers to *an in-depth and analytical examination of something, often with the intention of understanding its meaning, purpose, or significance.* Critique can also be negative or positive but typically emphasizes context, processes, and intentions behind an object or experience. In other words, criticism is often surface-level, focusing on the external features of a work, while critique is more in-depth, focusing on the underlying meaning-making mechanisms at work in an object or experience.

Whereas criticism typically concerns the shortcomings of something, critique considers the expressed intent and internal cohesion of an object or experience. Is the object or experience authentic to itself? Could it have been expressed in a more powerful or fruitful manner? Critical theorist Irit Rogoff states that in a global, pluralistic age, when we are better attuned to the myriad cultural expressions that exist around the world, we can evaluate a cultural artifact by looking at its fidelity toward its underlying assumptions.[24] One should not, therefore, establish a universal set of criteria that is indiscriminately applied to every instance of a cultural artifact. Rather, one must come to understand the artifact's narrative context and see if it successfully accomplishes what it set out to do. In art criticism, one cannot judge an abstract expressionist painting against the criteria used to judge a work of performance art. There will be some overlap in criteria, but much of what deems one work successful will be irrelevant to the success of the other work. The same goes for congregational worship across traditions. What is an essential criterium for successful worship in one tradition may not be for another tradition. A narrative-hermeneutical approach is sensitive toward the

24. Irit Rogoff, "Academy as Potentiality," in *A.C.A.D.E.M.Y.*, ed. Angelika Nollert et al. (Frankfurt: Revolver Verlag, 2007), 17.

context-specific criteria of judgment that changes from tradition to tradition.

The so-called worship wars often consist of ill-suited judgments about worship. The worship wars comprise ongoing debates concerning the theological legitimacy of traditional hymnody and contemporary worship as it concerns their lyrical and musical styles.[25] The debates generally center around the question of what constitutes appropriate worship and can include issues such as the use of contemporary music versus traditional hymns, the role of preaching, the use of visual aids and technology, and the role of personal experience in worship. Although the term "worship wars" emerged in the 1990s, these sorts of arguments have been raging in earnest ever since the Jesus Movement of the late 1960s. The conflicts initially arose between traditionalists who favored hymns and a more formal liturgy, and those who preferred contemporary worship that utilized worship teams and praise choruses.

While these conflicts typically arise from differences in style or theology, ethnomusicologist Jonathan Dueck suggests that differences in aesthetics also contribute to these conflicts. While interviewing worshipers who dealt with these clashes, Dueck noticed that many of the issues people cited had less to do with style or theology than with the feelings and memories that were lost or set aside by the competing tradition of worship. The aesthetics of these conflicts involve the "experiential, embodied, practiced feelingful way[s] of encountering the world."[26] The worshipers Dueck interviewed cited differences concerning their "aesthetics of encounter" along with stylistic and theological concerns. This explains why the worship wars seem so deeply rooted—even

25. Lemley, *Becoming What We Sing*, 27. It's worth noting that the term "worship wars" implies a level of intensity that may not be present in all cases of disagreement over worship style and practice.

26. Jonathan Dueck, *Congregational Music, Conflict and Community* (London: Routledge, 2017), 4.

the legitimacy of a person's affections are challenged by those from other traditions.

The exclusivism that runs through both sides of these arguments lack, I believe, a genuine understanding of what worship means for the other tradition. The debate is often complicated by the fact that different generations and cultural groups have different contexts and expectations for worship. Using a narrative-hermeneutical method to evaluate congregational worship music allows us to gain a better understanding of the other worship tradition in order to respect its elements and critique them responsibly. Understanding is often succeeded by appreciation, so a thoughtful method for understanding and critique could even help foster a more gracious Christianity.

HOW TO USE THIS BOOK

This book is meant to be used as a tool by students interested in worship studies and by worship practitioners interested in strengthening their worship ministries. It establishes methods for evaluating worship in part 1 and demonstrates these methods in practice through case studies in part 2. This book utilizes a narrative-hermeneutical approach to affirm the existence of various narrative traditions and to understand the tradition's culturally delegated values. Rather than observing set rules, a narrative framework looks at story-based principles that guide value judgments. This approach can be used to better understand one's own narrative tradition and can be useful for cross-cultural interpretation. Since narratives give individuals in a community a ground floor for interpreting and ascribing value onto experiences, this book endeavors to feature the equitable judgment of congregational worship. In our global, pluralistic age when it becomes difficult to navigate competing narratives, this book can help Christians understand the many varied worship expressions of global Christianity.

Part 1 establishes the parameters of biblical, aesthetic, theological, and pastoral judgments. Starting with the various judgments seems to be a reversal of the narrative-hermeneutical approach described above that starts with knowing narratives before making judgments, but these chapters merely explain the parameters of judgment that will be utilized later. In other words, the chapters of part 1 are theoretical. It reviews the literature in the fields of aesthetics and art theory, biblical and theological studies, and ministry. It looks at various methods already in use, both explicit and implicit, developing approaches that are distinct but inclusive enough to approach congregational worship music from various Christian traditions. Since the development of this method is a communal endeavor, part 1 also utilizes the feedback from worship practitioners and scholars from the five traditions assessed.[27] This part ends with a chapter that weaves together all the data and insights from the previous chapters to offer a prescriptive outlook on how to assess and select worship songs for the reader's congregation in ways that are informed, generous, and fitting. It addresses each of the judgments (biblical, aesthetic, theological, and pastoral) to help

27. In particular I interviewed twenty-one worship practitioners and scholars from various denominations between 2023 and 2024. I interviewed four Reformed (one from the Presbyterian Church in America, two from the Presbyterian Church [USA], and one from the Christian Reformed Church), four Pentecostals (two from the Foursquare Church, one from the Assemblies of God, and one brought up in a Charismatic nondenominational Filipino Immigrant Church), four Black Gospel practitioners (one from a Missionary Baptist Church, one from the National Baptist Convention, one from a nondenominational church with a Pentecostal orientation, and one from a nondenominational church with Church of God in Christ roots), four Evangelicals (three from the Southern Baptist Convention, and one from a progressive CBS [Community Bible Study]-aligned mainline Baptist church), and five Catholics (two from parishes in the United Kingdom and three from the United States in Georgia, Michigan, and Washington). The interviewees chosen are diverse in a few ways: they hail from different parts of the US (Alabama, Arkansas, California, Florida, Georgia, Indiana, Michigan, Nevada, New York, Pennsylvania, Virginia, and Washington), and two from England; they are racially varied (eleven white, five African American, three Hispanic, two Asian); and they are a mix of genders (fourteen men, seven women).

readers choose worship songs that are biblically faithful, aesthetically rich yet appropriate to the context, theologically sound and robust, and pastorally sensitive but challenging. Each chapter also has key words, discussion questions, and sidebars to help readers review important concepts and synthesize the information covered.

The chapters of part 2 are entirely observational and analytical, comprised of data collected through on-site ethnographical research at various churches. These chapters assess five churches from various worship traditions in North America utilizing our narrative-hermeneutic approach. In particular these chapters assess the congregational worship music of a Reformed church (Pillar Church in Holland, Michigan), a Pentecostal church (Life Church in Lancaster, California), a Black Gospel church (St. John African Methodist Episcopal Church in Fairburn, Georgia), an Evangelical church (Park Avenue Baptist Church in Titusville, Florida), and a Charismatic Catholic prayer group (from the Diocese of Colorado Springs, Colorado). These case studies all start by getting to know the worshiping community's narrative and then subject the community's congregational worship to biblical, aesthetic, theological, and pastoral evaluation.

By intention, part 2 identifies five worshiping communities from different denominational backgrounds, worship styles, geographical locales, and theological traditions, and it then utilizes the critical approaches of part 1 to make appropriate judgments of their congregational worship music. Part 2 includes ethnographical data from the worshiping communities, including interviews and focus group discussions with pastors and congregants from the various churches. It also assesses the structure, song selections, and aesthetic choices made throughout the worship services. This part of the book extends significant insight into real-life worship practices by comparing and contrasting the similarities and differences between worship traditions.

Finally, the book's conclusion provides closing remarks that weave together all the data and insights from the previous chapters. It draws informed conclusions and offers ways forward for engaging congregational worship music in ecumenical dialogue.

By addressing multiple modes of discernment in worship design, this book is devised to support church practitioners in their biblical, aesthetic, theological, and pastoral deliberations concerning congregational worship. It provides a hermeneutical dimension to the practical theology that is involved when designing a worship service, and it looks to utilize hermeneutical tools to gain deeper insight into one's own worship tradition and the worship traditions of others. Thus, this book bears immense pastoral and theological significance as it has the potential to lead practitioners to a deeper understanding of the worship traditions they lead and, ultimately, to help them facilitate an encounter between the community and the living God

CONCLUSION

This introduction defined terms and discussed the many ways meaning is made through congregational worship, especially worship music. While lyrics are significant for establishing rational meaning in song, the embodied acts of musicking create affective and communal meanings as well. Furthermore, religious meanings are expressed when musicking occurs in liturgical spaces. After considering these various modes of meaning-making, this chapter sought to establish a narrative-hermeneutical method for understanding and evaluating congregational music. This method pays attention to the context-specific criteria traditions produce for judgment. Appropriate biblical, aesthetic, theological, and pastoral judgments can only be made once the tradition's narrative is sufficiently understood.

STUDY QUESTIONS

1. What are some of the ways music can express meaning?
2. Have you experienced an instance when the worship song performed was unintentionally dissonant? How did the congregation respond?
3. Can you identify your worshiping community's guiding narrative? If so, how does worship music help to reinforce the narrative?
4. Have you experienced a situation where the context of a song's performance altered its meaning? How did it change?
5. Have you experienced any "worship war elitism" from another worship tradition toward your own? How did you respond?

KEY TERMS

Criticism: the act of evaluating or judging something, often with the intention of pointing out its faults or shortcomings.

Critique: an in-depth and analytical examination of something, often with the intention of understanding its meaning, purpose, or significance.

Hermeneutics: the branch of knowledge that deals with interpretation, looking at how meaningful human interaction is interpreted.

Judgment: the critical assessment of something to determine its value or significance.

Languages: entire systems of organized or organizing thought.

Lyrical dissonance: when the tone of the music contrasts with the theme of the lyrics.

Meaning: the relationship between signifiers (signs and symbols) and what they aim to express.

Musicking: the act of engaging music as a social activity, which involves interaction and participation from all those present, not just the performers.

Narrative knowledge: knowledge that is rooted in the formational stories we tell, the activities we participate in, and the affections evoked by those stories.

Narratives: stories told by storytellers who make sense of the world through narration.

Private worship: what happens between an individual and God as he or she responds to God through private acts of worship like prayer or devotional reading.

Public worship: what believers do when they gather together in a church community as they collectively respond to God.

Religious meaning: the religious significance we place on events, practices, texts, or beliefs.

Semiotics: the branch of knowledge that considers how signs are used to make meaning.

Worship: the relational act of connecting with the living God through the power and presence of the Holy Spirit. This happens by turning one's heart toward God as a response to God's self-revelation.

PART 1

Principles for How to Worship

CHAPTER 1

How to Use Biblical Judgment

Scriptural Faithfulness in Worship

One day after a university chapel service, I overheard a student dissenting to his peer that one of the worship songs performed during chapel was "biblically unsound." The worship team had performed Travis Greene's 2015 Gospel hit "Intentional." In this song, Greene repeats the lines:

> All things are working for my good
> 'Cause He's intentional, never failing.[1]

Throughout the lyrics, Greene paraphrases Romans 8:28, which states, "We know that all things work together for good for those who love God, who are called according to his purpose." The student had a problem with the fact that the song quotes only part of the biblical verse. The paraphrasing implies, he reasoned, that God works for everybody's good, not specifically for those who love God and are called according to God's purposes. Thus, the

1. "Intentional," words and music by Travis Greene © 2015 Sony Music (administrated by RCA Inspiration).

song implies a theological universalism when the biblical verse clearly refers only to those who are in covenant with God.

At the outset, after a quick reading of the biblical verse and the song lyric, it seems that the student has a point! Is it a misuse of Scripture to quote only part of a verse in a song lyric? Are we, therefore, teaching a biblically unsound doctrine implicitly through song? Maybe. But perhaps something else is going on. Could it be that the student was not understanding something about the song's context? What if Greene is doing something pastoral that conveys a specific meaning to those he is ministering to? There could be a context-specific "pastoral" use of the biblical text that eluded my student.

Greene wrote "Intentional" for a Black Gospel musical context. Black Gospel music often repeats phrases over and over again in order to confer new identities over the congregants.[2] The use of repetition serves a number of purposes, both musical and spiritual. Repeated elements in music create a sense of continuity and familiarity, which in turn helps generate expectancy before an emotional release. Repetition is often utilized through a call-and-response, where the choir or congregation repeats a phrase or a line of the song. In this way, the listener becomes an active participant in the music, which fosters a sense of community. Spiritually, repetition is utilized to reinforce the message of a song and to help listeners internalize and remember the lyrics. As the repeated words wash over the worshiper, the blessing seeps into his or her sense of self. The Bible verse in "Intentional" is paraphrased because the song is performed in a context where the recipient of God's promise is implied—the congregants *are* those who love God and are called according to God's purposes. Considering this, my student's judgment seemingly misunderstood the specific aesthetic and pastoral ways "Intentional" expressed biblical truth.

2. E. Patrick Johnson, "Black Performance Studies: Genealogies, Politics, Futures," in *The SAGE Handbook of Performances Studies*, ed. D. Soyini Madison and Judith Hamera (Thousand Oaks, CA: SAGE Publications, 2006), 450.

Rather than striving to understand the contextual fit of a worship song or style, critics from specific traditions (my student in this case) might apply the criteria of evaluation from their own ecclesial traditions indiscriminately to another tradition's expression of worship. For my student, it was inappropriate to apply the multifaceted standards of his didactically oriented Pent-evangelical tradition to a contemporary Black Gospel song.

This story demonstrates how claims to being "biblically sound" can be a bit dubious. Since the Bible is interpreted by individuals in community, biblical soundness can mean different things to different groups. Conservative Evangelicals might think being biblically sound means holding fast to a **plain-text reading** of Scripture (*interpreting Scripture in a straightforward, face-value way without looking for symbolic, allegorical, or theological interpretations*), whereas more progressive mainline Christians might see it as enacting the ethical mandates to love and bring about reconciliation. Furthermore, some traditions might see the liberative narratives of Exodus as normative for Christian living, whereas others might see sacrifice, as on the cross, as the foundational biblical motif to base all Christian living on. While every tradition reads the whole Bible, each tradition comes at the text from a different vantage point. The **reception** of Scripture refers to *how the Bible is received, interpreted, and utilized by individuals and communities over time*. Traditions implicitly apply the insights of certain texts over others and receive biblical texts differently depending on their context.

All of this leads us to an important question: Given our many contextual differences, what does it mean to be biblically faithful in worship? To answer this question, we'll explore the biblical foundations of worship. First we'll consider how the Bible is a record of God's revelation to humanity. We will then consider the Bible's general narrative and see how worship fits this narrative. We'll see that the heart of worship stays the same even as biblical contexts change. In the same way, the heart of worship must remain the same for the church even as various biblical expressions of worship shift and change depending on context.

A BIBLICAL VISION OF WORSHIP

Throughout this book, when we refer to Scripture, we mean the Christian Scriptures—the Holy Bible.[3] Theologically speaking, **Scripture** is *the God-breathed, authoritative record of God's revelation*. Scripture gives confessing Christians a glimpse of the experiences, communities, traditions, and rationale of God's historical interaction with humanity and creation. Since Christians view the Bible as a divinely inspired witness to God's interaction with human beings, they can look at it as an authoritative footing for all Christian thought and practice. Thus, Christians read Scripture devotionally to help guide their holistic formation. A **formative reading** of Scripture can be understood as *a process of spiritual formation* and can be contrasted with **informative reading** that *principally looks at the transmission of information*. Guided by the Holy Spirit, formative reading aims for the transformation of vision and desire with the end result of experiencing God and becoming like Christ.

Two additional terms to note when discussing biblical meaning in worship are *biblical exegesis* and *biblical hermeneutics*. **Biblical exegesis** is *the study of biblical texts in order to uncover their original, intended meanings*. Exegetes analyze the historical, contextual, linguistic, and literary makeup of a biblical text to try and unearth what the passage meant in its original context.

3. The Bible is a collection of sacred texts that are central to the religious beliefs of Christianity. It is divided into two main sections: the Old Testament and the New Testament. The Old Testament is otherwise known as the Hebrew Bible and consists of the Torah (or Pentateuch), narratives, prophetic literature, wisdom literature, and poetry. The New Testament focuses on the life and teachings of Jesus and the early church and consists of gospels, narratives, letters (or epistles), and apocalyptic literature. Different Christian denominations have variations in the biblical canon, with the Catholic and Orthodox churches including additional books known as the Apocrypha or Deuterocanonical books.

Thus, exegesis is primarily a historical task[4] that attempts to hear Scripture the way its original recipients would have heard it.[5] Biblical hermeneutics is closely related to exegesis but differs in some important ways. Recall the introduction, where I defined the broad field of hermeneutics as studying the way any meaningful human interaction is interpreted. **Biblical hermeneutics** is a more specialized form of the broader field of hermeneutics, one that *studies the principles used to interpret biblical texts*. While exegesis does the work of interpreting texts, biblical hermeneutics zooms out and looks at how one should go about interpreting these texts in the first place.

In their masterful work *How to Read the Bible for All Its Worth*, Gordon Fee and Douglas Stuart contend that biblical hermeneutics can be understood in a narrower sense where interpretation concerns seeking contemporary relevance of biblical texts.[6] Thus biblical exegesis asks what a text meant in its day and biblical hermeneutics asks what a text means to us today. Good hermeneutics, they contend, starts with exegesis. The original meaning of a text is the "point of control" for its contemporary meaning.[7] In other words, one cannot haphazardly read anything back into a biblical passage—our contemporary interpretations of a text must align with what it meant in the first place. Nevertheless, Fee and Stuart admit that it might be possible for a text to have a fuller or

---

4. It should be noted that Gordon Fee and Douglas Stuart define exegesis as a primarily historical task, but some modern and postmodern exegetes might push back against that notion. They might say the gap between the original author and the biblical text is unbreachable completely by any scholar. See Douglas Estes, "Introduction: The Literary Approach to the Bible," in *Literary Approaches to the Bible*, ed. Douglas Mangum and Douglas Estes, (Bellingham, WA: Lexham, 2018). Some might also argue that the literary task of exegesis distances itself from historical emphasis. See Clarissa Breu, ed., *Biblical Exegesis Without Authorial Intention? Interdisciplinary Approaches to Authorship and Meaning* (Leiden: Brill, 2019). These notions also begin to blur the lines between exegesis and hermeneutics as defined later in this chapter.

5. Gordon Fee and Douglas Stuart, *How to Read the Bible for All Its Worth*, 4th ed. (Grand Rapids: Zondervan Academic, 2014), 27.

6. Fee and Stuart, *How to Read the Bible for All Its Worth*, 33.

7. Fee and Stuart, *How to Read the Bible for All Its Worth*, 34.

deeper meaning beyond its original intent, but such interpretations run up against some difficulties.[8] Specifically, by whose authority can a fuller meaning of Scripture be legitimized? Catholics have a magisterium vested in the official teaching of the church, but Protestants have to rely on personal revelations or the authority of chosen individuals. Without accountability, a charismatic leader can find followers to adopt heretical, even cultish, teachings and practices. Yet with proper communal accountability and some epistemological humility, fuller interpretations could benefit a worshiping community. We'll see later in this chapter that this point is significant for assessing the way traditions use the Bible in worship—variances in biblical judgment often concern hermeneutical differences. Before diving into that point, let's consider what biblical judgment entails.

What Biblical Judgment Determines

Biblical judgment depends on *Scripture's ability to shape one's conceptions about God and the world by negotiating the veracity of confessional witness*. While we are spiritually formed by reading Scripture, we also determine if our personal experiences line up with the biblical account. As Kevin Vanhoozer states,

> Who do we say that he (Jesus) is and how do we determine what it means to follow him here and now? In each case, *judgment*—the ability to tell true from false, good from bad, valid from invalid, beautiful from ugly, part from whole—is the operative category. My wager is that attending to biblical form and content helps form sinners into mature disciples who learn how to exercise good theological judgment and practice what we may call *scriptural sapience* as they grow up in every way into Christ (cf. Eph. 4:15).[9]

8. Fee and Stuart, *How to Read the Bible for All Its Worth*, 35.

9. Kevin Vanhoozer, "Love's Wisdom: The Authority of Scripture's Form and Content for Faith's Understanding and Theological Judgment," *Journal of Reformed Theology* 5, no. 3 (2011): 251.

This sort of judgment entails thinking biblically about Christian discourse "in ways that both (propositionally) inform the mind's thoughts and (poetically) form the heart's desires."[10] In other words, biblical judgment bears the pastoral component of ministering faith's understanding in both the minds and hearts of confessing Christians.[11] It negotiates our experiences with the biblical form of the Christian faith.

The biblical form of the Christian faith first begins with the revelation of God to humanity. After all, God spoke before any Scriptures were ever written down. **Revelation** refers to *the disclosure of knowledge that comes directly from God*. This can take many forms, including the revelation of God's character (Deut. 7:9; 1 John 4:8), the revelation of God's will for humanity (Mic. 6:8; 2 Cor. 5:18–20), and the revelation of future events or prophecies (Matt. 24:3–14; Rev. 21:1–4). The ultimate revelation of God is the incarnated Christ (John 1:14). Through Jesus' life, ministry, death, resurrection, and outpouring of the Spirit, God's very nature, character, and plan for humanity are fully revealed (Col. 1:15–20). Furthermore, the Spirit continues to reveal God's truth and presence in the world today (1 Cor. 2:10–12). Thus, Scripture, too, is revelation as it further extends the revelation of Christ.

Theologian Karl Barth sees the Bible not just as a collection of human writings about God but as a form of divine revelation.[12] According to Barth, God is fully and uniquely revealed in Jesus Christ, and the Bible is a form of the Word of God as it bears witness to that revelation. He writes, "The direct identification between revelation and the Bible which is in fact at issue is not one that we can presuppose or anticipate. It takes place as an event when and where the biblical word becomes God's Word, i.e., when

10. Vanhoozer, "Love's Wisdom," 249–50.

11. Vanhoozer, "Love's Wisdom," 250.

12. Karl Barth, *Church Dogmatics*, vol. 1, *The Doctrine of the Word of God*, pt. 1, trans. G. W. Bromiley (1936; repr., Peabody, MA: Hendrickson, 2020), 119.

and where the biblical word comes into play as a word of witness."[13] The words of the Bible become the Word of God when they are heard in faith, which gives it the power to transform people's lives and bring them into a deeper relationship with God.[14] Like others throughout the church's history, Barth also emphasizes the importance of the Holy Spirit in the reading and interpretation of Scripture. The Spirit enables believers to understand and apply the message of Scripture to their lives, so without the Spirit's guidance, the Bible would remain a closed book. All in all, the Bible is a record of God's revelation, but it becomes revelation itself when it is proclaimed by the church under the Spirit's guidance.[15] The Bible preserves an account of God's historical revelation to humanity and becomes fresh revelation when its words are heard in faith.

The Content and Form of the Bible

The Bible's content, when properly (and faithfully) understood, can help guide us in our Christian lives. Vanhoozer points out that both the Bible's content and form work together to form our Christian thinking. We can view the form of Scripture through the Bible's various genres. **Form criticism** is *the exegetical task of identifying and analyzing the literary forms and genres of biblical texts*. Form criticism dictates our rules of engagement with a specific text of Scripture. Analyzing the form of a Scripture passage is important for understanding its content because the passage's form determines the way its information is processed.[16] The form of Scripture organizes the details of the content into meaningful patterns, so when we read the Bible we see how it connects to the greater Christian narrative. According to Vanhoozer, this point is essential for biblical judgment:

13. Barth, *Church Dogmatics*, I.1, 113.
14. Barth, *Church Dogmatics*, I.1, 121.
15. Barth, *Church Dogmatics*, I.1, 121.
16. Vanhoozer, "Love's Wisdom," 256.

> Scripture exercises authority over the various domains of personal and ecclesial judgment. *Form and content work together both to teach us concepts (i.e., convey information) and shape our conceptions (i.e., process information).* Biblical authority means that we are answerable *to* the God speaking in Scripture *for* our judgments about God, the good, and the gospel. The Bible's authority is not only propositional, then, but judgmental: its authority is a matter not only of discrete bits of information but of the ways in which we group them into meaningful patterns, evaluate, and look through them. *It is for the sake of forming right judgments that we must view biblical authority in other than merely propositionalist terms.*[17]

Hence, Vanhoozer argues that we shouldn't look at Scripture merely as propositional content but as a vehicle for presenting the overarching gospel message.

Vanhoozer believes the general form of Scripture is best described as a **theodrama**—*an approach to biblical interpretation that considers the dramatic conception of theological doctrine.*[18] We can see ourselves as actors that fit into a larger dramatic work. If we are to participate in Scripture's drama, our speech and action must fit with Scripture and our contemporary situation.[19] Theodrama is a helpful framework for thinking about biblical authority and interpretation because it looks at both the informative and affective facets of the gospel. It recognizes Scripture reading as a matter not merely of cognition but of affect and action too.[20] In other words, when we participate in the Bible's theodrama, we bridge the gap between comprehension and Christian practice. Biblically guided living entails a holistic formation that enriches the mind,

---

17. Vanhoozer, "Love's Wisdom," 266, italics in original.
18. Kevin Vanhoozer, *The Drama of Doctrine: A Canonical Linguistic Approach to Christian Theology* (Louisville: Westminster John Knox, 2005), 22.
19. Vanhoozer, *The Drama of Doctrine*, 111.
20. Vanhoozer, "Love's Wisdom," 267.

touches the heart, and motivates the actions of believers. When we look at Bible reading in this regard, we'll see it as a tool that helps Christians remain faithful in worship.

INTERPRETING THE BIBLE'S GENERAL NARRATIVE

After establishing what faithful Bible reading entails, we can now explore the Bible's general narrative, or theodrama. It's important to keep the whole biblical narrative at the forefront of our minds when reading Scripture because it establishes the overarching context from which we will interpret individual passages. When we know the full story of the Bible, we will avoid reading passages out of context. For instance, it is difficult to know what Jesus is talking about when he says, "This cup that is poured out for you is the new covenant in my blood" (Luke 22:20), without understanding pivotal biblical themes like covenant and redemption that run all the way through the Bible. Readers might miss the theological significance of what's happening—Jesus is claiming that his death and resurrection will establish a new covenant with God as the old covenant is fulfilled. This passage is also significant because it encapsulates the core message of Christianity that is centered around the life, death, and resurrection of Jesus Christ. We will see this core message present in the worship practices of every worship tradition assessed throughout this book.

For a concise summation of the Bible's general narrative, we must look no farther than John 3:16, one of the Bible's most famous passages that many of us were asked to memorize as children: "For God so loved the world that he gave his only Son, so that everyone who believes in him may not perish but may have eternal life." This verse says salvation is made available to humanity through Christ's sacrifice. There are, of course, other primary beliefs that flesh out the Bible's theodrama (i.e., God is creator, God is triune, humanity is fallen, Jesus is God incarnate, Jesus atoned for our sins and enabled salvation, the Spirit indwells believers, the Spirit empowers the church, and Christ will return to make all things new),[21] but everything in the Bible points to the crucial moment of redemption on the cross—the drama's climactic event. We'll see below that some traditions portray the general biblical narrative a little differently,[22] but all agree that it is this crisis event, the cross, that makes our religious narrative Christian.

Knowing the Bible's general narrative is practically important in worship because it helps us understand the biblical meaning of the songs we sing, the prayers we recite, and the rituals we perform. All that we do in worship is intended to deepen our faith and nurture our relationships with God and God's people. As such, knowing the biblical narrative also helps us see our own lives as part of God's ongoing story. When we sing praises about God's great deeds or reflect reverently about God's good character, we claim the truths of the Bible as our own. In worship we recognize our part in the narrative, and the stories of Scripture transform from mere history to *our* history. When the Bible's general narrative is affirmed and reaffirmed in worship, worshipers adopt a common identity as God's people—covenanted members of a larger story that transcends social and cultural divisions.

Worship in the Biblical Narrative

In the introduction, I defined worship as the relational act of connecting with God by turning one's heart toward God as a response to God's self-revelation. While this is a good summative definition of worship as a theological concept, in this chapter we'll see what in particular the Bible says about worship. This line of inquiry is important because it helps us determine if our worship practices are biblically faithful. The Bible utilizes several images

21. These primary beliefs will be discussed in further detail in chapter 3.

22. To cite just two examples, Pentecostals emphasize Pentecost as part of the crisis event that began with the cross, and the Reformed tradition utilizes a "redemptive-historical" approach that focuses on creation, fall, redemption, and restoration.

that conceptualize worship as a response to God's self-revelation to people in covenant. Our ability to love God and to express our love to God comes from the fact that God first loved us (1 John 4:19). The notion that worship is best understood as a response is evidenced by David when he recognizes his own praise as a response to God's steadfast love:

> Because your steadfast love is better than life,
> my lips will praise you.
> So I will bless you as long as I live;
> I will lift up my hands and call on your name.
>
> —*Psalm 63:3–4*

Moreover, the Bible describes several worshipful postures of response to God: adoration (Ps. 95:6), thanksgiving (Ps. 100:4), joy (1 Thess. 5:15–18), reverence and awe (Heb. 12:28), sacrifice (Rom. 12:1), and even lament (Ps. 6:8–9). Beyond demonstrating worshipful postures, the Bible also describes worship as obedience to God's voice (1 Sam. 15:22), which results in a life of worshipful, holy living (Col. 3:17; 1 Peter 1:15–16). Hence, the Bible sees worship as a lifestyle of response to God's love. This is what can be understood as the biblical heart of worship.

While in general the Bible views worship as service and loving postures before God, Scripture also recognizes the forms and methods of worship as shifting and changing when the narrative context changes. For instance, some of the earliest forms of worship in the Old Testament revolved around altars and sacrifices and were conducted by patriarchal heads of families like Abraham, Isaac, and Jacob (Gen. 12:7–8). Altars—site-specific places that accommodated ritual sacrifice and prayer[23]—were common during the patriarchal period.

---

23. Andrew Hill, "Old Testament and Worship," in *Theological Foundations of Worship: Biblical, Systematic, and Practical Perspectives*, ed. Khalia J. Williams and Mark A. Lamport (Grand Rapids: Baker Academic, 2021), 6.

WORSHIP AS A DIALOGUE

Rev. Rachel Klompmaker, an associate pastor for congregational care at First Presbyterian Church, Spartanburg, South Carolina, pointed out that responding to God is an appropriate way to think about congregational worship in the Reformed tradition because it highlights the fact that worship is a dialogue between God and the people of God:

> Reformed worship at its best is a discernible dialogue between God and the people. And things can transcend style—it can happen in any music style and in any kind of space. My favorite thing to do, whenever there's a bulletin or a worship order, is to draw arrows to look at who's speaking to whom in the service. I think Reformed worship at its best is a balanced dialogue between God and the people. And so a song can be God's speaking to us. A song can be us speaking to God, or it can actually be us speaking to one another. So in my tradition, a song can fit in any one of those categories and serve the function of that dialogue. A song can call us to confess our sins. It can be a word of assurance from God. It can be a song of gratitude and thanksgiving for our forgiveness. Functionally it's a chance for the people to speak, either to one another or to God.

Klompmaker also noted that worship songs give people "a way to speak their faith in a language that's familiar to them." Since the whole worship service is a relational flow of revelation and response, the words sung are just as theologically formative as the words of a sermon.

Then, after the exodus from Egypt, the Israelites built the tabernacle—a portable sanctuary—that housed the presence of God. Bezalel and Oholiab, two skilled craftsman who were gifted and empowered by the Holy Spirit, were tasked with overseeing the construction of the tabernacle (Exodus 31). Worship in the tabernacle was conducted by the priests and Levites (Exodus 29), and a full-fledged sacrificial system was developed (Leviticus 1–7). The Israelites also introduced major feasts and festivals of worship like the Passover during this time.[24]

During the monarchial period, the Israelites further solidified their worship practices by building Solomon's temple (1 Kings 6) and centralizing worship in Jerusalem. During this era, the king took on the role of a religious functionary; this was further solidified when David brought the ark of the covenant to Jerusalem.[25] Later, after a series of occupations, many Israelites were forced into exile during Babylonian captivity. Because the Israelites were now disconnected from the land of covenant promise,[26] they wrote a lot of the oral tradition down to preserve the faith, and worship shifted from ritual-based worship in the temple to a more didactic-based worship in the synagogue. Finally, the postexilic period saw older forms of worship restored as the temple was rebuilt (Ezra 3), but other elements of the didactic-based worship in synagogues, like prayer, Torah study, and instruction, were retained.[27]

Theologically, the biggest change in worship in the New Testament was the affirmation that Jesus, who is fully God, is worthy of worship (Matt. 28:17). With this revelation, the form of worship also shifted and changed as worship moved from the temple and synagogues to house churches.[28] Unlike worship in the Old Testament, worship in the New Testament found its footing quickly by merging various influences. Bruce Shields and David Butzu describe this merging as the integration of three patterns of worship.[29] First, the earliest Christians still retained much

---

24. Hill, "Old Testament and Worship," 8.
25. Hill, "Old Testament and Worship," 10.
26. Hill, "Old Testament and Worship," 12.
27. Hill, "Old Testament and Worship," 15.
28. Pheme Perkins, "New Testament and Worship," in *Theological Foundations of Worship: Biblical, Systematic, and Practical Perspectives*, ed. Khalia J. Williams and Mark A. Lamport (Grand Rapids: Baker Academic, 2021), 21.
29. Bruce Shields and David Butzu, *Generations of Praise: The History of Worship* (Joplin, MO: College Press, 2006), 35.

of the synagogue-style worship that revolved around Scripture reading and study. Many early Christians visited the temple to worship but brought these practices to their homes as well.[30] Early Christian worship was also influenced by a charismatic-style worship that was prevalent among the Hellenistic churches. Here Christians rejected elements of pagan worship such as animal sacrifice but adopted others like dramatic reenactments of the gospel narrative and highly emotional expressiveness.[31] In fact, some of Paul's pastoral guidance concerned the extent to which these worship practices were to be adopted (1 Corinthians 12–14). Hence, the inclusion of the Gentiles into the church was a major catalyst for change in the forms and methods of worship. Third and finally, the early church adopted elements of an apocalyptic-style worship that was modeled after the heavenly worship described in the book of Revelation, specifically chapters 4 and 5. Here we have the inclusion of music as a primary medium of praise in worship.[32] One of the major innovations in worship instituted by the early church was celebrating the Lord's Supper, which became a central element of early Christian worship.[33]

The Bible is also concerned about false worship and idolatry. One of the ways we learn from the Bible how to worship is by seeing how not to do it. The golden calf narrative in Exodus 32 is perhaps the most prominent biblical illustration of idolatrous worship. Driven by impatience, the Israelites regressed to familiar practices, emulating the worship customs of Egypt and neighboring regions in the ancient Near East. During Moses' absence, the Israelites turned to Aaron, seeking a physical representation of Yahweh to worship (vv. 1–5). By constructing a golden calf, they sought to honor Yahweh through a graven image, thereby breaking both the first and second commandments. In Acts 17,

30. Shields and Butzu, *Generations of Praise*, 36.
31. Shields and Butzu, *Generations of Praise*, 37.
32. Shields and Butzu, *Generations of Praise*, 47.
33. Perkins, "New Testament and Worship," 26.

Paul similarly cautions that idols are false representations of God (vv. 24–25) and urges the Athenians to abandon those false gods in favor of worshiping the living God, who, through Christ, will ultimately judge the world (vv. 30–31). Both the Old and New Testaments demonstrate how God alone should be worshiped, and that putting anything ahead of or in place of God is idolatry. G. K. Beale defines an idol as "whatever your heart clings to or relies on *for ultimate security*."[34] Hence, whatever is hindering one's total reliance on God is also an idol.

As can be seen in this brief summary of worship throughout the Bible, the foundational core that understands worship as responding to God's self-revelation never changed. The goal of worship was and is always to encounter God as God's covenantal people. Yet even the Bible demonstrates that context matters for adequately understanding and judging worship. Without knowing what was going on historically and socially, we would not know *how* the biblical writers maintained the heart of worship through varying customs. In the same way, the form and methods of worship might vary throughout the world today, but the foundational core of worship remains the same. By establishing broad-based standards of biblical judgment, we can both come to understand how Christian traditions practice biblical faithfulness in worship and celebrate the many varied ways God is worshiped across traditions around the world.

Standards of Biblical Judgment

As mentioned earlier, differences in worship often concern the ways in which traditions approach biblical texts hermeneutically. For instance, the order and elements in worship can vary depending on whether a tradition uses a liturgical calendar or whether they engage in spontaneous expressions of worship based

34. G. K. Beale, *We Become What We Worship: A Biblical Theology of Idolatry* (Downers Grove, IL: IVP Academic, 2008), 17.

on a direct interpretation of Scripture. But while the lived experience of worship changes from tradition to tradition, we can still establish general standards of biblical judgment to evaluate the biblical faithfulness of worship across all traditions. We can distill three broad benchmarks: (1) Worship practices should veer closely to the general biblical narrative; (2) worship practices should resemble the biblical heart of worship; and (3) our personal experience in worship should line up with Scripture. While these three standards are helpful to determine biblical faithfulness generally, I must reiterate that various worship traditions have used the Bible in different ways. Knowing these differences helps us understand how the standards of biblical judgment should be contextualized by tradition.

Greg Scheer recounts four approaches to how the Bible is used to form worship practices: the three-legged stool principle, the regulative principle, the normative principle, and direct revelation.[35] The oldest of these principles is the **three-legged stool principle**, which states that *Scripture, tradition, and church authority equally determine the content and contours of worship.*[36] For Catholics the sacred tradition consists of teachings passed down through the ages, starting from the time of the apostles. While these teachings were not written down as part of the canonical biblical texts, they are regarded as just as authoritative because they stem from Jesus. Church authority refers to the teaching authority of the magisterium, which is comprised of the pope and the bishops. The magisterium is also regarded as authoritative as Scripture because they are divinely instituted by Jesus and tasked to authentically interpret and safeguard Scripture and the teachings of the church.

Some high church Protestant traditions have adopted a version

35. Greg Scheer, *Essential Worship: A Handbook for Leaders* (Grand Rapids: Baker, 2016), 34–36.

36. *Catechism of the Catholic Church: Complete and Updated* (New York: USCCB Publishing, 1995), para. 95.

of the three-legged stool principle but replaced church authority with "reason." Unlike Catholics, Protestants believe Scripture holds primary authority for the Christian faith, and all Christians are given the freedom to interpret the Bible. They uphold the importance of tradition but define it broadly as the ecclesial work of the historic church. Reason refers to the experience and critical inquiry of Christians. While tradition and reason are important, they are secondary to the Bible's authority.[37] Nevertheless, these three are often viewed as the main sources for biblical worship in high church Protestant traditions.

One of the key particularities of the Reformed tradition is that it generally follows the "regulative principle" to govern the worship practices of the church. The **regulative principle** holds that *everything done in worship must be based on explicit commands or examples in Scripture*. This means that worship practices should be regulated by the Bible, and anything not commanded or explicitly allowed in Scripture is not permissible in worship.[38] *The Westminster Confession of Faith*, which is a central document in Reformed theology, affirms the regulative principle. Chapter 21, section 1, states, "But the acceptable way of worshiping the true God is instituted by himself, and so limited by his own revealed will, that he may not be worshiped according to the imaginations and devices of men, or the suggestions of Satan, under any visible representation or any other way not prescribed in the Holy Scripture."[39] Thus, music in Reformed worship bears a strong emphasis on teaching the faith to proclaim the gospel.

A similar but less restrictive principle is the **normative**

---

37. Although sometimes disputed, this Protestant formulation is often credited to Richard Hooker in the sixteenth century. See Richard Hooker, *Lawes of Ecclesiastical Politie*, bk. 5, ch. 8., accessed April 24, 2025, https://archive.org/details/oflawsofeccles00hook/page/n5/mode/2up.

38. R. J. Gore Jr., *Covenantal Worship: Reconsidering the Puritan Regulative Principle* (Philipsburg, NJ: P&R, 2002), 9–10.

39. Derek Thomas, "Through the Westminster Confession: Chapter 21.1, 2," June 3, 2013, www.reformation21.org/confession/2013/06/chapter-211-2.php.

principle, which states that *whatever is not explicitly prohibited by Scripture is permissible in worship*. This principle upholds scriptural boundaries while allowing for flexibility in how worship is conducted. Tradition can be upheld in worship as long as it does not contradict Scripture. Hence, Martin Luther upheld the basic structure of the Catholic Mass, eliminating only elements that he thought clashed with Scripture.[40] The normative principle is used by Lutherans, Methodists, and other mainline denominations. Many Evangelical traditions also follow this principle implicitly.

Direct revelation states that *God will reveal the truths of Scripture through the Holy Spirit's direct inspiration*. Because the Spirit is viewed as immediately available to believers, reason and tradition are deemphasized as necessary for interpreting Scripture. However, adherents will typically state that a recounted experience or content of a worship song or sermon must align with a plain-text reading of Scripture. This approach is utilized by Pentecostals and many in the Evangelical and Black Gospel traditions. Adherents to direct revelation state that the Spirit addresses Christians in ways that transcend human reason. Rickie Moore says it well:

> We know that there is a vital place for emotion as well as reason, for imagination as well as logic, for mystery as well as certainty, and for that which is narrative and dramatic as well as that which is propositional and systematic. Consequently, we appreciate Scripture not just as an object which we interpret but as a living Word which interprets us and through which the Spirit flows in ways that we cannot dictate, calculate, or program. This means that our Bible study must be open to surprises and even times of waiting or tarrying before the Lord.[41]

---

40. Jordan Cooper, *Liturgical Worship: A Lutheran Introduction* (Watseka, IL: Just and Sinner, 2018), 16.

41. Rickie D. Moore, "A Pentecostal Approach to Scripture," in *Pentecostal Hermeneutics: A Reader*, ed. Lee Roy Martin (Leiden: Brill, 2013), 11.

Direct revelation might at times have difficulties determining how to screen out illegitimate interpretations of Scripture. Yet adherents believe such an approach is needed to be open to what the Spirit is doing in the world today. In other words, the lived experience of believers is vital for knowing the biblical truth about God. *Knowing about* God and *experiencing* God directly inform each other in the lives of believers.[42]

Each of these approaches contextualizes how biblical judgment is used in worship. For instance, the Catholic rendition of the three-legged stool principle would view veering closely to the biblical narrative in conjunction with how tradition and the magisterium interpret the narrative. Thus worship practices cannot be determined by an individual worshiper's reading of the biblical text. Furthermore, tradition and the magisterium play a significant role in determining whether worship practices resemble the heart of worship and whether our personal experiences line up with Scripture. Individual judgments concerning worship are therefore checked by a historical structural authority within the tradition.

The regulative principle would take a more limited approach to biblical judgment. Not only would a worship song, for example, need to veer closely to the general biblical narrative, but it would need to quote Scripture directly. Thus, worship music will inevitably resemble the biblical heart of worship because it often *is* the texts of Scripture put to music. Hence a worshiper's experience of worship music would, as a matter of course, align with Scripture.

While the regulative principle does not leave much room for subjective judgments concerning worship music's biblical fit and function, the normative principle does. Because it allows for anything not prohibited in Scripture to be considered for worship, the normative principle must look closely at the standards

42. Moore, "A Pentecostal Approach to Scripture," 12.

detailed above to see if the worship song or practice veers closely to the general biblical narrative. This gives worship practitioners a metric to screen out something that may not go directly against Scripture but still doesn't fit the biblical narrative. For instance, some seeker-sensitive churches have adopted the practice of starting services with secular songs in order to help newcomers feel welcome at church. This practice would likely be condemned by adherents of the three-legged stool principle or of the regulative principle. But the normative principle could justify this practice since it's not condemned outright in Scripture. Yet many adherents of the normative principle would use biblical judgment here to say, "Even though this practice isn't condemned in Scripture, because the secular song veers so far away from the general biblical narrative, we'll avoid performing it." These standards can also be used when determining if a song or practice resembles the biblical heart of worship or if personal experiences in worship line up with Scripture. Applying these standards affords worship practitioners the possibility to screen out what is not biblically fit for worship.

Similarly, the direct revelation approach greatly benefits from using these standards of biblical judgment. Sometimes when worshipers are "caught up in the moment," it is difficult to tell if something is coming from God or only from the euphoria of the experience. Because the Spirit is revealing the truths of Scripture directly to worshipers, it is crucial to have a mechanism that allows worshipers to screen out what could just be an emotional response. What many Pentecostal practitioners instruct worshipers to do is make sure the experience they're having lines up with Scripture. They typically take a normative approach, but rather than only permitting things that complement Scripture, they give prophetic weight to what is revealed in worship. Yet even experiences that are deemed prophetic should veer closely to the general biblical narrative. It should speak the language of God's story and not express something distant from the biblical narrative. For instance, the second-century Gnostics and the modern Mormons both uphold extrabiblical revelations that veer far away from the general biblical narrative and into heterodoxy. Biblical judgment is thus crucially important to help safeguard against worship practices that lead people away from the faith. Furthermore, when worship practices are highly affective, it's important to make sure they resemble the biblical heart of worship and lead to a life of discipleship. Thus, adherents of direct revelation must periodically step back and make sure their personal experiences in worship line up with Scripture.

Now that we've established a sense of what biblical judgment entails in terms of a cohesive biblical vision amid shifting contexts, we can look a little deeper at the particular biblical commitments and starting points held by the five worship traditions we engage in part 2 of this book. To this task we now turn.

CONTEXTUAL PERSPECTIVES ON BIBLICAL JUDGMENT IN WORSHIP

The contents of this section are drawn from published scholarship and from a series of interviews conducted with scholars and practitioners from Reformed, Pentecostal, Black Gospel, Evangelical, and Charismatic Catholic traditions. What follows is in no way comprehensive but offers some firsthand accounts of practical, real-world experiences from cultural insiders. Reformed worship typically holds to a balanced gospel narrative that consists of the **creation-fall-redemption-consummation motif**. This motif provides *a lens for understanding the biblical narrative and God's plan for humanity and the world*. It is often used in Reformed theology to help Christians get a full sense of how the biblical drama unfolds.[43] It emphasizes God's sovereignty over all things, the brokenness of the world as a result of sin, and the hope of

43. Gordon Spykman, *Reformational Theology: A New Paradigm for Doing Dogmatics* (Grand Rapids: Eerdmans, 1992), 10.

redemption and restoration through Christ. It also emphasizes the importance of faith in Christ as the means of salvation and the ultimate hope of believers in the consummation of all things. While sometimes Reformed worship services zero in on particular biblical themes, they typically aim to reiterate the creation-fall-redemption-consummation motif weekly to foster a well-rounded biblical formation.

In worship Pentecostals emphasize the continuing work of the Holy Spirit in the lives of believers. In particular they read Luke-Acts as principally normative for Christian living. It does not merely recount the early church's story but recounts the start of *their* story as Spirit-empowered Christians today.[44] While they uphold the primacy of the cross's redemption narrative, they also believe that Christ poured out the Spirit on all flesh at Pentecost, who continues to be present and active in the world today. The experience of the Spirit is seen as a foretaste of the coming kingdom and a sign of its present reality.[45] Yet because the kingdom of God is not yet fully realized, the world remains in a state of brokenness, and the consummation of the kingdom is still to come. Narratively, Pentecostals emphasize that they live as a people in between the "now and not yet" of the kingdom of God. The **now and not yet** is *a theological framework used to explain the present and future realities of God's reign*. The crucifixion, resurrection, ascension, and Pentecost are all part of the same eschatological event that mediates between the present and future kingdom. In this age, Pentecostals view themselves as people who have been saved, healed, and empowered to proclaim and enact the message and deeds of the kingdom. Thus, in worship Pentecostals emphasize an eschatological reading of Luke-Acts.

Black Gospel worship practitioners commonly say that their

---

44. See Martin Mittelstadt, *Reading Luke-Acts in the Pentecostal Tradition* (Cleveland, TN: CPT Press, 2010), 2.

45. Frank Macchia, *Baptized in the Spirit: A Global Pentecostal Theology* (Grand Rapids: Zondervan, 2009), 143.

worship is hope oriented and biblically focused on the gospel. Hence, Black Gospel worship emphasizes the words and deeds of Jesus found in the four Gospels. However, the Black Gospel tradition reads the Bible hermeneutically from a unique perspective of the Black experience initially demarcated by the transatlantic slave trade and European colonization. While the term **Black experience** is *a multifaceted concept that encompasses the varied lives, histories, cultures, and struggles of Black people around the world*, one defining factor of Bible reading in the North American Black Gospel tradition is drawn from the social location of enslaved persons in the United States.[46] This social location prompted Black Christians to read soteriological passages through the lens of "Christ as liberator."[47] Thus, the exodus account, prophetic passages that focus on justice (e.g., Isa. 1:17; 40:1–5; 58:6–7; Jer. 22:3; 29:11; Ezek. 37:1–14; et al.), and the liberative passages from the Gospels—those that emphasize liberation, justice, and the upliftment of the marginalized (Matt. 5:3–12; 25:31–46; Mark 2:27; 10:1–31, 46–52; Luke 4:18–19; 6:20–21; John 8:31–32; 10:10; et al.)—become biblically foundational for Black Gospel worship.

Evangelical worship, preaching, theology, and personal devotion are all shaped by what Stanley Grenz calls the **Evangelical Scripture principle**. This principle *emphasizes the authority of the Bible as the ultimate guide for faith and practice*.[48] Evangelicals view the Bible as both a primary source for correct doctrine and a source for spiritual sustenance.[49] Narratively, Evangelical worship tends to view the gospel accounts of the crucifixion as represent-

46. Esau McCaulley, *Reading While Black: African American Biblical Interpretation as an Exercise in Hope* (Downers Grove, IL: IVP Academic, 2020), 17.

47. James Cone, *The Spirituals and the Blues: An Interpretation* (Maryknoll, NY: Orbis, 1992), 60.

48. Stanley Grenz, "Nurturing the Soul, Informing the Mind: The Genesis of the Evangelical Scripture Principle," in *Evangelicals and Scripture: Tradition, Authority, and Hermeneutics*, ed. Vincent Bacote, Laura Miguélez, and Dennis L. Okholm (Downers Grove, IL: IVP, 2004), 22.

49. Grenz, "Nurturing the Soul, Informing the Mind," 23.

ing the cornerstone of the biblical narrative. While many biblical themes are often expressed in worship, they typically point back to Jesus' work on the cross. The cross is often seen as a call to discipleship and a challenge for Christians to follow in Christ's footsteps as they bear their own crosses and strive to live lives of service and sacrifice. For Evangelicals the cross is not just a historical event but an ongoing reality that shapes their beliefs and daily lives.

To understand how Charismatic Catholic worship utilizes the Bible, we must first get a sense of how Roman Catholicism uses Scripture in worship generally. The Mass is divided into two main parts: the Liturgy of the Word and the Liturgy of the Eucharist.[50] The Liturgy of the Word focuses on hearing and reflecting on Scripture. The Bible readings are organized according to its liturgical calendar, which ensures that the entire Bible is read over a three-year cycle. While the Liturgy of the Word is pivotal for educating and forming worshipers in the teachings of the faith, the Liturgy of the Eucharist provides spiritual nourishment and grace through ritual acts of worship. **Eucharist** is *a Greek word that literally means "thanksgiving" and is used to describe Communion where the bread and wine become the body and blood of Christ through the power of the Spirit.* The **Liturgy of the Eucharist** is *the central part of the Catholic Mass where worshipers commemorate the Last Supper along with the death and resurrection of Christ by participating in the celebration of the Eucharist.* It focuses on biblical passages that highlight the theological and liturgical significance of the Eucharist.[51] Because Charismatic Catholics are fully integrated within the broader liturgical life of the parish, they, along

50. *Catechism of the Catholic Church*, para. 1346.

51. These include specific biblical references concerning the act of the Eucharist (Matt. 26:26–28; Mark 14:22–24; Luke 22:19–20; 1 Cor. 11:23–25), references to the Eucharist (Luke 24:30–31; John 6:51–58; Acts 2:42; 1 Cor. 10:16–17), passages that deal with the Eucharist's theological foundations (Gen. 14:18; Exodus 12), and eschatological eucharistic imagery (Isa. 6:3; John 1:29; Rev. 4:8).

with all Catholics, can be viewed as using the Bible holistically in worship with a special emphasis on the Eucharist passages.[52]

From these interviews and other sources, we see that each worship tradition focuses biblically on the crisis event of the cross but in unique ways. Reformed worship utilizes the creation-fall-redemption-consummation motif to robustly understand God's redemptive plan for humanity and the world; Pentecostal worship emphasizes a now-and-not-yet reading of Luke-Acts; Black Gospel worship focuses on the liberative foundations of the gospel message; Evangelical worship highlights the crucifixion as the cornerstone of an authoritative biblical account; and Charismatic Catholic worship reads the Bible holistically in worship, placing special emphasis on the Eucharist passages. Even in this limited sample, we can see ways in which these worshiping traditions add their own idiosyncrasies to the broad landscape of Western congregational worship. Uncovering similarities and distinctions between traditions helps us understand both our own traditions and theirs.

CONCLUSION

Considering the biblical foundations of worship, this chapter looked at biblical judgment as the first form of evaluation we can use to see how songs express a community's understanding of the gospel. We saw that the Bible's general narrative, punctuated by Christ's work of redemption on the cross, extends across every tradition of Christian worship. Yet the way in which the Bible is received changes from tradition to tradition. Accordingly, biblical expressions of worship change depending on context. To evaluate the biblical faithfulness of worship across traditions, three broad

52. The Catholic Church also prescribes the Liturgy of the Hours as its official prayer cycle. This is a set of daily prayers to be recited at specific times of the day. One could say, therefore, that the Psalms also play an important part in Catholic worship. See *Catechism of the Catholic Church*, para. 1174.

benchmarks are useful: Worship songs and practices should veer closely to the general biblical narrative; worship songs and practices should resemble the biblical heart of worship; and our personal experience in worship should line up with Scripture. These benchmarks can help us see how biblical judgment is contextually applied in worship even as the foundational core of worship as a response to God's self-revelation remains constant.

STUDY QUESTIONS

1. What difficulties can arise when seeking a fuller or deeper meaning of Scripture beyond its original intent?
2. Why is it important for worshiping communities to maintain proper communal accountability in interpreting biblical texts?
3. Why is it important to keep the whole biblical narrative in mind when reading individual passages?
4. How does affirming and reaffirming the Bible's general narrative in worship contribute to the common identity of God's people?
5. Explain the three broad benchmarks for biblical judgment in worship. Can you think of any other useful benchmarks to add?

KEY TERMS

Biblical exegesis: the study of biblical texts in order to uncover their original, intended meanings.

Biblical hermeneutics: the study of the principles used to interpret biblical texts.

Biblical judgment: a type of judgment that considers Scripture's ability to shape one's conceptions about God by negotiating the veracity of confessional witness.

Black experience: a multifaceted concept that encompasses the varied lives, histories, cultures, and struggles of Black people around the world.

Creation-fall-redemption-consummation motif: a biblical motif used in the Reformed tradition to help understand the biblical narrative and God's plan for humanity and the world.

Direct revelation: a principle that states God will reveal the truths of Scripture through the Holy Spirit's direct inspiration.

Eucharist: a Greek word that literally means "thanksgiving" and is used to describe Communion where the bread and wine become the body and blood of Christ through the power of the Spirit.

Evangelical Scripture principle: a principle that emphasizes the authority of the Bible as the ultimate guide for faith and practice.

Form criticism: the exegetical task of identifying and analyzing the literary forms and genres of biblical texts.

Formative reading: reading Scripture as a process of spiritual formation.

Informative reading: reading a text as transmission of information.

Liturgy of the Eucharist: the central part of the Catholic Mass where worshipers commemorate the Last Supper along with the death and resurrection of Christ by participating in the celebration of the Eucharist.

Normative principle: a principle that states whatever is not explicitly prohibited by Scripture is permissible in worship.

Now and not yet: a theological framework used to explain the present and future realities of God's reign.

Plain-text reading: interpreting Scripture in a straightforward, face-value way without looking for symbolic, allegorical, or theological interpretations.

Reception (biblical studies): how the Bible is received, interpreted, and utilized by individuals and communities over time.

Regulative principle: a principle that states everything done in worship must be based on explicit commands or examples in Scripture.

Scripture: the God-breathed, authoritative record of God's revelation.

Theodrama: an approach to biblical interpretation that considers the dramatic conception of theological doctrine.

Three-legged stool principle: a principle that states Scripture, tradition, and church authority equally determine the content and contours of worship.

CHAPTER 2

How to Use Aesthetic Judgment

The Form and Fit of Worship

Years ago, I served as the contemporary worship leader of a United Methodist church in Central Florida. The church, having existed for more than a hundred years, grew accustomed to hosting traditional, hymn-style worship services every Sunday. A newly appointed senior pastor, however, envisioned adding a contemporary service to the Sunday morning programming.[1] Congregants were free to choose whichever service they wanted to attend. Most people stayed with the traditional service they were already familiar with, but several members opted to try out the new contemporary service. To help these congregants transition from hymn-style traditional to contemporary worship, we decided to perform at least one hymn in each worship set. With a praise team fully equipped with singers, guitars, bass, keys, and drums, we played hymns in the middle of our sets or as tags. We thought

1. At the time, I was already serving as the youth and college pastor, and I led contemporary-style worship for the student services. Naturally, the pastor sought me out to help launch a contemporary service for the church.

the hymns brought a familiarity that would help congregants engage with a new contemporary style.

One week I was planning the worship set and decided to include the great nineteenth-century Holiness hymn "Blessed Assurance" by Fanny Crosby and Phoebe Knapp. If you're familiar with the song, you know the time signature is 9/8—nine beats in a measure and the eighth note gets the beat. Like every form of popular music, contemporary worship songs are typically written in 4/4 or 6/8, so 9/8 was somewhat of an unusual time signature. "Blessed Assurance" feels like 6/8 initially, but the melody moves too quickly to encourage listeners to sway back and forth like they would listening to a song in 6/8. So I did what many contemporary worship pastors have done in the past—I converted it to 6/8! I told the worship team, "We're gonna let this song breathe a little bit by making it 6/8." We added short rests after the words "assurance," "mine," "divine," and so forth. We thought it sounded awesome and meditative, making it more singable and swayable!

When we performed the song, the congregants instinctually sang the next phrases during the rests. You could see confusion set in on some of their faces. *Do they even know how this song goes?* After the service I caught quite a bit of flack for changing the hymn, which taught me a valuable lesson: Don't mess with the structure of hymns! Changing the formal structure of the hymn disrupted its typical flow—a flow that has entered the congregants' prayer lives over and over again, in *that* way, throughout their many years of Christian devotion. Since the song had ministered to them throughout their lives, the song's aesthetic structure was imprinted on their memories.

What this incident taught me was that even aesthetic choices in worship carry significant meaning. To minister well in a congregational setting, musical worship leaders must be aware of what the aesthetics of worship mean to the congregation and why. This chapter looks at how aesthetic judgment is applied to congregational worship, especially music. As we look at the form of worship, we'll see that what is valued aesthetically shifts according to the worshiping community's guiding narrative. This leads us to consider aesthetic fit in worship and how particular aesthetic criteria are valued in different traditions. To flesh out this topic, we will look at contextual perspectives on aesthetic sensibilities in Reformed, Pentecostal, Black Gospel, Evangelical, and Charismatic Catholic worship.

STANDARDS OF AESTHETIC JUDGMENT

Have you ever been told that judging the arts is a purely subjective endeavor? Someone might say, "Either you like it, or you don't," and because it's your opinion, you don't really have to give a rationale for your judgment. This isn't really how we judge the arts, though. While there is certainly a subjective element to our aesthetic judgment, much of what we judge as good or bad has to do with how well an artwork achieves its formal goals. For the most part, if a drummer misses a fill, a portrait's proportions are off, or an actor flubs a line, we judge the artwork negatively. As we'll see below, the formal elements of art are not the only thing we judge, but they are aspects of the arts that we judge that have clear standards of judgment. Hence, aesthetic judgment utilizes both subjective and impartial deliberations. To get a better grasp of this, we'll look at how aesthetic judgments are made, and what are generally understood as the formal elements of art and music.

Making Aesthetic Judgments

When we make **aesthetic judgments**, we make *value judgments concerning our perceptions of objects or experiences.* Unlike other axiological fields like **ethics** where we *ascribe moral values onto actions*, or **religion** where we *ascribe ecclesiastical values onto rites*, **aesthetics** *ascribes values of appreciation onto sensed perceptions.* Aesthetic judgments happen in two ways: First, they classify or categorize our felt responses to sensory stimulation. Did you witness beauty when you gazed with admiration upon your lover's face? Did you feel disgusted when you saw and smelled the dripping sludge? When you stared out into the vastness of the ocean, were you struck by an overwhelming feeling of awe? Determining the category of a sensory response is already a judgment. When we deem something beautiful, disgusting, or sublime, we judge that a particular feeling corresponds with one specific classification over another.

Second, aesthetic judgment determines which response merits praise and to what degree. We would generally agree, for instance, that the sensation of beauty is an aesthetic response that merits high praise and signifies something we should strive for. On the flip side, we would likely agree that the feeling of disgust merits discontentment, signifying something we should avoid. Yet there is a contextual, narrative component to aesthetic judgment that values fit. If a horror film is funny, for instance, we would think it is aesthetically weak, not because the feelings of whimsy or comical playfulness are inherently wrong but because they do not fit the aesthetic mood of the film.

In his *Critique of Judgment*, Immanuel Kant lays out how aesthetic judgment should be understood. Aesthetics, for Kant, occurs in the contemplation of an experience. Aesthetic pleasure, therefore, is not the visceral experience itself but reflection on the visceral experience. Aesthetic judgment comes about through reflection and is free, disinterested, and nonconceptual. Kant talks about two types of judgement, **determinant judgment**, which is *categorically subject to law*, and **indeterminant judgment**, which is *free-flowing and conditional*.[2] When we say someone ought to act a certain way morally, we are making a determinant judgment, evoking Kant's categorical imperative—an impenetrable moral obligation. When we say someone

2. Immanuel Kant, *Critique of Judgment*, trans. J. H. Bernard (Mineola, NY: Dover, 2005), 17.

ought to think the sunset is beautiful, we make an indeterminant judgment—a conditional imperative that depends on whether a person agrees. We are saying not "I think this is beautiful because it is objectively so" but "I think this is beautiful, and I think you should think so too." There's freedom in disinterestedness; it is subjective and not absolute. Kant writes, "The *ought* in the aesthetical judgment is therefore pronounced in accordance with all the data which are required for judging and yet is only conditioned. We ask for the agreement of everyone else because we have for it a ground that is common to all; and we could count on this agreement, provided we were always sure that the case was correctly subsumed under that ground as rule of assent."[3]

When we ask for agreement, we want others to approve of our subjective judgments. If we see something that is beautiful, we can ask someone their opinion to see if they agree or disagree. We can try to persuade one another to think certain ways about aesthetic matters.

Yet even though our aesthetic judgment is free and subjective, that does not mean we eschew standards of judgment. After all, when we try to persuade others why a work of art is great, we don't simply say, "It's great because I like it." We back up our claims with evidence, such as "the composition is so dynamic, I can't take my eyes off it" or "the color scheme is really effective in creating a mood" or "the painterly brushstrokes create a great sense of energy and movement." Our standards of aesthetic judgment provide evidence for the soundness of our conclusions. When we find ourselves in these types of discussions, we look for areas of agreement as a basis for our conclusions. We might ask, "Do you agree that what's most important about this piece is to evoke emotion, and not to emulate realism?" If yes, then we might argue that the other person is misjudging the piece by overvaluing something that is not central to it. The point is, we are still utilizing standards to

---

3. Kant, *Critique of Judgment*, 55.

make aesthetic judgments but using them as markers that prove the rationality of our judgments, not as proofs of objectivity.

Formal Elements

While many standards of aesthetic judgment are contextual, critics have long judged works of art formally by looking at a work or performance's composition and technique, as well as the emotional and expressive qualities, such as mood, atmosphere, and message. The formal elements of visual art and design, for instance, include line, shape, texture, value, space, color, balance, contrast, movement, pattern, and proportion. These formal elements are used in combination to create a wide variety of visual expression, which often conveys meaning or emotion. When a person critiques an artwork's form, he or she may look to see if a portrait that is intended to be painted realistically is proportional or if the rendered light of an object is producing the appropriate value that corresponds with nature. The person is judging the artwork's form according to the foundational standards of aesthetic judgment.

Likewise, music has its own formal elements that are used to create compositions. The **formal elements of music** are *rhythm* (the arrangement of long and short sounds and periods of silence), *pitch* (the highness or lowness of sound determined by the frequency of the sound wave), *timbre* (the tonal quality or sounds determined by the harmonic spectrum of the sound wave), *dynamics* (the loudness or softness of sound), *texture* (the way the parts or the composition are arranged in relation to the others), *form* (the structure of a piece of music), *melody* (a sequence of single pitches that make up a musical line), and *harmony* (the sounding of two or more pitches at the same time).[4] These are the widely accepted foundational elements of music, so if a piece

4. See Catherine Schmidt-Jones, *The Basic Elements of Music*, Textbook Equity Edition (Morrisville, NC: Lulu, 2014).

of music is judged formally, it will be assessed by the successes or failures of these elements and their relations to one another.

Although these foundations are widely accepted by teachers and practitioners as formal elements of music, the way they are valued and used are contextually bound. While a classical guitarist emulates emotion through dynamics, a punk rock guitarist, for instance, might value loudness and sonic commotion over a full range of dynamics. It's not that the punk rocker believes dynamics are not a formal element of music but that he or she chooses to have a limited dynamic range in order to produce feelings of energy and chaos at a punk rock show. Contexts, therefore, determine how formal elements are used and to what extent. Thus, they render a judgment even on the formal elements. They judge the formal elements not in terms of good or bad or right or wrong but in terms of fit.

Philosopher Nicholas Wolterstorff describes aesthetic fit, what he calls "fittingness," as "cross-modal similarity."[5] It constitutes the relation between qualities both within and across modalities.[6] **Aesthetic fit** determines *how closely things relate to one another*. As an example, Wolterstorff states, "To say that *large* fits better with *loud* than with *soft* (in sound) is to say that the cross-modal similarity between *large* and *loud* is closer than that between *large* and *soft*."[7] In other words, there is a closer fit between the aesthetic concept of "largeness" with "loudness" than there is "largeness" with "softness." We assume there is a close, natural fit between loudness and largeness, and we view largeness and softness as not fitting, even dissonant. Fit is an important concept in aesthetics because it shows how elements are valued contextually. Saying a punk rock song has no place for elegant dynamics is not a condemnation of elegant dynamics. It's saying that this

---

5. Nicholas Wolterstorff, *Art in Action: Toward a Christian Aesthetic* (Grand Rapids: Eerdmans, 1980), 99.

6. Wolterstorff, *Art in Action*, 98.

7. Wolterstorff, *Art in Action*, 99, italics in original.

formal element (dynamics) does not fit the genre (punk) in this way (elegance). That is, a song is evaluated not solely on how well it utilizes formal elements but on how well it utilizes the formal elements that are valued by the community. Aesthetic fit pays close attention to context for evaluation.

Furthermore, Wolterstorff says that to appropriately evaluate art, we must understand how art functions in a society.[8] Throughout Western modernity, art was generally seen as that which produces aesthetic contemplation to bring about aesthetic satisfaction.[9] This is perhaps rooted in Kant, who believed art should be judged based on its form, not on its content or purpose, and that it has value in and of itself, separate from any practical or moral considerations. According to Kant, the purpose of art is to provide aesthetic enjoyment and to stimulate intellectual reflection and emotional expression.[10] Wolterstorff, on the other hand, recognizes aesthetic contemplation as a possible function of some art but not as the sole purpose of all art.

Wolterstorff believes every art form must be judged against its social function, which makes aesthetic fit a key determining factor for evaluating an artwork's worth. A grand narrative of art that determines the worth of art for an entire society is impossible.[11] Societies are comprised of many communities with their own aesthetic sensibilities. Artworks emerge from cultures and subcultures within societies, so no singular standard of judgment is ever possible for the arts. Additionally, many art forms carry functional worth that is tied to social practices. Wolterstorff cites several examples of arts as "social practices," including memorial

8. Wolterstorff, *Art in Action*, 11.

9. Wolterstorff, *Art in Action*, 40.

10. Kant, *Critique of Judgment*, 112. It should be noted that Kant was more concerned with aesthetics as indeterminate judgment than the nature of art, and that the definition of art played a relatively small role in his aesthetics.

11. Nicholas Wolterstorff, *Art Rethought: The Social Practices of Art* (Oxford: Oxford University Press, 2015), 56.

art, liturgical art, work songs, and social protest art.[12] In each of these cases, art is not appreciated disinterestedly for its own sake but is appreciated with a vested interest that transcends the formal elements of the artwork. These arts function in service to social practices yet are still identifiably works of art. Wolterstorff contends that understanding a work of art entails understanding the "social-practice meaning" of the work. The social-practice meaning of a work entails "the significance it has when engaged by the public in accord with some extant social practice."[13] Appropriate judgment must, therefore, recognize the context and social practice of a work of art. If an artwork is made for display in a museum, then disinterested contemplation is the appropriate engagement of it, and judgments are made according to its success in this regard. If an artwork is made for liturgical usage, then disinterested contemplation is not an appropriate engagement of it. Liturgical art must be engaged appropriately as an element of worship and must be judged accordingly. Judging art according to its social practice allows us to understand the artwork's meaning and significance within its narrative context.

AESTHETIC FIT AND AUTHENTICITY IN NARRATIVE CONTEXT

We engage art in many different contextually bound ways,[14] and since congregational worship is a form of liturgical art, it must be understood aesthetically in light of its liturgical community. Classification is an important first step that must be taken when it comes to judging worship. If we misclassify a piece of congregational worship music as a piece of concert music, then we misapprehend the contextually bound criteria that are used to judge

---

12. See chs. 4–7 in Wolterstorff, *Art Rethought*.
13. Wolterstorff, *Art Rethought*, 112.
14. Wolterstorff, *Art Rethought*, 86.

liturgical art. Furthermore, the specific narrative surrounding the work of liturgical art is essential for appropriately understanding and judging the art form. Our task, therefore, is to understand aesthetic fit within the art form's narrative context.

A Narrative Theory of Art

Philosopher Noël Carroll has developed a **narrative theory of art** that *seeks to identify and judge artworks by means of historical narration.*[15] First, when we identify something as a particular form of art, we are grouping it with other things that convey similar characteristics. For instance, we might observe that a contemporary song bears a strong resemblance to folk songs from prior generations. We would classify it as such because its characteristics clearly fall within the folk tradition. Cultural practices shift over time as they adapt to new social circumstances,[16] but they still look recognizably consistent. They conserve the same DNA, if you will, even as they adapt. For instance, while folk songs today deal with contemporary issues, they are recognizably consistent with folk songs from the 1960s or 1990s. If we dig deeper, we will be able to trace the narrative trails of the contemporary song historically through the folk-song tradition. This is what it means to identify a song through historical narration. As Carroll writes, "Since cultural practices tend to reproduce themselves and to negotiate their self-transformations in ways that sustain continuity between the existing tradition and expansions thereof, the modes of identifying new objects as art make essential reference, though in different ways, to the history of the practice. New objects are identified as artworks through histories of art, rather than theories of art."[17]

---

15. Noël Carroll, *Beyond Aesthetics: Philosophical Essay* (Cambridge: Cambridge University Press, 2001), 63.
16. Carroll, *Beyond Aesthetics*, 67.
17. Carroll, *Beyond Aesthetics*, 71.

The **classification** of art entails, therefore, *observing the cultural practice and grouping it within a narrative tradition.* Since narrative traditions have their own histories, classification entails linking a cultural practice to an existing history.

An artwork's "identifying narrative" is that which "establishes that a work in question emerged in recognizable ways from an acknowledged art-world context through an intelligible process of assessment, resolution, and action."[18] The historical narrative starts with a description of the historical context and ends with the work of art's contribution to the narrative. Everything in between is the second act of the story that ties the narrative together.[19] An artwork can modify the narrative by continuing or repudiating what has come before. For instance, Kendrick Lamar's "Alright" thematically concerns social justice by addressing issues such as police brutality, racism, poverty, and inequality. The song's chorus repeats the phrase "We gon' be alright" as a message of hope and resilience to Black communities in the face of these challenges. Although "Alright" uses references to current events, it adds to hip-hop's historical narrative by continuing an important theme of the genre (social justice) in an authentic way.

Sticking with the same genre, there are also instances when a hip-hop song repudiates something that has come before in its narrative, adding a new layer and dynamic to the broader narrative of hip-hop. An example of this is when Lauryn Hill called out hip-hop's proclivity toward misogyny in her 1998 release *The Miseducation of Lauryn Hill.* In particular Hill discusses how society's pervasive influence of misogyny harms women. By rejecting limiting stereotypes and expectations, she encourages women to value themselves and pursue their dreams. In "Doo Wop (That Thing)," for instance, Hill addresses the double standards and

18. Carroll, *Beyond Aesthetics*, 92.

19. Noël Carroll, *Philosophy of Art: A Contemporary Introduction* (London: Routledge, 1999), 260.

unrealistic expectations that society places on both women and men in relationships. She encourages women not to turn a blind eye to men who mistreat them. As a cultural insider, Hill confronts something about the narrative that she wishes to change. Regardless of its critical stance toward what went before, both artworks were identified by and added to the genre's historical narrative.

Carroll's narrative theory of art is akin to Ricoeur's notion of emplotment discussed in the introduction. Both theories see an experience (Ricoeur) or cultural practice (Carroll) being grafted on to a preexisting narrative. The emplotted event then helps to shape the narrative moving forward. In a narrative theory of art, therefore, the only necessary feature an artwork must have to be classified as such is emplotment within a narrative.[20] Art can look radically different from tradition to tradition, but we can still know it's considered an artwork by the way the community has historically viewed and classified similar pieces or practices in the past.

We also don't need to know the entire history of a narrative to determine its identifying narrative. For instance, we could determine a song is a Gospel song because of the way it uses call and response, vocal runs, and polyrhythmic drums for praise breaks, even if we did not trace its lineage all the way back to the Black spirituals of the American South. To determine its narrative comprehensibility, all we needed to establish was a sufficient context.[21] Carroll calls the limited but sufficient context a "narrative connection" where we see a series of events relating to one another in a connected sequence.[22] Narratives are not formed by a collection of random events; the former event must be causally related to the latter event.[23] All in all, what makes a work of art's classification

20. Carroll, *Beyond Aesthetics*, 86.
21. Carroll, *Beyond Aesthetics*, 109.
22. Carroll, *Beyond Aesthetics*, 119.
23. Carroll, *Beyond Aesthetics*, 125.

and content graspable by a community is its relation to its socio-historical context—its narrative.[24]

As we utilize a narrative theory of art to classify art, which determines what fits where, we can also look to narrative to evaluate art. Evaluating art through narrative entails assessing a work's "narrative fit." For instance, a contemporary worship song that is stylistically akin to pop-rock would not fit narratively in a high church liturgical setting. It does not matter if the song is aesthetically excellent as a pop rock song, for it will be deemed inappropriate for the worship set because of narrative fit. Making an aesthetic judgment by **narrative fit evaluation** entails considering *the particular contextualized formal elements that have been adopted by the arbitrating community*. It does not look at aesthetic excellence on its own but looks at aesthetic excellence within the narrative context of the work of art. Narrative fit is less concerned about technical mastery of formal elements and more concerned about authenticity—that fitting formal elements are utilized in narratively appropriate ways.

Authenticity and Genre

Authenticity is *an evaluative concept that, when applied to music, marks both the narrative fit and the contextualized aesthetic value of music*. Authenticity, according to sociologists Phillip Vannini and J. Patrick Williams, refers to "a set of qualities that people in a particular time and place have come to agree represent an ideal or exemplar."[25] It is context-specific and communally determined. To use the language of historical narration, authenticity refers to how well something fits the plot of the broader narrative. While a classically trained oboist might be able to rip through Strauss's Concerto in D Major for Oboe, her skills might not be valued highly in Pentecostal circles. It's not that

24. Stephen Davies, *The Philosophy of Art* (Malden, MA: Blackwell, 2006), 81.

25. Phillip Vannini and J. Patrick Williams, eds. *Authenticity in Culture, Self, and Society* (London: Routledge, 2009), 3.

Pentecostals lack taste or musical standards but that different contextually bound standards are valued over those of Romantic concert music. An oboe solo during "Awake My Soul" not only would eschew aesthetic fit but its inclusion would seem forced and inauthentic to the style and genre that has come to epitomize the community's aesthetic sensibilities.

Genre in music refers to *the categorization of pieces of music into a shared tradition*. It is determined by several factors, including a musical performance's location, time, cultural competency, and cultural origins.[26] Jonathan Dueck points out that while genre deals significantly with aesthetic, sonic qualities, it also "forms a kind of social currency *between* related groups."[27] Cultural insiders determine relationships between social groups through genre. One way communities interact with one another is by accepting or rejecting genres and by determining if a song fits into a particular genre. Furthermore, the performance of a song is measured against its genre boundaries, which relate to the tradition's valued characteristics. David Lemley says that popular music performances "are packed full of visible and audible signifiers and linked to the larger body of images, stories, and ethos of the performers present in the song. Authenticity is always being measured, in both the performer and listener, in terms of the unwritten rules of style."[28] Genre fit is thus a major determinant of authenticity in music, and authenticity is a major determinant of a song's worth. After conducting ethnographical research on congregational worship music, Nathan Myrick states, "I have been struck by how often authenticity is noted as the definitive criterion of 'good' music. For many authenticity

26. Nathan Myrick, *Music for Others: Care, Justice, and Relational Ethics in Christian Music* (Oxford: Oxford University Press, 2021), 111.

27. Jonathan Dueck, *Congregational Music, Conflict and Community* (London: Routledge, 2017), 125–26, emphasis original.

28. David Lemley, *Becoming What We Sing: Formation Through Contemporary Worship Music* (Grand Rapids: Eerdmans, 2021), 115.

means being vulnerable in Christian communities, being honest to your fellows about your loves, values, and convictions. It is no accident that this criterion of good music is also a central criterion of good relationships—*good realities*."[29] Authenticity is thus an integral part of aesthetic judgment. Music's ability to evoke emotion is part of its aesthetic function, but it is also tied to authenticity. When a song helps a person genuinely engage emotionally with the community's broader narrative, it aids the community through social habituation and holistic formation.[30]

IMPROVISATION AND AESTHETICS

In an interview, worship scholar and ethnomusicologist Nathan Myrick discussed worship from his perspective as a scholar and Baptist congregant. He explained that aesthetics play an important part in shaping a community's identity: "Aesthetics and aesthetic preferences do drive the relational and communal development of a community. I think that is an important part of it, but within that I recognize a slippage or a messiness between the projected aesthetic outcomes or desires of a community from whatever power position it's projecting." Thus, Nathan went on to say that it is valuable to have a traditional sense of aesthetics for the identity formation of a community, but there should be "a lot of room for improvisation." He values that in the church he worships at, there is a permissive sense of aesthetic originality and individualism, even as the church extends a general sense of communal cohesion. Nathan sees communal aesthetic standards as flexible. A worshiping tradition looks, sounds, and acts in a way that indicates what is important for the community, but individual preferences play a part in augmenting the tradition's values.

29. Myrick, *Music for Others*, 117, emphasis original.
30. Myrick, *Music for Others*, 69.

Lemley puts it well, "Music is a catalyst for an interior experience that generates a vision of being in the world. The participant has the opportunity (only as long as the proscenium curtain is drawn back) to perform the life indicated by the music's projected affect and to try on its meanings."[31] Music is formative as it is deeply relational, merging both meaning and emotion.[32] As such, authenticity as a value in music could be understood both as a song's contextual fit and as its ability to help adherents express authentic emotions, which grafts them deeper into narrative identity.

CONTEXTUAL PERSPECTIVES ON AESTHETIC JUDGMENT IN WORSHIP

Now that we've established a sense of what aesthetic judgment entails in terms of form and fit, we will look broadly at the aesthetic criteria that are valued across the five worship traditions we engage throughout this book. Once again, what follows is not comprehensive or meant to be definitive; it is, however, informative since it is drawn from sources that include the insights of scholars and practitioners from these worshiping traditions. While every tradition views aesthetic components of worship (musical style, production quality, architectural style, style of dress, church décor, etc.) as importantly formative for their community, each tradition cites different ways that these components are formational.

The Reformed tradition has a firm sense of how aesthetic sensibilities shape congregants. Aesthetic sensibilities help worshipers determine appropriate postures for various expressions of worship. That is, they help worshipers understand who

31. Lemley, *Becoming What We Sing*, 102.

32. Myrick, *Music for Others*, 120.

God is, who they are, what they are doing in that place, and what is the appropriate way to behave in worship. Particular worship elements (i.e., the placement of the pulpit and the lectern, the look and placements of the Communion table and baptismal font, and the architecture of the church) help situate congregants into their tradition. Hence, the church's aesthetic sensibilities portray to the congregants how and to what end worship is enacted by the particular community. According to the Reformed interviewees, "accessibility" is especially important, and churches must be careful not to make things overly high art and ungraspable but to make them accessible enough to allow people to enter in. There must be a balance, however, since access shouldn't diminish the depth of what is being portrayed theologically. On matters of music, production, and tone, excellence is significant, along with the clarity and warmth of tone from worship leaders.

Pentecostals view the aesthetic components of worship as formative in reinforcing the community's shared religious identity and theological commitments. Because the worship practices are embodied practices, they inherently teach congregants about the essential elements of communal life and faith through the performative actions of prayer, Scripture reading, fellowship, and musical worship. Pentecostals tend to embrace contemporary, popular music styles because music powerfully mediates worship, especially when the music resonates with people in a particular (sub)culture. Pentecostals aim to show both God's accessibility and mystery portrayed in the way the elements of worship appear user-friendly, nevertheless, puzzling and mysterious to outsiders. Even as church aesthetics are, at times, inscrutable, the primary goal of church aesthetics is to help congregants enter the presence of God. As such, aesthetic sensibilities help create an atmosphere of spiritual openness for the congregants. Since Pentecostals come to worship with an expectation to encounter God, they utilize aesthetics to foster and enrich their expectation. Part of creating a space to encounter God is making sure that it authentically expresses the worshiping community's positionality. While matters of production, décor, style of dress, and architecture all help to create a reverent atmosphere of worship, they also communicate the importance of worship for the community. Aesthetic excellence communicates to the congregation that worship is a central aspect of their holistic formation.

Aesthetic formation significantly shapes the Black Gospel tradition, and this can be seen in churchgoers' style of dress. They typically wear their "Sunday best" to church. Men often wear tailored suits, ties, and polished dress shoes, and women wear elegant dresses or skirts, blouses, pearls, and ornately crafted hats. These aesthetic choices indicate the social importance worship services hold in Black communities. Black churchgoers present themselves in their best attire to bring reverence to a sacred space. One interviewee speculated that this might have to do with the historical importance of church meetings during slavery. In an era of profound oppression and dehumanization, church meetings represented a spiritual refuge where enslaved individuals could find solace, hope, and strength. Younger, contemporary Black Gospel churchgoers also dress in their Sunday best, but they do so in informal ways, blending smart casual attire with stylish urban trends. Formative aesthetic sensibilities also shape the way the worship service is conducted. While the preaching and music are often distinct in other worship traditions, in the Black Gospel context they are entirely integrated. Christian proclamation emerges from the music; they're one and the same. Those two parts of the ministry work in tandem to create an interactive space of proclamation, reception, and response.

Many Evangelical churches tend to have multiple services with different aesthetic styles. At traditional services, people often dress formally, and the musicians tend to use traditional sheet music and have traditional-style choirs. Contemporary services, on the other hand, frequently utilize full worship bands, and congregants dress casually. Because Evangelical churches have multiple, at times blended, services, it can be difficult to discern in what way the aesthetics are formative. Are the aesthetic components leading congregants to reaffirm a sense of traditionalism or a sense of newness in community? Since many Evangelical churches blend traditionalism and contemporary aesthetic sensibilities, it is evident that generational blendedness is vital in Evangelical worship. Evangelicals want to stay connected with who they have been historically even as they respond to changing times. Furthermore, because Evangelicalism is a tradition that is centered on the preached word, musical excellence is often determined by how well a song sets up or reinforces the sermon and how little it diverts from the didactic content of the overall exhortation.

The aesthetic sensibilities of Charismatic Catholic worship can best be described as a flow state between testimonial sharing, to prophecy, to singing in the Spirit, and to meditating on Scripture. There isn't much differentiation between the music and the overall worship experience; it all blends together. Each element helps worshipers discern how God is moving in their midst. The goal is to praise God until there's an experience of God's presence, at which point worshipers reflect and respond to God's presence corporately. While mainstream Catholic services utilize a traditional hymn structure—structures that have been around for hundreds of years—Charismatic Catholics use popular contemporary worship songs from major groups like Hillsong Worship and Bethel Music. These songs bear a simpler structure and are easier to pick up, which encourages the participants to be more physical in worship (e.g., raising hands). Younger gatherings even dance and jump around during worship. In terms of performance, contemporary worship utilizes improvisation, which enables times of singing in tongues. One interviewee said Charismatic

Catholic worship sees a greater degree of letting the Holy Spirit take control of the experience, rather than relying on tradition to guide worship. Charismatic Catholic worship is designed to foster a mystical encounter with the Divine.

From the interviews, we got the sense that Reformed worship uses aesthetic components to situate worshipers firmly into the life and practice of the Reformed tradition; Pentecostal worship utilizes aesthetic components to create a porous atmosphere for an experiential response of worship; Black Gospel worship views the meeting as a sacred space where preaching and music are intertwined, creating an interactive space of proclamation and response; Evangelical worship utilizes aesthetic components in worship to bridge the historical gap between generational expressions of Evangelicalism; and Charismatic Catholic worship creates a flow state between various elements of worship to foster Divine encounters. There is, of course, overlap between traditions, but each worshiping community brings some aesthetic elements that are totally unique, making way for specific forms of ministry to take place.

CONCLUSION

This chapter considered aesthetic judgment by looking at the general and contextual criteria for judging congregational worship music. We saw that both form and fit must be narratively understood to get a good grasp of what is valued by a community and why, and of how the aesthetic sensibilities create meaning. Evaluating worship through narrative fit involves considering how well the worship element fits within its narratively appropriate context. Hence, authenticity, marked by narrative fit and contextualized aesthetic value, is an integral part of aesthetic judgment. Worship is both aesthetically meaningful and emotional, and the aesthetic decisions that are made in shaping worship can play a formative role in the lives of believers.

STUDY QUESTIONS

1. Do you view aesthetic components of worship (musical style, production quality, architectural style, style of dress, church décor, etc.) as formative for your community? If so, in what way are they formative?
2. What aesthetic components are important for your worshiping community? Why do you think they're viewed as important?
3. What genres of music authentically fit your worshiping community?
4. What aesthetic responses do the songs in your worship sets typically evoke (i.e., sadness, triumph, adoration)?
5. Does your worshiping community's typical worship elements correspond well with its foundational standards of aesthetic judgment for liturgical art? Why or why not?

KEY TERMS

Aesthetic fit: determining how closely things relate to one another aesthetically.

Aesthetic judgment: a value judgment concerning one's perceptions of objects or experiences.

Aesthetics: the axiological field that studies the way in which values of appreciation are ascribed onto sensed perceptions.

Authenticity (aesthetics): an evaluative concept that, when applied to music, marks both the narrative fit and the contextualized aesthetic value of music.

Classification (aesthetics): observing the cultural practice and grouping it within a narrative tradition.

Determinant judgment: a Kantian term for judgment that is categorically subject to law, as in moral judgment.

Dynamics (music): the loudness or softness of sound.

Ethics: the axiological field that studies the way in which moral values are ascribed onto actions.

Form (music): the structure of a piece of music.

Formal elements of music: elements used to make musical compositions, which include rhythm, pitch, timbre, dynamics, texture, form, melody, and harmony.

Genre (music): the categorization of pieces of music into a shared tradition.

Harmony (music): the sounding of two or more pitches at the same time.

Indeterminant judgment: a Kantian term for judgment that is free-flowing and conditional, as in aesthetic judgment.

Melody (music): a sequence of single pitches that make up a musical line.

Narrative fit evaluation: evaluating something against the particular contextualized formal elements that have been adopted by the arbitrating community.

Narrative theory of art: art theory that seeks to identify and judge artworks by means of historical narration.

Pitch (music): the highness or lowness of sound determined by the frequency of the sound wave.

Religion (philosophy): the axiological field that studies the way in which ecclesiastical values are ascribed onto rites.

Rhythm (music): the arrangement of long and short sounds and periods of silence.

Texture (music): the way the parts or the composition are arranged in relation to the others.

Timbre (music): the tonal quality or sounds determined by the harmonic spectrum of the sound wave.

CHAPTER 3

How to Use Theological Judgment

The Confession and Content of Worship

Have you ever experienced a situation where the poetic imagery in a worship song was theologically confusing? I have. A little while back, a student in my songwriting class wrote a really fantastic worship song that expressed his adoration for Jesus. The chorus had a cool, repetitive, rhythmic flow where the lyrics quickly listed some names of God. The lyrics read, "I know a man named Jesus, *El Shaddai*, *Elohim*, *Jeshua*." I commended my student on the song in general—the structure, melody, flow, and concept where all really great! I suggested, however, that the words he used to describe Jesus were better associated with the Father, and this could be confusing for some worshipers. *El Shaddai* is first used in Genesis 17:1 and means the God who is sovereign and almighty.[1] *Elohim* is an Old Testament name for the God of Israel.[2] *Jeshua* is also Hebrew. It's a boy's given name and means savior. While *Jeshua* clearly references Christ (it's the Hebrew root

1. "El Shaddai," in J. D. Douglas and Merrill C. Tenney, rev. Moisés Silva, *Zondervan Illustrated Bible Dictionary* (Grand Rapids: Zondervan, 2011), 415.

2. "Elohim," in Douglas and Tenney, *Zondervan Illustrated Bible Dictionary*, 414.

for the name Jesus), *El Shaddai* and *Elohim* are typically associated with the Father.

Although the Father and Son are unified in Trinitarian relationship, certain names and characteristics align closer with particular persons of the Trinity. Names, concepts, and titles regarding Creator, provider, Almighty, protector, ruler, Father, and so on all associate closely with the first person of the Trinity. Savior, Redeemer, Christ, Messiah, Lamb, brother, Son, and so on associate closely with Jesus, the second person of the Trinity. Wind, dove, cloud, fire, presence, purity, empowerment, Holy Spirit, and so on associate best with the third person of the Trinity. Some images overlap (e.g., "Shepherd" and "King" are commonly associated with both Jesus and the Father, often to show Christ's oneness with the Father), but keeping imagery consistent throughout the song helps shape a worshiper's theological imagination in a way that is clear yet compelling. After taking my suggestions, the student changed the lyrics to be more consistently Christocentric. The chorus now says, "I know a man named Jesus, Emmanuel, Risen One, *Jeshua*."

In cases like this, it would be wrong to call the song theologically unsound, even in its first iteration. Confusion on how best to express something doesn't mean the meaning of the song contradicts orthodox theological beliefs. Some Christians are too quick to deem something heretical (beliefs opposing traditionally accepted church doctrine), especially when the theology is merely unclear. Furthermore, while the above case shows how a song could be theologically confusing, one might also find instances when a song's lyrics are inconsistent with some of the theological claims of his or her own particular tradition, but that doesn't make the song heretical either. After all, theologically different doesn't mean theologically wrong. As members of the same confessing church, it's important for us to approach a person's expression of worship with dignity and grace. If we assume anything, we should assume that the song came about as a deep expression of the writer's devotion to God.

Nevertheless, we can utilize hermeneutical tools to help us judge the theological fit of a congregational worship song. The theological judgment I propose here is not a divisive form of **heresy hunting**, by which some *Christians seek out faults in other Christians' theological reasoning to deem them unfit for the faith*. Rather, we will differentiate between primary, secondary, and tertiary doctrines of theology to help us delineate what topics are essential and universal for the church and what topics are malleable as they are expressed in various contextualized ways. This can help increase understanding between theological traditions and will, hopefully, increase one's appreciation toward other traditions of worship. This chapter starts by defining the confessional witness of theology and what sorts of questions theology seeks to engage. We'll discuss the main sources of theology and the primacy of Scripture for theological deliberation. We'll also look at how various beliefs are articulated uniquely in narrative context before I offer contextual perspectives on theological judgment drawn from interviews of practitioners from Reformed, Pentecostal, Black Gospel, Evangelical, and Charismatic Catholic traditions.

SOURCES OF THEOLOGICAL JUDGMENT

Does theology exist just to clearly and comprehensively explain Christian doctrine? Is it subservient to practical ministerial needs? While it does and is both of these and more, we can also understand theology as a tool that helps Christians stay faithful in worship. Theology helps us understand and express what and in whom we believe. This articulation is present internally in our prayer, praise, and preaching of the gospel within the church. It is also present externally in our bearing of the gospel to those outside the church through words and deeds. Theology helps us know what is essential for being God's community, and it helps us determine what is an acceptable range of beliefs and practices within the Christian faith. Theology shapes the content of worship, and worship helps form Christians as they think theologically. Worship both reinforces theological ideas and contextualizes confessional witness when it is grafted into a Christian tradition. In this section, we will look at what Christian confession entails and how theology shapes the content of congregational worship.

Confession and Confessional Witness

Throughout church history, Christian groups have written various **confessions**—*formal statements concerning their religious beliefs*. Broadly speaking, however, the theological concept of confession refers to the declaration of Christ's lordship and the affirmation of the gospel. In this book, we use the term "confession" in the latter, broader sense. As such, **confessional witness** can be seen as *the public testimony and proclamation of the gospel*.

When someone presents a witness to a worshiping community, worship and theology work together to help situate the witness into the broader Christian story. Before looking at theological judgment in worship, let's consider the sorts of questions that concern confessional witness and theological thought. Once we get a sense of what theological judgment entails, we can consider judging theology in worship.

In his book *Vision and Discernment*, theologian Charles Wood contends that we do not merely ascribe to some "universally valid statement" of witness.[3] Rather, we make theological judgments about claims of confessional witness through various modes of inquiry. He writes, "Judgment presupposes criteria. Whether one is attempting to judge the adequacy of some former instance of witness, or deliberating on a course of action for the future, one needs standards by which to judge. The search for what is

3. Charles Wood, *Vision and Discernment: An Orientation in Theological Study* (Eugene, OR: Wipf and Stock, 2002), 40.

constitutive of valid confessional witness is thus ingredient in the critico-creative inquiry, in each of its three basic dimensions."[4] To determine what standards of judgment are commonly used, Wood delineates what sorts of questions and disciplines constitute theological inquiry. He sees three comprehensive aims, or dimensions, surrounding theological study. These aims can be understood as clusters of questions that form theological disciplines.

The first set of questions concerns the "Christianness" of the allegedly confessional witness.[5] Is the set of beliefs truly Christian, or should it be categorized as something else? Are these experiences and reflections on experiences consistent with the Christian narrative? This sort of inquiry interests historical theologians as they seek to situate occurrences of confessional witness within a historical narrative.[6] This also corresponds with our notion of classification, discussed in chapter 2, as a mode of aesthetic judgment. Just as one already judges a work of art by classifying it as such, one also judges an instance of confessional witness by classifying it as such. When we categorize something as confessional witness, we affirm (1) that it meets all the criteria of classification thereof, and (2) that it is a genuine expression of the Christian faith. We can refer to Wood's first cluster of theological inquiry as **historical classification**.

The second set of questions concerns the veracity of the confessional witness. Is that witness really true? What truth claims is the witness implicitly making?[7] This sort of inquiry corresponds with philosophical theology because it aims to uncover the logic of the claims made through the witness and uncover the commitments operant behind the claims.[8] This parallels our discussion in chapter 2 on aesthetic evaluation.

---

4. Wood, *Vision and Discernment*, 40–41.
5. Wood, *Vision and Discernment*, 39.
6. Wood, *Vision and Discernment*, 41.
7. Wood, *Vision and Discernment*, 39.
8. Wood, *Vision and Discernment*, 45.

As in aesthetic evaluation, the claims here are judged against the narrative framework from which they emerge. In other words, the theological claims are contextually true. Saying "God is faithful in covenant" means nothing to a nontheistic naturalist. To a Reformed Christian, however, that sentiment reflects his or her theological framework and describes an appropriate attitude toward life's circumstances. The truth of the claim is narratively bound. We can refer to this cluster of theological inquiry as **epistemological evaluation**.

Finally, the third set of questions concerns theological fit. Is the witness appropriately related to the context? Is it fittingly enacted?[9] Not only do these questions look at the context surrounding a witness but they determine how well it fits into a narrative framework, practically speaking. Wood sees these questions as dealing with enacted practices—the actions of a Christian community. Since it considers how theology is enacted in Christian practices, this type of inquiry corresponds with practical theology.[10] Wood writes, "Christian witness is borne by the actions of Christians and Christian communities, and by their very being *as* Christians and communities. It is both official and unofficial, formal and informal, explicit and implicit, verbal and nonverbal."[11] Practical theology looks deeply at what the church does and judges it against its guiding narrative. In this regard, judging for theological fit is similar to judging for authenticity in aesthetic evaluation. Both consider fittingness as an important evaluative criteria. We can refer to this cluster of theological inquiry as **authenticity judgment**.

Connecting Theology to Worship

While historical evaluation, epistemological evaluation, and authenticity judgment help us determine the appropriate location

9. Wood, *Vision and Discernment*, 40.
10. Wood, *Vision and Discernment*, 47.
11. Wood, *Vision and Discernment*, 47.

of a confessional witness, we still must determine what sorts of sources or authorities these evaluative tools are measured against. Many theological methods recognize the following tools, sources, authorities, or contexts that play into theological reflection: **Scripture** (the Holy Bible, which is recognized by all Christian traditions as inspired by God), **reason** (*the principles of logic but also tools from both the sciences and humanities, such as philosophy, sociology, and psychology*), **experience** (*individual, or common human phenomenon*), **tradition** (*the ecclesial tradition, or any kind of faith tradition*), and **community** (*the faith community that surrounds the confessional witness*). Considering these sources, theological judgment discerns the truth and fit of confessional witness in a broader Christian context. Since confessional witness concerns the public testimony and proclamation of the gospel, **theological judgment** *considers past, present, and prospective instances of witness and determines if they genuinely express the Christian faith.*[12]

Theology and worship exist in a mutually coextensive relationship. Theology provides the intellectual foundation for worship since it is based on the narrative principles that inform how Christians understand and relate to God. Theology also informs the content and structure of worship when it helps shape the liturgy and order of worship, as well as the selection of Scripture readings and music. Worship expresses theology through its use of preaching, prayer, music, and other liturgical elements to express beliefs about God and Christian living. It provides a platform for Christians to put their theological beliefs into practice and to deepen their understanding of God.

It should be noted, however, that the theology expressed in worship is narratively and contextually bound. We reinforce through worship not only general theological beliefs but also tradition-specific theological beliefs. The way God is imaged

---

12. Wood, *Vision and Discernment*, 73.

in worship varies among traditions.[13] Theologian and worship scholar Don Saliers puts it well: "Human beings pray and worship out of received traditions of practice and thought. Just as any reading of Sacred Scripture inherits ways of reading and interpretation, so ways of worship and prayer inherit a history of practices. These are always embedded and embodied in cultural forms: music, language, gesture, images, and particular ritual actions."[14]

Not only does theology inform our worship but what we believe about God is shaped by how we worship and why, which is determined in large part by our specific Christian tradition.[15] A community's worship is thus a generative practice that is borne out of tradition—it's a negotiation between what has been taught and new instances of witness.[16] Having considered how theology is judged and how this connects to worship, we will next distinguish between the primary, secondary, and tertiary beliefs of Christian traditions to determine which beliefs are essential and should thus be safeguarded and which are flexible.

PRIMARY BELIEFS IN NARRATIVE CONTEXT

Espoused theology refers to *explicitly proclaimed theological beliefs*.[17] Truly, I cannot recall a single instance where the espoused theology of a contemporary worship song was heretical. I've experienced, as indicated in the introduction of this chapter, instances of theological confusion or theological particularity in the lyrics

13. Don E. Saliers, "God and Worship," in *Theological Foundations of Worship: Biblical, Systematic, and Practical Perspectives*, ed. Khalia J. Williams and Mark A. Lamport (Grand Rapids: Baker Academic, 2021), 53.

14. Saliers, "God and Worship," 58.

15. Saliers, "God and Worship," 57.

16. Saliers, "God and Worship," 57.

17. Glenn Packiam makes the helpful distinction between "espoused" and "operant" theology. While espoused theology is explicitly stated, operant theology is what is implicitly encoded in the worship. See Glenn Packiam, *Worship and the World to Come: Exploring Christian Hope in Contemporary Worship* (Downers Grove, IL: IVP Academic, 2020), 105.

of congregational worship songs, but heresy? No. For a worship song to be heretical, it would have to deny one of the basic beliefs of the Christian faith. I'm reminded of a story a worship pastor friend of mine told me about his friend who was an evangelist. This young, trendy evangelist was the main speaker at a youth conference. He came up toward the end of the worship set to lead the students further into a time of ministry as they transitioned to the sermon. The evangelist was fired up by what was happening. The students were highly engaged with raised hands and joyous shouting, and the band played a prolonged "trash can ending" to wrap up the worship set. The evangelist started shouting, "Jesus is alive!" And the students responded with loud cheers. He repeated, "Jesus is alive!" The crowd got even more frantic. Then, in a moment of pure, adrenaline-filled ecstasy, he blurted out, "Jesus never died!" The crowd responded with a mixture of excitement and confusion. *Did he just say Jesus never died?*

The next day, after realizing what he had done, the evangelist made a social media post apologizing for getting caught up in the moment and failing to recognize the theological impact of his words. Fundamentally, if Jesus never died, then he never atoned for the sins of humanity and salvation would not be possible. The evangelist knew this, but he had a major slipup! Although this didn't come about in the lyrics of a congregational worship song, this was an actual instance of heresy during a worship set. The evangelist denied (seemingly by accident) a primary doctrine of the Christian faith. This was an instance of heresy because it denied the cross, and a denial of the cross renders the Christian faith erroneous. After all, Paul tells us that if Christ did not die and resurrect, then our proclamation and faith are in vain (1 Cor. 15:14).

We can laugh about the accidental outrageousness of what the evangelist said, but it demonstrates how serious we take the denial of a primary Christian belief. While differences with secondary and tertiary beliefs should be met with toleration as we seek further dialogue, differences with primary beliefs are necessarily discordant. To be a Christian, one must be a devoted follower of Christ. This is a relational matter that entails loving God with all our heart, soul, and mind (Matt. 22:37). Doctrinally speaking, however, a Christian must affirm and confess the primary Christian beliefs of the faith. Put succinctly, **heresy** constitutes *a denial of a primary Christian doctrine*. We should bear in mind, however, that some Christians have difficulty expressing their theological beliefs. We must recognize that discipleship also entails intellectual growth in the faith. It would therefore be better to deem heresy as the intentional denial of a primary Christian belief. It is intention that separates the wolf from the confused sheep. This leads us to an obvious question, what are the primary Christian beliefs?

The Creeds and Theological Triage

In his book *Finding the Right Hills to Die On*, pastor and theologian Gavin Ortlund helpfully differentiates primary, secondary, and tertiary beliefs through what he calls "theological triage." Triage is a medical term that refers to the ordering of medical care by urgency. **Theological triage** *orders doctrines according to their significance for the Christian faith*.[18] Ortlund describes a fourfold schema for understanding the importance of beliefs: first-rank doctrines, which are essential to the gospel; second-rank doctrines, which are urgent for the church but not essential; third-rank doctrines, which are important but not essential or urgent; and fourth-rank doctrines, which are indifferent and theologically unimportant.[19] To determine what rank a doctrine falls under, Ortlund suggests asking four questions:

---

18. Gavin Ortlund, *Finding the Right Hills to Die On: The Case for Theological Triage* (Wheaton, IL: Crossway, 2020), 17–18.

19. Ortlund, *Finding the Right Hills to Die On*, 47. Throughout this section, we will consider only the first-, second-, and third-rank doctrines since fourth-rank doctrines are, by Ortlund's own admission, not theologically important.

1. How clear is *the Bible* on this doctrine?
2. What is this doctrine's importance to *the gospel*?
3. What is the testimony of the *historical church* concerning this doctrine?
4. What is this doctrine's effect upon the *church* today?[20]

The questions here determine the biblical, theological, historical, and practical weight of the doctrine. If the doctrine has little bearing on any of these concerns, then it is likely not a primary doctrine. While Ortlund's insight is helpful, another way to determine primary Christian beliefs is to look at the church's ancient confessions. In particular the church has historically codified primary Christian beliefs through its ecumenical creeds.

In theology, a **creed** is *a formal statement of beliefs that is used to express the foundational tenets of the faith*. The so-called ***ecumenical* creeds** refer, typically, to *three of Christianity's oldest creeds: the Nicene-Constantinopolitan Creed (381), the Athanasian Creed (c. fifth century), and the Apostles' Creed (its final form is c. sixth century).*[21] They're called ecumenical because they are thought to encapsulate the faithful witness of all Christians. These creeds functioned as a means of summarizing biblical material and providing normative exegesis against what were deemed, at the time, heretical interpretations. They also provided Christians a starting point and grammar for discussing and reflecting on theology. They functioned as signposts inviting people to reflect on Scripture and eventually functioned as an important part of early church corporate worship.

Today the creeds help us consult the wisdom of Christians from the past as we look out to the church's contemporary needs.[22]

---

20. Ortlund, *Finding the Right Hills to Die On*, 79, emphasis original.

21. See Christian Reformed Church, *Ecumenical Creeds and Reformed Confessions*, 2nd ed. (Boca Raton, FL: CRC Publications, 1987).

22. J. V. Fesko, *The Need for Creeds Today: Confessional Faith in a Faithless Age* (Grand Rapids: Baker Academic, 2020), 15.

The creeds weren't meant to confine or restrict church doctrine toward a rigid fundamentalism but are broad enough to allow for "doctrinal flexibility," which makes room for differing opinions on theological topics.[23] This helps us avoid "majoring on the minors" as we differentiate what is essential to the faith.

Primary, Secondary, and Tertiary Beliefs

The creeds also help us distinguish between primary, secondary, and tertiary theological beliefs. **Primary beliefs** are *basic beliefs that are fundamental to the Christian faith*. The basic Christian beliefs professed in the ecumenical creeds are the following: God created all things; God is one and triune; humanity fell; Jesus is God incarnated; Jesus atoned for our sins on the cross; Jesus' death and resurrection enable our salvation; the Holy Spirit indwells believers; the Holy Spirit empowers the church for ministry; Christ will return and make all things new; God's people will resurrect in glory and reign with Christ forever. These are primary, first-rank doctrines because a denial of any of these basic Christian beliefs would be a denial of the Christian faith.

Secondary beliefs constitute the *doctrinal variations that underlie the primary declarations*. For instance, that God is Creator is a primary theological concern, but how God went about creating (i.e., fiat creationism, progressive creation, theistic evolution) is a secondary concern. That Christ atoned for our sins on the cross is a primary theological concern, while how atonement works (i.e., propitiation, substitution, moral exemplar) is a secondary concern. That Christ will return is a primary theological concern, but when Christ will return (i.e., premillennialism, postmillennialism, amillennialism) is a secondary concern. Secondary theological concerns are crucially important for fleshing out a tradition's theological leanings. While primary theological concerns determine if a person should

23. Fesko, *The Need for Creeds Today*, 87.

be classified a Christian or not, secondary theological concerns determine what Christian tradition (e.g., Eastern Orthodox, Roman Catholic, Lutheran, Reformed, Anglican, Baptist) the believer subscribes to.

Since secondary beliefs are contextually bound by tradition and shift around according to context, they have caused many schisms in the church. Splits happen when important secondary theological issues are observed as primary concerns. For instance, many Pentecostals and Black Gospel worshipers view Spirit baptism and the continuation of spiritual gifts as a matter of primary theological concern. Many Evangelicals view biblical inerrancy as a primary theological concern. Many Reformed Christians view penal-substitutionary atonement as a primary theological concern. Catholics believe baptism is necessary for salvation and thus a primary theological concern. Each of these issues is essential for the respective tradition's theological narrative, so the traditions have good reason to elevate them to primary theological concerns.

Is it accurate, however, to say that the more particular beliefs in Spirit baptism, biblical inerrancy, penal-substitutionary atonement, or baptism are necessary to classify a person as a Christian? What if the person already affirms the Holy Spirit, scriptural authority, Christ's atonement, and the importance of baptism in broader terms? In other words, must a person believe these particular versions of the primary doctrine to be considered a Christian? Many Pentecostals would say Christians who do not believe in Spirit baptism are theologically lacking, but they would refrain from saying they are not Christians. Likewise, many Evangelicals would say a denial of biblical inerrancy is dangerous and can lead to a slippery slope of unbelief, but that does not mean they're not Christians. Many Reformed Christians see penal substitution as the best way to describe the atonement but not necessarily the only way. Many Catholics even recognize the validity of properly administered baptism from other traditions, a key step for ecumenical dialogue across traditions.[24] All this is to say that secondary theological beliefs are important and should be held securely but with a relaxed grip. They should not be elevated to a degree of primary concern that makes ecumenical dialogue and partnership impossible.

Finally, **tertiary beliefs** constitute *doctrinal variations within a secondary doctrine*. For instance, a tradition that subscribes to the secondary theological belief of premillennialism might argue about (and often does!) when Christ will return in relation to the great tribulation. The pretribulational, midtribulational, and posttribulational views of the rapture only make sense in a dispensational premillennial framework. This tertiary theological debate is important to many Evangelicals and Pentecostals, but most Reformed and Catholic Christians are post- or amillennial. In other words, this premillennial argument has little theological bearing on a Presbyterian or Catholic's eschatology. Tertiary issues are hardly worth splitting over, so holding these views with an open hand allows us to maintain a humble disposition as we show grace toward one another. A lot of Christian infighting can cease when we perform theological triage in this way.

People serving in ministry might notice that while these neat categories are helpful for understanding theological judgment, they often get very messy in real-life settings. How do we respond to the blurring of primary and secondary issues? How should, for instance, the universal church, which is predominately Trinitarian, take Unitarian and Oneness views of the Godhead? They may deny the Trinity but still see salvation as only available through Christ crucified. **Heterodoxy** refers to *beliefs that differ from those officially sanctioned by the Christian faith*. Does the

24. See *Catechism of the Catholic Church: Complete and Updated* (New York: USCCB Publishing, 1995), pt. 2, sec. 2, art. 7, para. 1271–72. These paragraphs recognize the validity of baptism from other traditions as long as they are done with water and in the name of the Father, Son, and Holy Spirit.

heterodoxy of Unitarians and Oneness Pentecostals equate to heresy? Furthermore, if you were to poll congregants from your church, how many of them could actually describe the Trinity without accidently falling into heresy? The analogies we use to describe the Trinity (e.g., God is like an egg with three parts or God is like H_20) tend to portray heresies like tritheism or modalism rather than the post-Athanasian formula of one *ousia* in three *hypostases*. The point is, theological triage gets messy in ministerial practice, and we best serve our congregations when we are open to dialogue and mutual development. Nevertheless, as ministers we have a duty to balance this open dialogue with faithful guidance. Relationships require mutuality and trust, and too often theological judgment is used to create division or forced indoctrination. We must utilize theological judgment to bring clarity and confidence to our congregants, not to stifle dialogue and suppress originality in thought.

Thinking in terms of primary, secondary, and tertiary beliefs, we can use theological judgment for congregational worship music in three ways: First, we must assure that the espoused theology in a worship song's lyrics demonstrates faithfulness to primary Christian beliefs. It is here where the worship pastor as shepherd protects the flock from the wolves of false doctrine. Any doctrine that intentionally denies a primary Christian belief must be discarded lest we open the door for cultic sectarianism. As mentioned before, it is hard to find this sort of error in contemporary Christian worship—most points of disagreement occur between secondary and tertiary beliefs. Nevertheless, the worship pastor must use theological judgment well to safeguard primary Christian beliefs in congregational worship.

Second, we must assure that the espoused secondary beliefs align authentically with the worshiping community's theological tradition. Here theological judgment concerns evaluating the fit of a song's theology against its tradition. The espoused secondary belief may not be wrong in itself, but if it differs enough from the worshiping community's theological tradition, then it could cause theological confusion for the community. If the theological motif is too unfamiliar to the tradition's guiding narrative, the worshiping community might have trouble engaging with it.

THEOLOGICAL FIT OF WORSHIP SONGS

Andrew Ray Williams, a Pentecostal theologian and senior pastor from Virginia, has admitted to vetoing songs because of theological fit. In particular he chooses to avoid songs that champion "an over-realized eschatology" or songs that are overly triumphalistic. At times, however, Andrew provides his church with reasoning for why a particular song is included in the worship service:

> Sometimes I will provide commentary on a song before or after it is sung during the worship song set. The song "King of My Heart," for example, has a bridge that repeatedly states, "You're never gonna let me down." Before singing this part of the song, I will state that this is indeed not a truthful and honest disposition before God. Indeed, God will let us down. But if we are going to sing this at all, we must sing it eschatologically—we must sing it recognizing that in the end, all letdowns will be righted in light of God's transformation of the cosmos and all things therein. I give that framing, or I don't allow us to sing the bridge.

Here the pastor is choosing to reframe the content of the song so it does not become theologically confusing for the congregants. This is also a good pastoral device because explaining the lyrics of a worship song can help boost understanding, encourage participation, deepen spiritual connection, and build community among the congregants. Instead of avoiding the song outright, the pastor has created an opportunity for a richer dialogue concerning a pertinent theological theme.

Worse, because the secondary belief is alien to them, the congregants may think they are performing something heretical when in actuality the belief is only theologically different. Realizing the contextual nature of secondary beliefs can help worship practitioners appreciate the nonprimary differences in other worship traditions. The worship pastor must use theological judgment well to know what his or her congregation is able to receive and how.

Third and finally, we must avoid the inclusion of divisive tertiary beliefs in congregational worship music. Since tertiary beliefs are those we hold with open hands, they should not enter our liturgies. Liturgies are spiritually formational, so we must be wise to include only theological concepts that aid in both our individual formation and our communal fellowship. While tertiary beliefs are interesting to discuss and debate, they do not bear on a person's salvation or spiritual formation, and they tend to cause division or unnecessary sectarianism in worshiping communities. The worship pastor must use theological judgment well to know what beliefs are divisive and unnecessary and ultimately unfit for congregational worship. When theological judgment is used in these three ways, worship pastors can protect primary beliefs, affirm contextual secondary beliefs, and discard divisive tertiary beliefs in congregational worship.

CONTEXTUAL PERSPECTIVES ON THEOLOGICAL JUDGMENT IN WORSHIP

Now that we've established a sense of what theological judgment entails in terms of confessional witness and content, we will look at some of the particular theological values of the five traditions assessed throughout this book. In particular we will look at the distinctive approaches of the various communities' theological narratives and how they are expressed in worship.

"Covenant" is an important theological theme in Reformed worship. Calvinists see covenant as providing a framework for understanding salvation, the relationship between God and the people, and the significance of the sacraments. In other words, much of the language of the creation-fall-redemption-consummation motif discussed in chapter 1 is understood through the framework of a covenantal theology. Many Reformed ministers use denominationally endorsed hymnals, so the songs have already been scrutinized and accepted. In these cases, what is most important is selecting songs that demonstrate theological balance so a full range of the Christian story is portrayed throughout the worship service. However, the Reformed churches that perform contemporary worship typically sing songs that are general enough that congregants don't really scrutinize the lyrics. Yet when songs implicitly demonstrate second-rank theological issues from other theological traditions, ministers will either avoid performing those songs or will edit the songs to be more resonant with their own community's theological convictions.

As discussed in chapter 1, Pentecostals tend to engage a "now-and-not-yet" approach to worship. They see the Spirit's presence in worship as an eschatological inbreaking. While the cross is pivotal for establishing discipleship, there is a connection between the cross, Pentecost, and the eschaton, as future possibilities are seen in a believer's present reality through worship. Spiritual gifts and divine healings (physical, emotional, and social) are all understood in this frame as foretastes of the ultimate healing that is to come. Throughout Pentecostalism, now-and-not-yet theology is closely linked to the experience of the Holy Spirit. Christoforming discipleship happens when the Spirit breaks into the present and believers are subsumed into life in the Spirit. Because Christ and the Spirit are inextricably linked, Pentecostals generally perform songs that are expressive and theologically focused on both the Spirit and Christ. And because they tend toward a theology of encounter, Pentecostals can tell from the congregation's response when a song is noticeably not theologically fitting.

While the Black Christian tradition is not monolithic, a consistent theme is that every rendition of Black theology clearly demonstrates the importance of context when interpreting biblical texts and religious experiences. In particular Black theology is deeply rooted in the lived experiences, struggles, and communal expressions of Black Christians. Biblical scholar Esau McCaulley refers to *the distinctive theological approach that emerges from the experiences and perspectives of Black church communities* as **Black ecclesial theology.**[25] Accordingly, Black Gospel worship expresses orthodox theological beliefs from the context of the Black lived experience. Songs, therefore, tend to inspire hope and resilience in the midst of both societal and everyday struggles. One interviewee said songs are like sermons or altars: They encourage and minister to worshipers in many different ways throughout their day-to-day lives. Participation in worship allows congregants to reframe their social circumstances in light of God's redemptive, liberative work and promises. Similar to Pentecostalism, when a Black Gospel worshiping community finds a song not theologically fitting, they might respond politely by continuing to sing but will refrain from responding expressively.

Evangelical worship focuses on Scripture, discipleship, and Christocentrism. Singing Scripture is seen as a powerful way to engage with God's Word, deepening the congregants' relationships with God and others. This emphasis helps congregants internalize biblical truth, which reinforces the faith and promotes unity within the church. Because Evangelical worship is generally Christocentric, some popular worship songs may be omitted from a church's repertoire, not because they're unbiblical or untrue but because they're not centered on Jesus. But if the song is clearly rooted in a biblical passage and focuses on Christ, Evangelicals

25. Esau McCaulley, *Reading While Black: African American Biblical Interpretation as an Exercise in Hope* (Downers Grove, IL: IVP Academic, 2020), 5.

will feel comfortable performing it in worship even if the song was written by a believer outside Evangelicalism.

Theologically, Charismatic Catholic worship seems to embrace an eschatological vision of worship. Theologian Scott Hahn argues that the Mass is best understood as an experience of heaven on earth. In worship, Catholics participate in heavenly worship, and through the Eucharist, Catholics receive in the present a forestate of what will become of them. He writes, "In the Eucharist we receive what we will *be* for all eternity, when we are taken up to heaven to join with the heavenly throng in the marriage supper of the Lamb. At Holy Communion, we are already there."[26] Hahn sees the act of Communion as literal participation in the marriage supper of the Lamb recounted in Revelation 19:6–9. Charismatic Catholics put a Pentecostal spin on Hahn's eschatological insight, emphasizing the active and ongoing presence of the Spirit in the lives of believers, similar to the experiences described in Acts. Hence, while Charismatic Catholics look forward to the future fulfillment of God's kingdom, they also emphasize experiencing God's kingdom in the here and now through the power and work of the Spirit. This reflects a realized aspect of eschatology where the blessings and presence of the kingdom are partially realized in the present. **Realized eschatology** *interprets certain eschatological events as already having been fulfilled, at least partially, in the present rather than awaiting entirely on future realization.* There are also ecumenical reasons for enacting a realized eschatology in worship—when Catholics and Protestants join together in worship, they experience a foretaste of what is hoped for in Revelation when every tribe and tongue join together in worship before the Lamb (Rev. 7:9).[27] Ecumenical outreach across denominations is important for Charismatic

26. Scott Hahn, *The Lamb's Supper: The Mass as Heaven on Earth* (New York: Doubleday, 1999), 56–57.

27. William Kangas, "Worship in the Charismatic Renewal: A Case Study in the Word of God Community" (PhD diss., Catholic University of America, 2022), 307.

Catholics, which is evidenced by the joint prayer meetings they often host where outside denominations are invited to join in worship. These meetings emphasize unity in the Spirit through common worship practices.

Throughout this section, we saw that the five worshiping communities assessed all utilize theological judgment to affirm their own tradition's beliefs while discarding beliefs that veer too far away from what their communities validate. We saw that Reformed worship utilizes a covenantal framework and the creation-fall-redemption-consummation motif to understand its liturgical expressions; Pentecostal worship operates in a now-and-not-yet theology that sees the Spirit's presence in worship as an eschatological inbreaking; Black Gospel worship embodies orthodox theology through the lens of the Black experience; Evangelical worship theologically focuses on Scripture, discipleship, and Christocentrism; and Charismatic Catholic worship seeks to experience God's kingdom in the present through the Eucharist and gathered worship. Although we will often find overlap and agreement between these church traditions, especially as they express primary theological beliefs, we can see how each tradition has a distinctive theological framework that guides its confessional witness.

CONCLUSION

This chapter looked at theological judgment first by discussing the sorts of proclamations that constitute Christian witness. Theology and worship are closely connected—theology provides the foundation and shapes the content and structure of worship. Worship expresses theology and reinforces tradition-specific beliefs. Our understanding of God is shaped by how we worship in our particular Christian traditions. Utilizing the concept of theological triage, we distinguished between primary, secondary, and tertiary doctrines to see what sorts of theological ideas should guide the lyrics of congregational worship music. We saw that differences primarily arise in secondary and tertiary beliefs, so pastors and worship leaders must evaluate whether a song aligns with the worshiping community's theological tradition. By using theological judgment effectively, pastors can safeguard primary beliefs, affirm contextual secondary beliefs, and discard divisive tertiary beliefs in worship.

STUDY QUESTIONS

1. How can worship music express theological convictions implicitly and explicitly?
2. Have you experienced any songs in your church's worship set that have theologically confusing lyrics?
3. Have you experienced any songs in your church's worship set that explicitly portray theological ideas from a different theological tradition than your home church?
4. Do the worship songs you are familiar with primarily portray primary or secondary theological beliefs?
5. Does your worshiping community strive to engage a broad Christian audience or a specific tradition within Christianity?

KEY TERMS

Authenticity judgment (theology): determining how well a confessional witness fits into a theological narrative framework.

Black ecclesial theology: the distinctive theological approach that emerges from the experiences and perspectives of Black church communities.

Community: the faith community that surrounds the confessional witness; often recognized as an authoritative source for theology.

Confession (theology): a formal statement concerning one's religious beliefs.

Confessional witness: the public testimony and proclamation of the gospel.

Creed: a formal statement of beliefs that is used to express the foundational tenets of the faith.

Ecumenical creeds: three of Christianity's oldest creeds, including the Nicene-Constantinopolitan Creed (381), the Athanasian Creed (c. fifth century), and the Apostles' Creed (its final form is c. sixth century).

Epistemological evaluation (theology): uncovering the logic of the claims made through the witness, and the commitments operant behind those claims.

Espoused theology: explicitly proclaimed theological beliefs.

Experience: individual or common human phenomenon; often recognized as an authoritative source for theology.

Heresy (theology): the intentional denial of a primary Christian doctrine.

Heresy hunting: when Christians seek out faults in other Christians' theological reasoning to deem them unfit for the faith.

Heterodoxy: beliefs that differ from those officially sanctioned by the Christian faith.

Historical classification (theology): categorizing something as a confessional witness by affirming it is a genuine expression of the Christian faith.

Primary beliefs (theology): basic beliefs that are fundamental to the Christian faith.

Realized eschatology: a theological view that interprets certain eschatological events as already having been fulfilled, at least partially, in the present rather than awaiting entirely on future realization.

Reason: the principles of logic and tools from both the sciences and humanities such as philosophy, sociology, and psychology; often recognized as an authoritative source for theology.

Revelation (theology): the disclosure of knowledge that comes directly from God.

Secondary beliefs (theology): doctrinal variations that underlie the primary declarations.

Tertiary beliefs (theology): doctrinal variations within a secondary doctrine.

Theological judgment: a type of judgment that considers past, present, and prospective instances of witness and determines if they genuinely express the Christian faith.

Theological triage: the ordering of doctrines according to their significance for the Christian faith.

Tradition: an ecclesial tradition, or any kind of faith tradition; often recognized as an authoritative source for theology.

CHAPTER 4

How to Use Pastoral Judgment

The Ministry and Formation of Worship

I remember talking to a worship pastor friend about what songs his church currently had in rotation for their Sunday morning worship services. He mentioned that his congregation was not doing Cory Asbury's "Reckless Love," a song released through Bethel Music, a Charismatic music label that originated out of Bethel Church in Redding, California. This caught me by surprise because, at the time, "Reckless Love" was one of the most popular contemporary worship songs, winning two GMA Dove Awards in 2018 and being nominated for a Grammy in 2019. It's still played regularly in churches across the globe today. Because of the song's immense popularity, and because my friend leads contemporary worship at a Pentecostal church, I figured the song's exclusion must have had to do with the controversy surrounding the song's title.

For a season, "Reckless Love" provoked controversy because of its use of the word "reckless" to describe God's divine love. Some argue that it is theologically inappropriate to call God's love reckless.[1]

1. See John Piper, "Should We Sing of God's 'Reckless Love'?" Desiring God, May 25, 2018, www.desiringgod.org/interviews/should-we-sing-of-gods-reckless-love; Joshua Pelletier, "Reckless Love: Theological Review," Ratio Christi, July 23, 2019, https://

I have argued elsewhere, however, that the use of "reckless" in the title is metaphorical, not literal.[2] It is, in fact, a qualifying metaphor, purposefully qualifying the noun "love" with an adjective that doesn't fit well with it. But that's the point of metaphors—they cause friction between concepts to produce new ways of understanding ideas. By qualifying love this way, we get a sense that God's love is passionate and zealous, and that God, out of love, would even go into harm's way for us.

While one might agree that "reckless" describes God's love fittingly in a metaphorical sense, my friend told me that the theological controversy was not why he didn't include it in his repertoire. In fact, my friend liked the song and agreed with my defense of its title. He chose to leave it out of the rotation for a pastoral reason, not a theological one. He told me that his particular congregation was made up of many ex-addicts, and using the word "reckless," metaphorically or not, would conjure up images of irresponsible behavior that the ex-addicts knew all too well. Recklessness for an addict means acting selfishly and dangerously to feed their addictions. This is not what Asbury meant when he wrote the song and not what most of us take away from it when it is performed. My friend didn't think the song was theologically wrong, but rather he thought it would be pastorally irresponsible to include the song for his particular congregation. In other words, my friend used pastoral judgment to discern the song's fit for his church's congregational worship.

What this episode reveals is that beyond biblical, aesthetic,

---

ratiochristi.org/blog/reckless-love-theological-review/?gclid=CjwKCAjw_YShBhAiEiwAMomsENzSKgeYJYdx8pDxMCBMHg22OkBMr26PySCsThmr5TWrf6GydJU_6BoCiRUQAvD_BwE; Will Young, "Is 'Reckless Love' an Accurate Depiction of God?" *Liberty Champion*, April 24, 2018, www.liberty.edu/champion/2018/04/reckless-love-accurate-depiction-god/; Georgi Boorman, "Sorry, Bethel Music, but God's Love Just Isn't 'Reckless,'" The Federalist, December 28, 2018, https://thefederalist.com/2018/12/28/sorry-bethel-music-gods-love-just-isnt-reckless/.

2. See Steven Félix-Jäger, *Renewal Worship: A Theology of Pentecostal Doxology* (Downers Grove, IL: InterVarsity, 2022), 171–75.

and theological judgment, a fourth form of judgment is needed to assess congregational worship: pastoral judgment. Pastoral judgment in worship involves discerning what songs and worship elements will be most beneficial and meaningful for the worshiping community, while also remaining true to the traditions and teachings of the church or ministry. This chapter profiles pastoral ministry to get a sense of what pastoral judgment entails. It discusses the holistically formative functions of pastoral ministry, especially as it concerns spiritual and moral formation. This chapter also looks at the various titles and responsibilities musical worship leaders are given and how this differs across denominations. Finally, this chapter offers contextual perspectives on pastoral judgment as we once again consider the interviews that were conducted for this book.

PASTORAL JUDGMENT IN SPIRITUAL AND MORAL FORMATION

Before we consider pastoral judgment, it is important for us to define the role of a pastor in pastoral ministry. A **pastor** is *a spiritual leader who serves and leads a congregation of believers in a church or ministry*. Pastors are responsible for guiding the congregation's religious sensibilities, which concern both spiritual and moral formation. Led by the Holy Spirit, pastors seek to foster the holistic development of the congregants as they all grow together in community. Since pastors have been called by God to serve and lead their faith community, they should seek to faithfully fulfill that calling with humility, dedication, and compassion.

In John, Jesus refers to himself as the Good Shepherd to describe his own role in caring for his followers. In John 10:11 he says, "I am the good shepherd. The good shepherd lays down his life for the sheep." This passage emphasizes the sacrificial nature of pastoral ministry, as well as the importance of caring for and protecting the members of one's congregation. The type of authority given to a pastor is like that of a shepherd—it's noncoercive and based on "covenant fidelity, caring, mutuality, and the expectation of emphatic understanding."[3] Thus "shepherding" becomes the pivotal analogy for contemporary pastoral ministry as it's modeled after Christ's own ministry on earth.

The shepherding analogy draws from the image of a shepherd who cares for and tends to a flock of sheep, providing protection, guidance, and nourishment. As theologian Thomas Oden writes,

> This is the vocation of the pastor: to know the parish territory, its dangers, its green meadows, its steep precipices, its seasons and possibilities. The pastor leads the flock to spring water and safe vegetation. The flock recognize their own good through the shepherd's voice. They do not see it in their interest to follow strangers. They know their own shepherd will not mislead them. The shepherd is able to anticipate their needs in advance and is willing to deal with each one individually.[4]

Similarly, **pastoral ministry** *involves providing spiritual care and guidance to a community of believers*. A pastor is responsible for leading and guiding the congregation, just as a shepherd leads and guides the flock. Pastors provide spiritual nourishment through preaching and teaching, offer pastoral care and counseling, and create a sense of community and belonging within the church. A pastor also safeguards the congregation from spiritual dangers and provides a safe and welcoming environment for all members.

According to Oden, pastors serve their worshiping communities both as priests and as prophets. Pastors operate in priestly roles when they serve as chief liturgists for their worshiping communities. A **liturgist** is *someone who leads the worship service and*

---

3. Thomas Oden, *Pastoral Theology: Essentials of Ministry* (New York: HarperCollins, 1983), 53.

4. Oden, *Pastoral Theology*, 52.

is responsible for planning and leading the order of worship for the church. Liturgists organize, interpret, and preside over the worship of their communities. As liturgists, pastors must be prepared for worship and must help others prepare for worship as well.[5] Pastors also operate in prophetic roles when they speak on behalf of God to the congregants. Preaching and interpreting Scripture is a prophetic task as it aligns people to the will of God and motivates them toward action.[6] One distinctive aspect of pastoral ministry is that both the priestly and the prophetic offices are merged into the same ordained public office.[7] Pastors lead congregants in prayers, preaching, Scripture readings, pastoral counseling, and more as they provide moral, spiritual, and religious guidance to their congregants.

Pastoral Roles in Worship

As we consider the profile of pastoral ministry detailed above, it becomes evident that the musical worship leader's role is fundamentally pastoral. I am using the somewhat cumbersome title **musical worship leader** here to demarcate *the minister who leads a church's congregational worship music.* As we'll see next section, different churches use specific titles for the musical worship leader depending on how their tradition defines their liturgical structures. Nevertheless, what can be said is that the musical worship leader's role is that it functions pastorally in a significant way. This point frames our sense of what constitutes pastoral judgment. **Pastoral judgment** refers to *the process of evaluating and making judgments about the holistic (spiritual, physical, and emotional) needs of individuals in a worshiping community.* It constitutes determining the best course of action that helps someone in their spiritual or emotional journey and making judgments about the corporal and moral direction of the whole community.

5. Oden, *Pastoral Theology*, 90.
6. Oden, *Pastoral Theology*, 86.
7. Oden, *Pastoral Theology*, 86–87.

Pastoral judgment is thus based on the application of biblical and theological principles to the specific circumstances and needs of the individual or group.

While biblical, aesthetic, and theological judgments have determinable criteria for adjudication, pastoral judgment is less descript as it entails a musical worship leader's ability to foster spiritual and moral growth through congregational worship. This sort of judgment is weighed against its results. Are the congregants growing spiritually and morally? Do the songs we choose to sing together powerfully aid the congregants' spiritual formation? What "waters and pastures" should we lead our congregants to? These sorts of questions determine the pastoral strength of congregational worship music.

Worship scholar John Witvliet points out that to lead others toward spiritual and moral formation through musical worship, a worship leader must first see their task as a Spirit-led calling. He writes, "Worship leadership requires spiritual maturity and a desire to grow in the knowledge and love of the Lord. . . . As with any other ministry or vocation within the church, it is a calling. The Spirit gifts some for this ministry. It is our challenge to cultivate those gifts and refine them for the building up of the church."[8] By grace the Spirit makes each movement of worship possible, so the Spirit has the leading role in our worship.[9] Thus, the task of the musical worship leader is to be sensitive to the Spirit's leading. To lead the congregation, the musical worship leader must first follow God's lead. This requires humility, spiritual maturity, and obedience to God. To faithfully serve in this capacity, the musical worship leader must be prayerful and guard against emotional, spiritual, or political distractions. If the musical worship leader wishes to aid the congregation's holistic formation, he or she must first be invested in their own holistic

8. John Witvliet, *Worship Seeking Understanding: Windows into Christian Practice* (Grand Rapids: Baker Academic, 2003), 271.

9. Witvliet, *Worship Seeking Understanding*, 274.

formation. One can give only what he or she has, so faithful leadership can flow only from being a faithful disciple of Christ.

From the stage, the musical worship leader plays a major role in the congregants' spiritual formation. The musical worship leader facilitates the affective side of the liturgy. As the pastor seeks to connect the mind and the heart through preaching, the musical worship leader punctuates and reaffirms the content of worship by leading the congregants through multisensory engagement. Furthermore, the musical worship leader often models expressive responses to worship from stage, teaching the congregants how to respond bodily in worship.[10] Thus, the musical worship leader displays the postures of worship by encouraging congregants to interact communally with the music. From the stage, musical worship leaders discern the needs of the congregants[11] and, like shepherds, lead them to fresh (spiritual) waters and green pastures.

The musical worship leader's role extends beyond the stage, however, and into the weekly life of the believer. What was shared from stage by the preacher, and rearticulated and enriched by the musical worship, stays with the congregants as they reenter the marketplace throughout the week. As David Lemley puts it, "Worship shapes a way of life, and the concrete lives of worshipers. *Lex vivendi* (the way of life) determines the ultimate authenticity and efficacy of our worship."[12] We should evaluate the authenticity of worship not only by its aesthetic fit or theological content but also by the quality of discipleship the worship produces in the lives of believers.[13] Worship aids discipleship as it shapes and forms people into the image of God, the object of worship.

Although worship services typically happen on Sundays, the

10. To think about how embodied action in worship forms us, see W. David O. Taylor, *A Body of Praise: Understanding the Role of Our Physical Bodies in Worship* (Grand Rapids: Baker Academic, 2023).

11. David Lemley, *Becoming What We Sing: Formation Through Contemporary Worship Music* (Grand Rapids: Eerdmans, 2021), 219.

12. Lemley, *Becoming What We Sing*, 28.

13. Lemley, *Becoming What We Sing*, 28.

musical worship leader's role is not only bracketed by Sunday but extends out to the everyday formation of worshipers. Kaemingk and Willson, in their book *Work and Worship*, argue that a holistic theology of the church's mission in worship would recognize that workers make up the **priesthood of all believers**—*the biblical idea, based on 1 Peter 2:9 and Revelation 1:6, that all believers have a part to play in the ministry of the church, including its worship (even if we still have distinct roles), and all have the responsibility to grow in their faith.*[14] Workers bring "their priestly bodies" both to the church and the workplace to glorify God.[15] Kaemingk and Willson write, "On their way into the sanctuary, they carry their whole lives—their fish and their grain—into the presence of the Lord. On their way back out to the city, worshipers carry the grace of Christ, the law of God, and the power of the Holy Spirit into the world. Gathered and scattered. Welcomed and sent. This is the heartbeat of healthy Christian worship."[16] Musical worship leaders must be cognizant of the everyday lives of the congregants, recognizing that *they* are the ministers of God's local mission. Worship is not just for Sundays but for every day. We gather in God's name so we can later scatter and proclaim God's name.

Moral and Holistic Formation Through Worship

Congregational worship also aids the moral formation of congregants in a worshiping community by establishing a context where members grow in holiness.[17] **Moral formation** concerns *the shaping of an individual's ethical values, principles, behaviors, and decision-making abilities.* Orthodox theologian Vigen

---

14. Matthew Kaemingk and Cory Willson, *Work and Worship: Reconnecting Our Labor and Liturgy* (Grand Rapids: Baker Academic, 2020), 51.

15. Kaemingk and Willson, *Work and Worship*, 51.

16. Kaemingk and Willson, *Work and Worship*, 18.

17. Vigen Guroian, "Moral Formation and Christian Worship," *The Ecumenical Review* L9, no. 3 (1997): 374.

Guroian is quick to point out that worship is not merely a tool for "conscientization or moral formation."[18] Rather, moral formation is a second-order thing that emerges from our holistic spiritual formation into holy, set apart members of the kingdom of God. As Guroian writes,

> All of our ethical reflection and moral behaviour [*sic*] as Christians exceeds the minimalism of the second-order language of moral community and moral formation. We are destined to grow into holiness. Thus while the church might make use of the language of moral formation to interpret itself to the world and to the unconverted, or to explain the needs for social reform, and to instruct the unformed within the church, this language simply does not comprehend the fullness of the church as the holy people of God and the sacrament of a new and renewed creation.[19]

In other words, the language of moral formation is a useful way to talk about our holistic formation in the church, but it's only an effect of our holistic formation, not the cause. We might say things like "Jesus helped me grow in kindness" or "God has been working on my self-control," but these are effects of becoming more like Christ. Positive moral formation is not the end goal, or *telos*, of Christian living. Rather, the end goal of Christian living is **cruciform discipleship**—*Christian living that emulates Christ's self-sacrificial love, humility, and obedience to God*. In other words, Christians are to follow Jesus in a way that is "cross-shaped." Holistically becoming like Christ means imitating Christ's self-giving nature even if it means enduring suffering or hardship. **Moral faithfulness** concerns *Christians committed to honoring God in their ethical lives and surrendering to the will of*

18. Guroian, "Moral Formation and Christian Worship," 373.
19. Guroian, "Moral Formation and Christian Worship," 375.

God.[20] Moral faithfulness is thus a natural outcome of cruciform discipleship, not the end goal.

Because moral formation is an effect of a person's holistic formation through worship, we can assess how musical worship in particular affects a person's moral formation. In his book *Music for Others*, Nate Myrick contends that music is inherently relational, which makes it bear an ethical dimension.[21] Music can be seen as an artistic expression of cultural values and identity, and as such, it can play a significant role in shaping a person's moral beliefs. Music has the power to evoke emotions and create connections between individuals, regardless of their cultural or social backgrounds. By bringing people together in this way, music can help to foster a sense of shared humanity and promote ethical values such as compassion, respect, and inclusivity. The aesthetic components of music are correlated to a person's way of relating to the world. The affective experience of music articulates and confirms to the listener how he or she should want to experience the world.[22] Music's formational power is not reducible to just one thing, and because music forms people in community, its formational power is both individual and relational. Music forms us affectively, emotionally, and intellectually, in both the private and public arena.[23]

Worship music functions morally when it uses its affective powers to bring about social bonding and healing. As Myrick writes, "Music is ethical when it heals; when it restores minds, bodies, and emotions to relational health; when it repairs broken and fractious relationships through its embodiment of the other, or through its symbolic representation of mutual values, or through its affective convictions of injustice."[24] Worship

---

20. Gary Tyra, *Getting Real: Pneumatological Realism and the Spiritual, Moral, and Ministry Formation of Contemporary Christians* (Eugene, OR: Cascade, 2018), 82.

21. Nathan Myrick, *Music for Others: Care, Justice, and Relational Ethics in Christian Music* (Oxford: Oxford University Press, 2021), 48.

22. Lemley, *Becoming What We Sing*, 114.

23. Myrick, *Music for Others*, 52.

24. Myrick, *Music for Others*, 124.

music helps congregations heal by affectively instilling a vision of a reconciled reality into the congregants. This vision functions proleptically as an inbreaking of what is to come. It motivates the congregants into action "by orienting the affections of the congregation toward generating those kinds of worlds that are centered on calling human beings to just and therefore healthy relationships with one another and by extension with God."[25] The worship songs we sing often contain messages of hope, redemption, and spiritual renewal, which inspire us to focus on God's reconciling work in the world, even in the midst of our difficult circumstances or personal challenges. Pastoral judgment in congregational worship entails assessing if and how worship songs bring about visions of hope and reconciliation as a morally formative aspect of our holistic formation.

While pastoral judgment entails the positive formation of congregational worship, it also entails assessing if and how worship songs are morally deforming. **Moral deformation** concerns *the promotion of harmful attitudes and behaviors*. Music can be morally deforming when it is used to exploit and oppress individuals and groups. It can reinforce harmful stereotypes, spread hateful messages, or promote unrealistic standards of beauty or success. Likewise, musical worship can legitimate or perpetuate unjust social arrangements that lead to moral decline.[26] Part of pastoral judgment in congregational worship is safeguarding against manipulative, morally deformative ideologies that could be present in congregational worship music. Musical worship leaders must use discernment to ensure music is utilized in properly formative ways. This is an important part of providing spiritual guidance and support for the worshiping community. In this way, the musical worship leader bears pastoral responsibilities for the congregation.

25. Myrick, *Music for Others*, 124.
26. Guroian, "Moral Formation and Christian Worship," 375.

PASTORAL TITLES AND ROLES IN NARRATIVE CONTEXT

In biblical, aesthetic, and theological judgment, there are distinctions between general and contextual principles. For instance, the elements of art and design are typically viewed as general principles for aesthetic judgment, but these elements are then contextualized and understood through narrative fit. Likewise, the primary Christian doctrines of the faith are typically viewed as general principles for theological judgment, and secondary and tertiary doctrines are viewed as contextual principles since they exist only within the narratives of particular theological traditions. The general principles of pastoral judgment discussed above consist of the pastoral role of shepherding toward holistic formation (spiritual and moral). Similarly, when these principles are applied to specific traditions, we begin to see the contextual fit of pastoral judgment. In this section, we'll look at how pastoral titles and roles vary across traditions. The musical worship leader's pastoral duties differ across traditions, which correspond to the worship leader's title.

Worship Leaders as Shepherds

Perhaps the greatest aspect of a worship leader's role is to help shepherd the congregation. In his book *The Worship Pastor*, Zac Hicks outlines the role of a worship pastor, emphasizing the importance of the pastor as a shepherd of the congregation through the acts of congregational worship.[27] Hicks argues that congregational worship should not be solely focused on music or production but should be viewed as a formational practice that shapes the congregation's understanding of, and relationship with, God.[28] Throughout his book, Hicks highlights the need for worship pastors to be theologians, pastors, and artists who lead their

27. Zac Hicks, *The Worship Pastor: A Call to Ministry for Worship Leaders and Teams* (Grand Rapids: Zondervan, 2016), 17.

28. Hicks, *The Worship Pastor*, 31.

congregations in authentic and transformative worship experiences. For Hicks "worship pastor" is the appropriate title for the musical worship leader as long as the role is appropriately pastoral. If the worship leader aids in the holistic formation of the congregants, Hicks contends, then the leader should be considered a pastor. Yet even if the word "pastor" isn't in the worship leader's title, we should still view the leader as functioning in a pastoral capacity.[29]

Some Evangelical, Pentecostal, and Black Gospel churches adopt the title of worship pastor, while others prefer to use worship leader or worship minister. Since Evangelical, Pentecostal, and Black Gospel churches are heavily influenced by the Free Church tradition,[30] they have no uniform approach regarding whether worship leaders can or should be referred to as pastors. It ultimately depends on the individual church or denomination's theological beliefs about pastoral ministry. For Catholics the priest is the presider of the liturgy of the Mass, and the person who coordinates the worship segments of a prayer meeting is simply called the leader of the prayer meeting.

While most Evangelical, Pentecostal, and Black Gospel churches require pastoral credentials to carry the title of pastor, some do not. Yet even if these churches require ordination, they tend to have moderate ordination processes that may not require formal ministerial training to attain pastoral licensing.[31] Conversely, Catholics and many mainline Protestant

---

29. Witvliet, *Worship Seeking Understanding*, 282.

30. The Free Church tradition is a Protestant Christian movement that emerged in the sixteenth century as a response to the perceived corruption of the institutional church. Free churches emphasize the autonomy of individual churches and reject the authority of hierarchical structures and creeds. They typically practice congregational polity, meaning that each church is self-governing and democratic, with decisions made by the congregation as a whole. Free churches often prioritize individual conscience and religious freedom, as well as a personal relationship with God. They also tend to emphasize the priesthood of all believers, which means that all Christians have equal access to God and can serve as ministers.

31. For instance, in the Southern Baptist Convention (SBC), pastors can become ordained by meeting certain criteria and going through a formal process of examination

denominations require pastors to be educated, either through a formal theological education or through other means of training and preparation. Catholics and many mainline denominations require pastors to have a master of divinity degree or its equivalent from an accredited seminary (e.g., the Episcopal Church, the United Methodist Church, the Presbyterian Church (USA), the Evangelical Lutheran Church in America, and the United Church of Christ all have these requirements), and some of these denominations also require residencies prior to receiving ordination.

It is worth noting, however, that many denominations that do not have formal education requirements still encourage their pastors to pursue theological education and provide opportunities for ongoing training and development. Witvliet maintains that every denominational tradition should encourage musical worship leaders to grow in theological knowledge.[32] Even informal educational endeavors like reading theologies of worship or attending worship conferences would do a lot to help musical worship leaders grow in pastoral wisdom.

Catholic and Reformed practitioners tend to define the role of the worship leader in an entirely different way than Free Church practitioners. The principal act of communal worship at a Catholic Church is the Mass, also known as the Eucharist. The **Mass** is *a liturgical service that includes the Liturgy of the Word (readings from Scripture, a homily, and prayers) and the Liturgy of the Eucharist (the consecration and reception of Communion).* Catholic churches typically celebrate Mass daily, but the Sunday Mass is considered central for the life of the church.

---

and approval. The SBC requires that candidates for ordination meet certain criteria, such as being a member of a Southern Baptist church for a minimum period of time, demonstrating a calling to ministry, and exhibiting a sound theological understanding of the Bible. The candidate must seek the approval of their local church and undergo an examination by the church's ordination council. The local church then recommends the candidate, who then goes through an examination by the state convention's credential committee. So while there is a process to attain pastoral credentials, there is no educational requirement.

32. Witvliet, *Worship Seeking Understanding*, 272.

WORSHIP PASTOR OR WORSHIP LEADER?

Some ambivalence toward calling a worship leader a pastor may have to do with the worship leader's lack of ministerial and theological training. A Pentecostal pastor-theologian I interviewed made this point:

> Worship leaders in the contemporary sense are a recent phenomenon, and in many ways they are given more latitude than they are probably trained/prepared for. I think we can have "song leaders" and pastors help lead the worship. However, no doubt, there are pastors who are also qualified and readied worship leaders. I tend to think, however, that a twenty-one-year-old who has little biblical or theological training and yet is talented musically and vocally might not be the best person to be picking out songs and exhorting the congregation during a worship set.

For this pastor-theologian, a worship leader should not be called a pastor because of the position, but he or she could be called a pastor if he or she is appropriately trained in Bible and theology to exhort a congregation. It has less to do with a formal process to obtain an official title than it has to do with appropriate pastoral preparedness.

While the pastors of Charismatic Catholic churches lead the liturgy of the worship service, "music ministry leaders" lead congregations in praise and worship through music.

Similarly, in the Reformed tradition, those who lead musical worship are typically called "song leaders" or "music directors," not pastors. The role of the "worship leader" is to facilitate and guide the congregation in worshiping God through the use of prayer, Scripture reading, music, and other elements of worship. Worship leaders are essentially liturgists, not mere leaders of music. While Evangelical, Pentecostal, and Black Gospel churches often refer to the musical worship of a service as "worship,"

Catholics and the Reformed tradition tend to refer to the whole liturgy as "worship." Since these traditions view worship leaders as liturgists, they typically preserve the title of worship leader for ordained pastors. Nevertheless, while there may be differences in approach and emphasis, the primary role of a musical worship leader in any church is to facilitate and guide the congregation in worshiping God. The specific methods and techniques used may vary depending on the context and tradition, but the goal remains the same: to help the congregation connect with God and to guide them in their holistic formation.

The Pastoral Function of Musical Worship

The pastoral function of musical worship differs depending on the tradition. In general all Protestant and Charismatic Catholic congregations place a strong emphasis on congregational singing, and music is often used as a means of fostering a sense of community and shared worship. Reformed worship music is often used to create a contemplative and reflective atmosphere. The pastoral function of music in the Reformed tradition is to help individuals connect with God and with the community of believers, to deepen their understanding of the faith, and to center their hearts and minds around the gospel.

Consistent with its revivalist roots, the Evangelical tradition places a strong emphasis on personal spiritual experience, so music helps create an atmosphere of worship and spiritual encounter. Music is often used to create a more informal and participatory atmosphere than in Reformed traditions, and there is often a greater emphasis on emotional expression and personal experience in the lyrics and performance of contemporary worship music. Like the Reformed tradition, the pastoral function of musical worship in the Evangelical tradition is to create a sense of community and belonging among believers. However, Evangelical worship also strives to help individuals connect with God on a personal level, and to express their faith in personally meaningful ways. Music is thus seen as a tool for creating an atmosphere of worship that draws individuals closer to God.

There is some overlap between Pentecostal, Black Gospel, Evangelical, and Charismatic Catholic worship as they pertain to their pastoral functions. All of these traditions utilize music to facilitate spiritual encounters with God, helping congregants connect with God on personal levels. Music is also seen as an important means of evangelism in each tradition. Through music, believers can share their faith with others and create opportunities for others to powerfully encounter God. One unique pastoral function of musical worship in these traditions is that they aim to create an atmosphere in which individuals can experience the presence of God in a tangible way. Music is seen as a means for facilitating spiritual encounters that stimulate the practice of spiritual gifts such as healings, tongues, prophetic utterances, and so on. The lyrics of these songs often focus on themes of personal transformation, faith, surrender, and spiritual empowerment.

Pastoral judgment in musical worship entails discerning what songs are appropriate for the particular worshiping community and why. Part of pastoral judgment is utilizing biblical, aesthetic, and theological judgment to see what fits the worshiping community. Perhaps the style of the song is so unfamiliar to the worshiping community that it would distract the congregants and throw them out of worship. The musical worship leader thus uses pastoral judgment to avoid doing the song, to change the style of the song, or to coach the congregation into understanding why the style is appropriate for their community's worship. Similarly, a worship song might be so theologically unique to another tradition that it could cause confusion among the congregants and also throw them out of worship. Here one uses pastoral judgment to avoid doing the song, to edit the song to better fit the worshiping community's theological tradition, or to explain the theological differences to the congregation and why it's still worth singing.

HOW GOSPEL MUSIC MINISTERS TO PEOPLE

Dr. Raymond Wise is professor of African American and African Diaspora Studies at Indiana University. He serves as the director of the African American Choral Ensemble and the executive director of the African American Arts Institute. He is also the president of Raise Productions, a Gospel production company that provides educational training and resources for the Gospel community. As Dr. Wise was pursuing his formal education, he saw that Gospel and classical music did not mix very well and that the two cultures did not really come together. Consequently, he has made it a life goal to teach people how to perform Gospel music in academic settings. He has developed pedagogy, curriculum, and new methodologies throughout various institutions that teach people about the African American sacred music traditions.

Dr. Wise sees that music in the Gospel tradition is used in many different ways to minister to people. He says,

> Music is used in multiple ways because the black church isn't monolithic. You can think of its worship practices as sitting within a continuum where on one end is an African aesthetic and on the other is a European aesthetic. Therefore, there's not just one way that music is used in the African American tradition; it is used based on that continuum and where people fall. However, there's also a pragmatic and functional way music is used in the African American church tradition. It's used to go through the entire process of worship, from confession, cleansing, and healing to adoration. Music can be used anywhere throughout the worship experience for all of those things. It's used to help congregants feel a release from the burdens they bring. It's used for community, to relate and connect with others. It's used to rejoice and celebrate. It's used throughout to move people from the place they enter to where they leave transformed.

Music, therefore, runs through the whole Black Gospel worship expression and is an inextricable part of the Black church tradition.

In each case, the musical worship leader must know the congregation well and use discernment to see what approach best aids their holistic formation.

Pastoral judgment is also used when the musical worship leader determines if the congregation is spiritually ready for something that is challenging but beneficial. Perhaps certain congregants are still spiritual infants. Paul dealt with this issue when he addressed the church in Corinth: "I fed you with milk, not solid food, for you were not ready for solid food. Even now you are still not ready" (1 Cor. 3:2). If we circle back to the example from the introduction of this chapter, we can think about my worship pastor friend's pastoral judgment in the same way that we'd consider Paul's pastoral judgment in 1 Corinthians. It's not that the solid food was bad for them but they were not ready to consume it. In the same way, it's not that the song "Reckless Love" was bad for them to sing but they were not ready to consider God's love in this way. It's not that my worship pastor friend will never do "Reckless Love" in his church but just that he will not do it at this time. As his congregation continues to grow in Christian maturity, perhaps he can revisit the song and explain to them why singing it is worthwhile.

Later on, in 1 Corinthians 8, Paul discusses eating food that was offered to idols. In chapter 8, Paul shows that that there is nothing spiritually wrong with eating meat that was offered to idols since his readers have the knowledge that no idol in the world represents a god who actually exists (v. 4). He mentions, however, that some people may be so steeped in their preconversion ways of life that even after they turn to Christ, seeing another Christian eat sacrificed meat may become a stumbling block. Paul writes,

> It is not everyone, however, who has this knowledge. Since some have become so accustomed to idols until now, they still think of the food they eat as food offered to an idol, and their conscience,

> being weak, is defiled. "Food will not bring us close to God." We are no worse off if we do not eat and no better off if we do. But take care that this liberty of yours does not somehow become a stumbling block to the weak. For if others see you, who possess knowledge, eating in the temple of an idol, might they not, since their conscience is weak, be encouraged to the point of eating food sacrificed to idols? So by your knowledge the weak brother or sister for whom Christ died is destroyed. But when you thus sin against brothers and sisters and wound their conscience when it is weak, you sin against Christ. Therefore, if food is a cause of their falling, I will never again eat meat, so that I may not cause one of them to fall.
>
> —*1 Corinthians 8:7–13*

Paul restricts an action that is not sinful, not to bolster a sense of legalism but for the sake of helping others avoid being needlessly confused or unsettled. Paul utilizes pastoral judgment as he deals with the church in Corinth, and in so doing, he gives us a good principle for ministry: Give the congregants only what they can handle, and be sensitive to where they are spiritually in their journey of holistic transformation. Worship pastors, as shepherds, must make sure the stream is flowing slowly enough that the sheep feel comfortable drinking the water.

CONTEXTUAL PERSPECTIVES ON PASTORAL JUDGMENT IN WORSHIP

After establishing what is involved in pastoral judgment, we will once again consider the five traditions assessed throughout this book. In particular we will explore how worship songs are used to minister to people in each church tradition.

Reformed worship sees musical worship as helping people practice appropriate postures of worship. The songs are performed to help carry the acts of liturgy from one moment to another and to help people respond to the next element of worship in the appropriate posture, whether the people are called to praise, confess, give thanks, or be sent out. Hence, worship songs and congregational prayers are used to encourage certain postures of worship (adoration, repentance, thanksgiving, supplication, lamentation, exhortation, invocation, imprecation, or confession). Music also helps people flow from one element of the worship service to another. This constitutes the nonlyrical way music connects the elements of worship. While songs could be a response to the sermon, they are not merely recapitulations. The congregants prayerfully reflect on the sermon and then respond to God in their own ways.

Pentecostal worship songs are used to minister to congregants by creating a space for divine encounter. Rather than rehearsing beliefs about God, worship songs are meant to put worshipers in contact with the living God. As I mentioned in the introduction, there is a relational kind of "knowing" that is different than rational knowing, and worship songs create the space to relationally know and be known by God. For Pentecostals worship music creates a charged space that engages a person bodily and emotionally, which helps people dwell in an atmosphere of vulnerability. When congregants allow themselves to be vulnerable in front of God, they are more open to experiencing a divine encounter. Music underscores many elements of worship, such as the ministry time, altar calls, and special presentations, in order to unify the flow of the service and to help people remain in a state of expectancy. Pentecostal worship often includes times of spontaneous prayer and intercession during which believers pray for the needs of others and seek God's guidance and direction. These moments of prayer and intercession are usually underscored by music, which helps create an atmosphere of expectancy for encountering God's presence.

Black Gospel worship utilizes music ministerially in a way that forms identities and emboldens a sense of perseverance.

In particular it helps to confer upon believers a new identity in Christ, one that stands in contrast to the images of subjugation that were forced upon oppressed Black people. The pastor's role goes beyond teaching and walking with people but also entails encouraging congregants, reminding them about God's promises, rekindling a passion for Christ, and keeping their spiritual fervor. The Black ecclesial tradition sees this pastoral role as belonging to everyone involved in worship. It's a communal endeavor that is guided by the pastor and reinforced by the music. One interviewee said the music is like a punctuation—an exclamation point—to what the pastor proclaims. The pastor carries the ideas in one way and the music does so in another way, but both are speaking the same language. The music and proclamation go so well together that it can be difficult to separate them and evaluate them individually. They seamlessly work in tandem to foster spiritual formation.

In Evangelical worship, songs are primarily sung to expand and confirm the content of the sermon. While the music helps congregants celebrate God's beauty and grandeur, the lyrical content is typically in line with the church's biblical readings of the week. Music, therefore, bears an educational focus where everything lines up in a cohesive frame. This didactic function of worship music supports the spiritual growth and education of a congregation by conveying biblical and theological messages through music. Hence, musical worship leaders minister to their congregants by choosing songs that faithfully demonstrate the gospel and align with the principal message of the worship service.

Similar to Pentecostal worship, Charismatic Catholic worship music is utilized to create a space to encounter God on personal and corporate levels. However, there are some key distinctions between the two traditions. Because Pentecostalism comes from revivalist roots, it puts a great emphasis on individual transformation. Conversely, Catholicism fosters a much stronger sense of communal formation. Specifically, prayer meetings are geared toward communal enrichment as the gathered body of believers seeks to comprehend what God is doing in their community and the world. Songs will typically be sung in the third person plural rather than the first. Ministerially, music makes the prayer meetings accessible to newcomers, provides avenues for active participation, and helps structure the worship environment.[33] Perhaps the greatest ministerial function of music is to facilitate prayer. The meetings are called "prayer meetings" rather than worship gatherings because prayer is the foundation upon which everything else is built.[34] Congregants are encouraged to pray and sing in tongues, and to pray over one another, because Charismatic Catholics believe God is actually listening and will respond.[35] Hence, music helps facilitate the prayers of a Charismatic community.

To summarize, Reformed worship sees congregational worship music as helping congregants enter into appropriate postures of worship. Worship music helps congregants rightly receive revelation from God and rightly respond to God. Pentecostal worship sees congregational worship music as helping to create an atmosphere where congregants can experience God's presence. Divine encounter is essential for Pentecostal spirituality, and the songs that are sung should help congregants center their minds and hearts on the Spirit. Black Gospel worship music is used to empower and shape identities. The pastor's role includes teaching, encouraging, and revitalizing congregants' faith, while music reinforces and punctuates what is expressed. Together, music and proclamation create a cohesive and impactful course of spiritual formation. Evangelical worship sees congregational worship music through a didactic lens—as extensions and affirmations of the sermon. Evangelical worship is aligned by Scripture, and the proclamation of the Word through preaching is central.

33. William Kangas, "Worship in the Charismatic Renewal: A Case Study in the Word of God Community" (PhD diss., Catholic University of America, 2022), 86.

34. Kangas, "Worship in the Charismatic Renewal," 93.

35. Kangas, "Worship in the Charismatic Renewal," 94.

Finally, Charismatic Catholic worship utilizes music to encounter God personally and communally, and facilitates prayer and communal formation.

CONCLUSION

This chapter looked at pastoral judgment first by defining the term "pastor" and seeing what constitutes pastoral ministry within a church. We then looked at how pastoral judgment is used in a worship service, particularly as it concerns choosing songs that minister to people where they are in their faith journeys. Since the pastoral goal of congregational worship is to lead people into God's presence, musical worship leaders must be aware of where God is leading the congregants at this point in their holistic transformation. This chapter also looked at the various titles musical worship leaders hold across traditions and what roles they carry. Even though there are many ministerial differences between these traditions, it's important to see that believers are nevertheless ministered to in all of them. Recognizing this allows us to see how believers across traditions are spiritually formed to be better disciples of Christ.

STUDY QUESTIONS

1. How do the worship songs that are performed at your church shape the congregation's understanding of, and relationship with, God?
2. Does your church's style of performed worship music fit aesthetically with your church's tradition and culture?
3. Have you ever experienced worship songs that promote harmful attitudes and behaviors for congregants?
4. Has your church ever avoided performing a song for pastoral reasons?
5. What terms does your church use for the musical worship leader? What term does it use for the worship service? What is the rationale for these terms?

KEY TERMS

Cruciform discipleship: Christian living that emulates Christ's self-sacrificial love, humility, and obedience to God.

Liturgist: someone who leads the worship service and is responsible for planning and leading the order of worship for the church.

Mass: a Catholic liturgical service that includes the Liturgy of the Word (readings from Scripture, a homily, and prayers) and the Liturgy of the Eucharist (the consecration and reception of Communion.

Moral deformation: the promotion of harmful attitudes and behaviors.

Moral faithfulness (Christian): Christians committed to honoring God in their ethical lives and surrendering to the will of God.

Moral formation: the shaping of an individual's ethical values, principles, behaviors, and decision-making abilities.

Musical worship leader: the minister who leads a church's congregational worship music.

Pastor: a spiritual leader who serves and leads a congregation of believers in a church or ministry.

Pastoral judgment: the process of evaluating and making judgments about the holistic (spiritual, physical, and emotional) needs of individuals in a worshiping community.

Pastoral ministry: involves providing spiritual care and guidance to a community of believers.

Priesthood of all believers: the biblical idea, based on 1 Peter 2:9 and Revelation 1:6, that all believers have a part to play in the ministry of the church, including its worship (even if we still have distinct roles), and all have the responsibility to grow in their faith.

CHAPTER 5

How to Plan Worship Well

Assessing and Selecting Worship

One of the courses I teach at my university centers around worship design. In this class, students learn how to create worship services that reflect different traditions, styles, and cultures. For their final project, students work in groups of three or four to design and lead a complete worship service. They lead their services in our campus prayer chapel, with each group having a full class period to carry out the service.

During these services, everyone is involved—we worship God together! Yet while we maintain a posture of worship, we also take notes of what we're observing and then hold class discussions after each service. The discussions are critical, but gracious—we highlight strengths and offer constructive feedback on how the service could have been strengthened. Even though we have different groups, this task truly feels like a collaborative class project since each service connects to the next.

A common thing we talk about after each service is "flow." **Flow** in worship refers to *the progression of a worship service, where each element of worship naturally leads to the next.* Flow is not just about the organization of the worship service but also helps foster a distraction-free environment, allowing worshipers to focus on God. After each service, we discuss the arrangement of worship elements, the transitions between them, how the congregation interacts with each part, and the overall flow of the service. Since the groups can implement insights from previous discussions, we often observe significant improvements from one service to the next.

One time when I oversaw this assignment, the service flow got noticeably better as the groups went on. After the final group's service ended, I asked the class, "Did any of you check your phones during the service?" They said no. "Did anyone get distracted from something in the room or leave for a moment?" Again, they said no. The flow was so good during the service that everyone was able to remain locked in to what was happening. Everything in the service made sense, and the transitions between elements were seamless. We saw that good flow allowed everyone to focus on who was being worshiped rather than on the individual elements of worship.

The goal of this chapter is to offer a practical outlook on how to plan a worship service in a way that is true to our Christian faith and aware of context. In this last chapter of part 1, we will draw together many of the things discussed throughout the previous chapters. We will explore how to design worship that is biblically faithful, aesthetically fitting, theologically sound, and pastorally focused. First, we will consider what planning the order of worship means broadly. We will identify what should be consistent throughout every Christian tradition's worship design. We will also look at the importance of flow in worship design. Finally, we will examine various perspectives on worship design and flow. In particular we will look at how the five traditions assessed throughout this book design their orders of worship and create flow. Thus, we will close out part 1 with practical, prescriptive insights before turning to part 2, where we assess particular churches from each tradition.

PLANNING THE ORDER OF WORSHIP

While there are many words that mean worship (or imply worship) in the Bible,[1] there are two primary groupings of words that describe worship conceptually. First, worship is often described as entering a state of reverence. The Hebrew words *shakhah* and *sagad*, for instance, mean to take on a posture of reverence like bowing down or prostrating oneself. Likewise, the Greek word *proskyneo* means to bow down and kiss toward the hand of a superior, like bowing down and kissing the ring of a king, and *sebomai* means to revere or adore. This first grouping of words expresses worship through the act of showing reverence, which includes a person physically bowing down to honor a subject. Second, worship is often described as a work of service. The Hebrew word *abad* is commonly used to describe service or work for another, and the Greek word *leitourgia* means the service of the people. This grouping of words is commonly associated with the work of priests and the clergy. When we talk about worship design, we're talking about this latter grouping—the work or service or worship. We are seeking, therefore, to design worship for God and the congregation faithfully as servants.

An excellent and widely used book on worship design is Constance Cherry's *The Worship Architect*. Cherry uses the image of house building to discuss designing biblically faithful and culturally relevant worship services. Just as a house's foundation ensures that every part of the house remains connected and aligned, so does the foundation of a worship service ensure all its elements are connected and aligned.[2] For Cherry the biblical foundation of worship rests on six major themes that can

---

1. For instance, the Old Testament contains various terms for praise and thanksgiving, including *barak*, *halal*, *shabach*, *tehillah*, *zamar*, *yadah*, and *todah*. Similarly, the New Testament makes use of several words, including *ainesis*, *epaineo*, *eulogia*, *halleluia*, *hymneo*, *latreuo*, and *therapeuo* to describe worship.

2. Constance Cherry, *The Worship Architect: A Blueprint for Designing Culturally Relevant and Biblically Faithful Services*, 2nd ed. (Grand Rapids: Baker Academic, 2021), 12.

be traced throughout Scripture. Worship should be (1) centered on God's acts of salvation, (2) patterned on a flow of revelation and response, (3) covenantally oriented between God and God's people, (4) corporate in nature, (5) related to every person of the Trinity, and (6) a transformational journey for worshipers.[3] These themes are great, but I would add "worship is Spirit-filled in nature." Some New Testament verses describe true worship as being "in the Spirit" (John 4:23–24) and filled with the Spirit (Eph. 5:18–19). These verses and others emphasize the importance of being guided and filled by the Spirit in worship, and of living a life that reflects true Spirit-led devotion. We'll see later in this chapter why sensitivity to the Spirit is crucially important for worship design. Nevertheless, Cherry's themes help us see the dialogical pattern of worship. A **dialogical pattern** refers to *a conversational structure characterized by a relational exchange between two or more participants*. Seeing worship as a dialogical pattern means it is a fundamentally relational act between God and God's people. This concept aligns with the definition of worship in the introduction of this book as a relational act of connecting with God by turning one's heart toward God in response to God's self-revelation.

According to Cherry, worship is most appropriately understood relationally as a rhythm of God's revelation and the worshipers' response to God. She writes, "True worship is the experience of encountering God *through the means that God usually employs*, a conversation built on revelation/response. Viewing worship as a conversation implies a relationship."[4] Any true biblical foundation must point back to the real, living relationship Christians have with God. If the Bible's primary devotional function is to point readers to God, then biblically faithful worship is that which fosters a person's relationship with God.

3. Cherry, *The Worship Architect*, 28.
4. Cherry, *The Worship Architect*, 20, emphasis original.

Cherry says that after establishing the foundation, every expression of worship should be structured by the "load-bearing walls" that help facilitate a community's worship.[5] These load-bearing walls create "four rooms" that represent the four primary movements of worship: the gathering, the Word, the table, and the sending. Cherry's metaphor is based on the **fourfold order of worship**—*a structured sequence of worship historically used in Christian worship to organize worship services.* These four movements provide a "balanced diet" that nourishes a healthy Christian life.[6]

The gathering is where God calls us, and we extend God's invitation to others. The Word is where Christ calls us to live transformed lives. We gather around the Word of God during worship and in Christian education, in small groups and individually. The table is where the Holy Spirit unites us with the Trinity and with one another.[7] As Cherry points out, Communion is often done as a table response, but when Communion isn't available or administered, there should at least be some intentional response to the Word.[8] Some of these alternate responses may include testimonies, moments of silence, responsive prayers or songs, altar calls, ministry times, and so on. Finally, the sending is where the church becomes Christ's partner in earthly ministry. Congregants exit the walls of the church and are commissioned to find ways to serve both the spiritual and material needs of the world.[9] These primary movements of worship structure the service so worshipers are aware of the dialogical pattern that's going on.

To use Cherry's architecture metaphor, she sees phase 1 as laying the foundation of worship and phase 2 as building the

5. Cherry, *The Worship Architect*, 49.

6. Greg Scheer, *Essential Worship: A Handbook for Leaders* (Grand Rapids: Baker, 2016), 50.

7. Scheer, *Essential Worship*, 80–81.

8. Cherry, *The Worship Architect*, 99.

9. Scheer, *Essential Worship*, 82.

structures of worship—building load-bearing walls that make the four rooms (movements) of worship. These movements help to align worship theologically as a dialogue between God and the worshiping community. Because these first two phases look at the biblical faithfulness and theological soundness of a worship service, they correspond with our notions of biblical and theological judgment (chapters 1 and 3, respectively). And while every worshiping tradition should follow the fourfold pattern of worship, worshiping traditions can contextualize how they choose to follow the pattern. In Cherry's metaphor, the next phases[10] are where these contextualizations may occur.

Phase 3 of a building project concerns choosing and installing functional elements like doors and windows.[11] Here a builder decides what kind of doors and windows will function well and fit in with the house and surrounding community. While these elements are needed, they can take on many different forms: Will the interior doors be panel, flush, barn, pocket, or French doors? Will the windows be single or double hung? Although the general function of these elements remains the same, making decisions about these elements will alter the way the house looks and feels. In the same way, worship designers will make decisions about how the prayer, music, preaching, and testimonials function in worship. Some questions worship designers might ask include, When in the service will prayers occur? Will prayers be corpo-

10. Cherry shifted the metaphor between the first and second editions of this book. In the first edition (released in 2010), phase 3 was the functional elements of worship (i.e., installing doors and windows in the building process), phase 4 was the style in worship (i.e., making design decisions in the building process), and phase 5 was about nurturing hospitality in worship. In the second edition (released in 2021), phase 3 refers only to windows and seems to combine phases 3 and 4 of the first edition; and phase 4 refers to opening doors, which reworks phase 5 of the first edition. For learning how to design worship, I will refer to the way the first edition describes phases 1–4, as these seem most explanatory and helpful.

11. Cherry, *The Worship Architect*, 141. In the second edition of this book, Cherry focuses only on the windows, but I think the metaphor works best when referring to any functional element.

rate, personal, or intercessory? What function does music serve in the service? Will music underscore other elements of worship? How will worship leaders or liturgists transition from element to element?

Furthermore, some traditions may follow the liturgical calendar to help structure their worship. The **liturgical calendar** is *a cycle of seasons and feasts observed by many Christian denominations to commemorate and celebrate key events in the life of Jesus and the church*. For many traditions, the liturgical calendar helps guide worship, readings, and rituals throughout the year. Even if a tradition does not follow the liturgical calendar explicitly, most traditions still design worship according to significant Christian seasons like Christmas, Holy Week, Easter, and Pentecost. The way a worshiping community arranges the elements of worship within the fourfold order of worship may vary from tradition to tradition. Because this phase looks at how a worshiping community worships God and ministers to its congregants, it corresponds with pastoral judgment (chapter 4).

While phase 3 concerns choosing and ordering elements of worship for functional reasons, phase 4 concerns choosing and ordering elements of worship for stylistic reasons. Harking back to the building metaphor, phase 4 entails making design decisions like choosing tiles, flooring, cabinets, paint colors, and so on. The designer wants to make sure the design elements work well with the structures of the house and fit authentically with the styles of the surrounding community. For instance, it may not be fitting to build a house with German-style architecture right in the middle of a Southwestern community where every building presents Spanish-inspired architecture. There's always the possibility of creating interesting fusions between styles, but designers typically strive to make sure the design of a house fits in the community and authentically represents the residents. In the same way, worship design should stylistically fit both the worshiping community and the surrounding community the church wishes to engage.

Worship designers would do well to assess the demographics of the broader community before determining what styles of worship should be adopted. The styles of worship are malleable but should authentically reflect the aesthetic sensibilities of the community.

Adapting worship styles to reflect the community's aesthetic sensibilities can foster in the congregants a sense of belonging. Worshipers can feel more connected to a worshiping community when the worship service evinces feelings of cultural continuity as current generations connect with the spiritual heritage of those who formed the community. Furthermore, when the musical style is familiar, worshipers will be more likely to participate, and the elements of the service will be more easily absorbed. For the purposes of outreach, people from the surrounding areas will likely feel more comfortable and welcomed by worshiping communities that feel culturally familiar to them.

While the content of worship should be fixed, worship styles are contextual and should reflect the community.[12] On the one hand, **content** refers to *the things we do to assist our dialogue with God* (i.e., Scripture reading, praying, preaching, and singing). **Style**, on the other hand, is *the way we deliver the content of worship*. In other words, content is the material of worship, whereas style is the manner in which the material is expressed.[13] Worshiping traditions can bear multiple styles (e.g., Evangelicals might do hymn-style traditional worship or contemporary worship), but the styles should fit the worshiping community's tradition, history, and surrounding community. Style should therefore be evaluated not as right or wrong but as fitting or not fitting to a community. This evaluative approach lines up with our notion of aesthetic judgment (chapter 2).

We can utilize our four judgments highlighted throughout this book to design worship that is biblically faithful, aesthetically

---

12. Cherry, *The Worship Architect*, 253.
13. Cherry, *The Worship Architect*, 253.

fitting, theologically sound, and pastorally focused. Worship designers can use biblical judgment to make sure biblical foundations of the worship service are set. Not only should the Word be biblically focused but the worship songs should be biblically faithful and contextually fitting. Designers can use aesthetic judgment to make sure the style of worship authentically expresses the aesthetic sensibilities of the worshiping community. Without compromising the content of worship, designers can present worship in a way that makes sense for the community. Designers can use theological judgment to make sure the movements of worship foster a dialogue with God that appropriately emulates the biblical narrative. They can make sure the worship focuses mainly on primary theological issues while thoughtfully espousing secondary issues that make sense for the community. Finally, designers can use pastoral judgment to make sure the worship elements function in a way that appropriately ministers to God and the people. They can be cognizant of how the chosen worship elements are forming the congregants.

Designing worship with our four judgments in mind helps us determine what should be constant and unchanging in worship and what can change depending on context. It helps us critically assess what we're doing in worship instead of relying only on intuition. This way we can have a fuller sense of how we corporately express our adoration to God and how congregants are being ministered to in worship.

CREATING FLOW IN WORSHIP

As we've been discussing, a crucial part of designing worship is creating flow. Practically speaking, flow helps unite the elements of worship so the service becomes a single cohesive expression of corporate worship. It's easy to see why flow is aesthetically important—good flow helps maintain an atmosphere of expectancy. It can build a sense of anticipation, elevate an emotional state, and bring people to a place of deeper, experiential connection. When worshipers are locked in, their experience of worship becomes distraction-free. When worshipers are drawn into a powerful aesthetic experience, they enter a heightened state of concentration that enables them to become fully immersed in God's presence during worship. According to theologian Lexi Eikelboom, when people enter a state of flow, they become so immersed in what is happening that their perception of time ceases to exist—they get caught up in the moment. They enter a "perfect state of concentration without struggle."[14] Ironically, when worship leaders and teams create good aesthetic flow, they help shift focus away from the top-tier musicianship and seamless transitions that created the flow and onto the content of worship. As Zachary Barnes writes, "Musical flow helps to create an atmosphere and environment that is conducive to awareness of God's presence."[15] In other words, good flow helps worshipers focus on who the elements of worship are addressing instead of on the elements of worship.

Good flow also supports worship ministerially. Flow helps people enter and stay in a dialogue with God. As worshipers work through the fourfold order of worship, they hear from and respond to God. When worshipers stay in a moment of worship, they are more attentive to what God is telling them. Thus, worship designers should be cognizant of how flow helps facilitate the narrative arch of a worship service. Flow helps guide the congregants through a structured spiritual journey that mirrors the elements of a story, with a beginning, middle, and end. The call to worship (gathering) sets the scene, and the rising action develops with musical worship and the presentation of the Word.

---

14. Lexi Eikelboom, "Flow and the Christian Experience of Time," The Rhythmic Theology Project, October 8, 2016, https://rhythmictheologyproject.com/2016/10/08/flow/.

15. Zachary Barnes, "How Flow Became the Thing," in *Flow: The Ancient Way to Do Contemporary Worship*, ed. Lester Ruth (Nashville: Abingdon, 2020), 20.

ONE HOPE PROJECT

One Hope Project is a collective of worshipers that formed out of the Charismatic Catholic worship tradition in the United Kingdom. Although the project started as a small gathering of young worshipers, it has grown to become a full-time charity with its own online worship school. They have written and recorded original worship music, performed at events and retreats all over the UK, and have engaged in many creative worship projects. One of the collective's goals is to help people encounter Jesus through worship and the arts.

In an interview with Joe Wells, the collective's cofounder, we discussed some of the particularities of worship in the Catholic Charismatic Renewal and how that worship can differ from the more traditional style of worship in the Catholic Mass. When asked about the role of flow in the design of worship, Joe offered some great insight:

> Flow is really important in worship. We're taking people on a journey from moment to moment. We want to serve people and see how we can facilitate a space so people can encounter God. From a Catholic point of view, they're used to the beauty of liturgy. Liturgy has a story arch that takes people on a journey from repentance to the word, and to Eucharist as the high point. There's a real depth in liturgy. So when we're leading a service, we're thinking of that arch, we're thinking about how to create that space. At the end of the service, there are moments of silence when people can reflect and encounter God. Catholics are comfortable with silence.

Joe noted that Catholics are comfortable with both the grandeur of praise and the quietude of contemplation, and Charismatic Catholics feel blessed to embrace that full range of dynamics to truly connect with the liturgy.

The spiritual peak of the service would be the table response, which then concludes with a benediction (sending). Good flow helps worshipers experience God through a coherent framing of events. Such framing helps us make sense of our spiritual encounters in worship and graft those experiences into the overall story of our lives.[16] Good flow, in other words, helps us make meaning in worship that is relevant for our whole lives.

Creating flow in worship is not a modern invention. Historically, Christian traditions have included set orders of prayers, readings, songs, and sacraments, all designed to lead worshipers through comprehensible spiritual experiences. The flow of these services was carefully crafted to guide the congregation through the Christian narrative. Significantly, worship historian Lester Ruth argues that contemporary worship has reintroduced certain historical aspects of worship that have been overlooked by traditional practices. Specifically, he states that early writings instructed worship leaders to create an open-ended approach to time that works in spontaneity while creating a sequence of essential activities that flow in an orderly manner.[17] The contemporary move to create space for response in worship is, as Ruth argues, an old but relevant move.

Flow is particularly affective in that it works counterculturally in a day and age that is oriented toward productivity and expediency. As we get caught up in the experience of worship, we set aside the pressures of a clock-driven, consumeristic society. As Barnes writes, "In a society driven by time—and its restraints and limits—the notion of flow evokes something heavenly and truly of God's presence. . . . The easy transition from one song

16. For more on this, see chapter 3 of Steven Félix-Jäger, *Renewal Worship: A Theology of Pentecostal Doxology* (Downers Grove, IL: InterVarsity, 2022).

17. Ruth roots these concepts in the description of worship provided by the second-century apologist Justin Martyr, which has seen a resurgence in contemporary worship settings. See Lester Ruth, "An Ancient Way to Do Contemporary Worship," in *Flow: The Ancient Way to Do Contemporary Worship*, ed. Lester Ruth (Nashville: Abingdon, 2020), 11.

to another doesn't break the atmosphere of worship; it thereby evokes within the congregation the feeling they are in heavenly places with God's eternal presence that has no end. Flowing in worship with songs creates this perception of the eternal in the midst of the congregation. One is caught up into the presence of God."[18]

When we are oriented toward the eternal God, we are properly realigned to God and the world. Flow helps us stay in the moments that truly matter—those moments saturated by the presence of God.

Having recognized the significance of flow in worship, we can now discuss the practical methods worship leaders can employ to create seamless worship experiences. First, we should appreciate the differences between what happens on Sunday morning services and what happens during midweek worship services. Sunday morning services are typically the main weekly gatherings of a worshiping community—hence they are often seen as a church's central meeting for corporate worship. Regardless of whether the tone is formal or informal, the atmosphere of a Sunday morning service is generally one of celebration, community, and reverence. It highlights the shared experience of worship as the congregation comes together. Midweek worship services, on the other hand, are often more intimate. They may focus on Bible study, prayer, or community building, or may be completely centered around musical worship. These services provide congregants an opportunity for spiritual renewal during the week, offering a different kind of spiritual nourishment that doesn't compete with, but complements, the Sunday service.

Because the purpose and focus of these services are different, worship design should also be approached differently. One way to think about designing worship is to consider what sort of anticipation worshipers enter with. For instance, many families struggle

18. Barnes, "How Flow Became the Thing," 21.

to get everybody ready for church in the morning. By the time the family arrives at church, checks in their children to the kids' ministries, and settles into worship, their focus may be scattered. Hence, many contemporary Sunday morning services start with loud, upbeat praise songs to get everyone in the room clapping and singing together. In other words, the first song functions in a way that orients people toward a posture of worship. Singing the same words and moving bodily together quickly helps people set aside the hassle it was to get to church and focus on God in community. More liturgical traditions start their Sunday services formally with a call to worship. Here speaking in unison is the bodily action that orients the worshiper toward openness.

Let's consider how a Sunday morning service moves through the fourfold order of worship by focusing on a contemporary worship service. These services typically start with a musical worship set that moves from fast praise songs to slower worship songs.[19] This movement shouldn't be seen as a rote formula for designing worship but as a means of taking worshipers on a journey: They gather and unite by singing the praises of God and God's wonderful deeds and then move toward a more intimate expression of worship that is both personal and communal. This posture of worship is characterized by openness, facilitating the worshipers' readiness to receive the Word, which in turn prompts them to engage with the Word through the table. After the response, the congregation is sent out with a charge, benediction, or closing song.

A typical Sunday morning service includes a welcome address, prayers, singing, Scripture readings, a time for tithes and offerings, a sermon, a response to the Word (i.e., Communion or an altar call), and a benediction. Many churches also incorporate testimonials and various artistic expressions, including dances, visual arts,

19. Contemporary worship traditions occasionally differentiate "praise" and "worship," interpreting praise as celebrating God's actions, while worship is viewed as a focus on God's character. See Félix-Jäger, *Renewal Worship*, 4–5.

and dramatic performances. It is essential for a worship designer to ensure a seamless flow among these components, which may involve underscoring them with music or facilitating transitions through prayers or readings. Announcements play a crucial role in any community; however, they can frequently disrupt the flow of worship. Hence, the placement of announcements in the order of service can be tricky. Some churches place announcements right after the first song while the band is still vamping, which is then followed by the rest of the worship set. Others place announcements after the musical worship right before the sermon. Some place announcements right at the start or right at the end of the service, but this seems to disrupt the gathering and the sending, respectively. While churches need to keep their communities informed with what is happening at the church, the goal for worship designers should be to place announcements in a way that preserves flow in worship.

The design of a midweek worship service varies from that of a Sunday morning service because of the distinct purposes inherent in each type of worship experience. The Sunday morning service is traditionally regarded as a gathering of the whole worshiping community, which leads to a worship style that generally resonates with a wider audience, and programming that is available for individuals of all ages. The midweek services typically attract a smaller group of worshipers, consisting primarily of dedicated participants who are deeply engaged in the church community. Because worshipers at these gatherings tend to come with a greater expectation for encounter, minimal effort is required to guide them into an appropriate posture of worship. Hence, midweek worship services can start with prayer, a soft worship song, or even a shared meal.

Years ago I led worship at a worship night for a college group I pastored. The event was scheduled to commence at 7:00 p.m., yet attendees began arriving around 6:45. They engaged in lighthearted conversations, filling the air with laughter and friendly exchanges. On this particular night, I decided to initiate worship without any prior announcement. I began to sing the chant-like worship song "Quiet My Mind" a cappella while the conversations continued. Gradually, the other members of the worship team joined in with harmonies, allowing the song to resonate throughout the gathering. Bit by bit, the audience became aware of the unfolding moment, turned their attention to the stage, and began to sing along. After several minutes of progressing through the verses, we reached the chorus, which was met with a sudden surge of energy. The drums crashed, the electric guitars soared, and the voices sang,

> Raise up my hands that are hanging down
> Strengthen my feeble knees.[20]

At this point, everyone was fully immersed in worship, resounding with shouts of praise and raised hands.

This story indicates a creative approach to worship that was possible only because of the worshipers' expectations. While certain worshiping communities can indeed foster an environment conducive to creative and spontaneous services on Sunday mornings, this largely hinges on the cultural context and anticipations of the community. Although there are no formal regulations dictating that worship must follow the formats described above, worshiping communities commonly maintain the distinctions outlined above between Sunday morning and midweek worship services.

One key principle that every worship designer must embrace is to be aware of the Spirit's guidance. This holds true irrespective of the worship style or tradition. As worship designers seek the Spirit's direction during the planning phase, it is essential

---

20. "Quiet My Mind," words and music by Tracy Orrison-Yoho, CCLI #491766 © 1991 Sound Truth Publishing (administrated by Calvary Chapel of Merritt Island).

for the worship leader to remain attuned to the Spirit's activity within the community at every moment during worship. God possesses the deepest understanding of what is going on in the hearts of everyone in the congregation; consequently, the Spirit may guide the worship leader to undertake an entirely new approach in the moment. Key to this dynamic is making sure the musicians and speakers are adept at navigating spontaneous musical shifts. They should be familiar enough with their instruments to facilitate a seamless flow of spontaneous worship. Such adaptability should be rehearsed in advance so it is engrained in the DNA of what is possible in worship. Worship leaders must educate worship teams and congregants not only about the Spirit but also about how to respond to the Spirit's leading. It is this sort of openness that allows for new possibilities of encounter in worship.

CONTEXTUAL PERSPECTIVES ON THE ORDER AND FLOW OF WORSHIP

We will end this chapter considering some of the worship design principles utilized by the five traditions assessed throughout this book. As in previous chapters, the information from this section is drawn from the interviews conducted with practitioners from each tradition. Although these principles should not be regarded as absolute within their respective traditions, they can be interpreted as endorsing general principles that are frequently employed in their specific contexts of worship.

Some Reformed worship services follow a prescribed liturgy that sets an order of worship; others follow a less formal liturgical pattern. The liturgical patterns typically include a call to worship, a prayer of adoration, a confession of sin, Scripture readings, songs, prayers of intercession, tithes and offerings, a sermon, Communion (if administered that week), and a benediction. This liturgical structure guarantees that each week the worship service encourages participants to engage in a variety of worship postures. Following the creation-fall-redemption-consummation motif, Reformed worship designers strive to choose songs that thematically fit a balanced gospel narrative each Sunday. Many Reformed churches perform traditional hymns, while others do contemporary worship songs, and some mix the two. There is no set of rules limiting the style of music at a Reformed service. As a secondary emphasis, Reformed worship designers aim to incorporate the seasons and feasts of the global historic church (i.e., Advent, Christmas, Epiphany, Lent, Palm Sunday, Maundy Thursday, Good Friday, Easter, and Pentecost) with their respective emphases. This approach not only enriches the worship experience but also deepens participants' connection with their historic faith.

Pentecostal worship designers aim to create a space for encountering the Holy Spirit in worship. The services typically start with a welcome, a worship set of three to five songs, a "ministry time" where the pastor connects the musical worship with either the sermon or other pertinent spiritual dynamics in the room, a moment for tithes and offerings, a sermon, a response to the Word (Communion, an altar call, prayer, or a closing song), and a benediction or charge. Often within this general structure there are spontaneous moments for prayers, Scripture readings, prophetic words, and testimonies. One practitioner said there's beauty in structure, but there's also beauty in releasing what is planned and letting the Spirit do whatever the Spirit wants to do in that moment. Hence, Pentecostal worship designers typically leave a lot of room for spontaneous responses. After the message, on weeks where Communion is not planned, the response often lends itself to spontaneity. There may be a call to repentance or for salvation or for recommitting of lives. Sometimes these responses come as altar calls, and other times members of prayer teams are made available to pray with people during a closing song. The songs are often chosen to fit a particular biblical theme or to go along with the theme of the service or sermon. Generally, Pentecostal worship services aim to foster a dynamic and responsive worship experience that encourages personal connections and spiritual encounters.

Because Black Gospel worship is transdenominational, it is difficult to determine singular principles that every church follows. After all, three of the most prominent Black church denominations come from entirely different traditions. The Church of God in Christ (COGIC) is Pentecostal, the National Baptist Convention (NBC) is Baptist, and the African Methodist Episcopal (AME) Church is Methodist.[21] Thus, these three prominent denominations come from entirely different Protestant streams and vary in worship practices. Yet while there are many Black denominations,[22] they are typically viewed as united by the Black experience, an affirmation of blackness, and by a public advocacy for justice.[23] Gospel music is rooted in the lived experiences of Black people. It emerges from their historical context, particularly the legacy of slavery and oppression, and is deeply influenced by those experiences. This foundation is what imbues the music with passion, emotion, and energy. The expressions of both pain and joy are integral to its essence. Music serves a deliberate and functional role within worship settings. Worship leaders employ music to facilitate the entire worship experience. The selected music can include processional pieces, hymns, or contemporary songs, all of which may embody a Gospel style. Various musical genres are often incorporated within the broader context

21. Esau McCaulley, *Reading While Black: African American Biblical Interpretation as an Exercise of Hope* (Downers Grove, IL: IVP Academic, 2020), 5.

22. Along with COGIC, NBC, and AME, there is the African Methodist Episcopal Zion Church (AME Zion), the Christian Methodist Episcopal Church, (CME) the National Baptist Convention of America, Inc. (NBCA), the Progressive National Baptist Convention (PNBC), the Pentecostal Assemblies of the World (PAW), the United Holy Church of America (UHCA), the Church of Our Lord Jesus Christ of the Apostolic Faith (COOLJC), and others.

23. McCaulley, *Reading While Black*, 6.

of Gospel expression as well. All of those elements are used to move worship forward and to help people enter God's presence. Regardless of the denomination, music is used instrumentally to guide individuals from their initial state upon arrival to a transformed state as they depart.

While Evangelical worship designers don't typically adhere or attend particularly closely to a lectionary or the liturgical calendar, they do strive to organize worship services around central themes that are typically highlighted in the sermon. Similar to Pentecostal worship services, Evangelicals utilize informal structures that typically begin with a welcome, a worship set of three to five songs, announcements and a time for tithes and offerings, the sermon, and a response to the sermon (i.e., Communion, an altar call, or a closing song). Worship designers consider the direction of the pastor's message, as well as the current needs of the congregation. For instance, if the congregation is experiencing challenges, the designer might aim to choose songs that resonate with those circumstances. Evangelical worship services often begin with an upbeat tempo in hopes of uniting all the congregants bodily and spiritually. As the worship set approaches the sermon, worship leaders transition to a more intimate and worshipful atmosphere, allowing the congregation to reflect deeply on the lyrics. This approach prepares the congregants' hearts for the message that God conveys through the pastor.

Catholic worship designers work in two different modes depending on whether they are designing worship for the Sunday Mass or for a midweek prayer meeting. In a way, worship isn't designed for the Mass, rather music directors serve a liturgy that preexists them. Planners are typically attentive to the lectionary readings of the day. Hence, much of the Mass is formed around Scripture readings or liturgical seasons. While much of what happens is prescribed by the liturgy, a lot can happen within the structure of the liturgy that looks and feels unique. For instance, there are places in the liturgy where songs can be chosen or slotted in: The entrance hymn, the offertory song, songs during Communion, and songs at the sending are all places where music directors exercise authority over what is sung. The rest of the liturgy is filled with musical moments that are prescribed. The midweek prayer meetings adopt a distinctly different strategy for organizing worship. In these meetings, worship planners select songs with an ecumenical perspective. While they frequently incorporate original worship music from Charismatic Catholic composers, they also include well-known contemporary Pentecostal and Evangelical songs. The chosen songs are designed to be congregational and easily singable, allowing them to be "prayed through" rather than simply performed. Given that Charismatic Catholics engage in prayer through music, they ensure that the lyrics align with their Charismatic Catholic beliefs.

To summarize, Reformed worship services are characterized by a structured liturgy that fosters diverse worship experiences while aligning with the overarching gospel narrative. Pentecostal worship designers focus on creating an environment that fosters an encounter with the Holy Spirit, balancing structured elements of worship with opportunities for spontaneous expressions and responses. Black Gospel worship, while diverse across various denominations, is fundamentally united by the shared experiences of Black people. The music plays a crucial role in transforming congregants through emotional communal expressions of solidarity in worship. Evangelical worship designers focus on creating services that align with the sermon's central theme, utilizing a flexible structure that fosters both communal engagement and personal reflection. Finally, Catholic worship designers adapt their approach based on the context of the service. The Sunday Mass focuses on a liturgical structure, while midweek prayer meetings utilize an ecumenical selection of contemporary worship songs to foster encounters with the Holy Spirit.

CONCLUSION

This chapter looked at worship design as a relational and dialogical act between God and the worshiping community. It emphasized the importance of a biblically grounded, aesthetically rich yet appropriate, theologically sound, and pastorally sensitive approach to worship that adheres to the fourfold order of worship. We also examined the significance of flow in worship design. The key to achieving good flow in worship is by bringing together different elements into a seamless experience that encourages deep connection with the Spirit, enabling worshipers to rise above the distractions of daily life and fully engage in God's presence. By thoughtfully crafting worship services with flow in mind, leaders can create an environment that allows congregants to encounter God. Lastly, this chapter discussed several principles that guide worship design across various traditions. While these principles may not be exhaustive, we will observe how they are implemented in the churches we evaluate in part 2 of this book. Part 2 consists of ethnographical studies of different churches throughout the United States. By evaluating the worship design of their worship services, we will be able to see how these principles were practically applied in real settings.

STUDY QUESTIONS

1. Does your worship ministry implicitly or explicitly follow the fourfold order of worship?
2. What style of worship is most fitting for your worship tradition?
3. In what ways can you create better flow in your worship services?
4. Of the five traditions assessed, what tradition does your church align most closely with? Do you find the principles of worship design from that tradition helpful? Why or why not?
5. Would you consider adopting any worship design principles used by other traditions? If so, which principles?

KEY TERMS

Content (in worship): the things we do to assist our dialogue with God.

Dialogical pattern: a conversational structure characterized by a relational exchange between two or more participants.

Flow: the progression of a worship service, where each element of worship naturally leads to the next.

Fourfold order of worship: a structured sequence of worship historically used in Christian worship to organize worship services consisting of the gathering, the Word, the table, and the sending.

Liturgical calendar: a cycle of seasons and feasts observed by many Christian denominations to commemorate and celebrate key events in the life of Jesus and the church.

Style (in worship): the way we deliver the content of worship.

PART 2

Case Studies of Evaluating Worship

CHAPTER 6

Evaluating Reformed Worship

Pillar Church, Holland, Michigan

In the heart of the quaint downtown area of Holland, Michigan, stands Pillar Church's historic building, a prominent architectural gem that captivates the attention of all who pass by. There is a timeless quality to the building's white and light gray exterior. Dominating the front façade of the building stand six large Doric columns, reminiscent of an ancient Greek temple. The columns—or "pillars"—are well known throughout Holland, and, one might say, symbolically represent the church's status as a pillar of the community, a stalwart dedicated to serving the city.

After a pivotal process of reconciliation, which will be discussed later in the chapter, Pillar Church reestablished and reimagined its role in the community, coming to understand itself as a "church for the city." As is noted on Pillar's website, "Pillar strives to be a church 'for the city,' a community of people who follow Christ in mission for the world God created, loves and redeems."[1] Throughout the twentieth century, Pillar identified itself as a neighborhood Christian Reformed church. But while

1. "Pillar Serve," Pillar, accessed June 24, 2023, https://pillarchurch.com/.

the surrounding downtown area, along with two prominent educational institutions (Hope College and Western Theological Seminary), developed all around the church property, the "neighbors" gradually moved out to the suburbs. Jon Brown, Pillar's current lead pastor, said, "The reestablishment was as much about reengaging the neighborhood as it is now—a downtown and college community. So that's why we say we're a church for the city; we want to evaluate ourselves according to the health of our community." Key to being a church for the city is an emphasis on reconciling the surrounding community back to God and one another.

This chapter explores how congregational worship music can be used to encourage reconciliation, and how Pillar Church, in particular, utilizes Reformed worship to foster its identity as a church for the city. The purpose of this chapter is to map the church's narrative framework to better understand its social and ecclesial context. Once this narrative is established, this chapter considers the church's tradition, history, communal impact, and aesthetic impressions. Having compared Pillar's congregational worship against its narrative framework, this chapter then assesses its biblical, aesthetic, theological, and pastoral value. This will allow us to make commendations and recommendations based on what Pillar's worship means in its narrative-hermeneutical context.

UNDERSTANDING: Mapping the Narrative Framework of Pillar Church

A mix of primary and scholarly sources, as well as ethnographic research conducted in April and June 2023 informed this chapter. I visited and observed the 10:30 Sunday morning service on June 18, 2023. I also conducted a series of interviews: an interview with executive pastor Rev. Chris Devos about Pillar's church history, an interview with lead pastor Rev. Jon Brown about worship and the life of the church, an interview with the pastor of worship arts, Rev. Jonathan Gabhart, about the church's worship practices, and an interview with a focus group of six church members who answered questions about the community and church identity. The remainder of this section utilizes these sources to analyze, respectively, the church's tradition, history, social impact, and aesthetic impressions.

Tradition

The Reformed tradition is rooted in the Protestant Reformation of the 1500s. Its primary leader was French pastor and theologian John Calvin, whose movement spread all over Europe and then to North America. The Reformed movement is theologically inspired by Calvin's 1536 publication ***Institutes of the Christian Religion***—*a foundational text that exposits, among other things, a broadly Augustinian view of grace and election, and a covenantal view of Christian living.* The main tenets of Calvinism are often summed up with the acrostic **TULIP**: *total depravity, unconditional election, limited atonement, irresistible grace, and the perseverance of the saints.* While not representative of all expressions of the Reformed tradition, this acrostic helpfully demonstrates that it is through divine election, rather than human free will, that people are saved. Calvinism can also be understood as a covenantal theology in which the concept of election is viewed as a framework for understanding God's relationship with humanity.[2] Worship and the sacraments are largely understood through this covenantal lens.

The three main associations of Calvinist groups are Reformed churches, Presbyterian churches, and Congregational churches. **Reformed churches** were *the principal Calvinist churches of continental Europe* and were particularly popular in the Netherlands.

2. David Steele, Curtis Thomas, and S. Lance Quinn, *The Five Points of Calvinism: Defined, Defended, and Documented*, 2nd ed. (Phillipsburg, NJ: P&R, 2004), 28.

Presbyterian churches *began under Scottish pastor John Knox, one of Calvin's students, who established Calvinist churches in Scotland.* Finally, **Congregational churches** *stem from the Calvinist Puritans who left England and headed to North America to flee religious persecution from the Church of England.*[3]

Pillar Church is a dual-affiliation congregation of the **Reformed Church in America (RCA)** and the **Christian Reformed Church in North America (CRC)**. The RCA is the oldest of these two denominations and was Pillar's original affiliation. The RCA was founded in a small colonial town of New Amsterdam (modern Manhattan, New York) in 1628 by a group of Dutch settlers. RCA churches formed throughout the 1600s and were all Dutch-speaking. The church started holding English-speaking services in 1764 prior to the start of the Revolutionary War.[4] The RCA's growth was bolstered tremendously in 1847 when a wave of Dutch immigrants settled in Pella, Iowa, and Holland and Zeeland, Michigan.

Holland, Michigan, was founded by a small Dutch colony led by Rev. Albertus Van Raalte, a Calvinist pastor from Arnhem, the Netherlands.[5] That same year, Van Raalte started and presided over a small church in a log cabin for the Holland community. By 1850 the church affiliated with the RCA, and the church came to be known as the Holland Reformed Protestant Dutch Church. By 1854, after substantial growth, the church decided to build a new building located centrally in downtown Holland, which was completed in 1856.[6] This same church building is still in use today.

A major schism took place in 1857 among the Reformed church communities of Holland. Several Holland congregations

---

3. "Calvinism," A Study of Denominations, accessed June 19, 2023, www.astudyofdenominations.com/denominations/calvinism/.

4. "History of the RCA," Reformed Church in America, accessed June 19, 2023, www.rca.org/about/history/.

5. "Michigan SP Holland Reformed Protestant Dutch Church," National Archives Catalog, sec. 8, p. 1, accessed June 18, 2023, https://catalog.archives.gov/id/25340374.

6. "About Us," Pillar, accessed June 18, 2023, https://pillarchurch.com/about/.

withdrew from the RCA and formed a new denomination named the Christian Reformed Church.[7] There were many reasons for the schism, including differences concerning Communion, hymnody, usage of the catechism, and most significantly, membership in secret societies such as the Freemasons. Holland Reformed Protestant Dutch Church retained its affiliation with the RCA until 1882, when the majority of the church decided to sever its ties with the denomination and join the CRC, changing its name to Ninth Street Christian Reformed Church. Those who wanted to remain with the RCA formed another church nearby with the name First Reformed Church.

History

As of 2023, Pillar Church has had twenty-two lead pastors in its long history.[8] In the 1980s the church was officially renamed Pillar Christian Reformed Church—a name congregants were already calling the church for many years. The church membership from 1910 until the mid-1950s held steadily at around one thousand people, but after the 1950s the church experienced a stark decline. By the early 2000s, only about two hundred members remained.[9] This decline is partly because of a post-WWII migration of families to the suburbs of Holland and partly because, according to former lead pastor and current executive pastor Chris DeVos, the church lost its perspective on how to engage with the demographics of the Holland area.

---

7. "Michigan SP Holland Reformed Protestant Dutch Church," National Archives Catalog, sec. 8, p. 3, accessed June 18, 2023, https://catalog.archives.gov/id/25340374.

8. The specific pastoral tenures are as follows: Albertus Van Raalte (1847–67), R. Pieters (1869–80), Evert Bos (1886–92), Kornelis Van Goor (1893–1902), Andrew Keizer (1902–10), Edward Tuuk (1911–19), James Ghysels (1919–25), John De Haan (1925–29), Nicholas Monsma (1929–40), George Gritter (1940–47), Thomas Yff (1947–52), Marvin Vander Werp (1952–58), Wilmer Witte (1958–65), Leonard Greenway (1966–69), Fred Van Houten (1970–74), Jacob Hasper (1976–86), Calvin Vander Meyden (1986–90), Clarence Reyneveld (1991–93), Michael De Vries (1993–2000), Christopher DeVos (2003–12), and Jon Brown (2012–present).

9. Chris DeVos, Zoom interview by Josh Edwards, April 28, 2023.

When DeVos was lead pastor from 2003 to 2012, he had a vision for Pillar CRC to be a catalyst for reconciliation in the city. One of the major steps to accomplish this vision was to reconcile the divisions made between the RCA and CRC. To this end, in 2012 Pillar was granted dual affiliation with both denominations—a major feat that took place after 130 years of division. The church brought in Jon Brown, who is licensed with the RCA, to become lead pastor and retained DeVos, who is licensed with the CRC, to be pastor of congregational mission.[10] The church then officially adopted the name Pillar Church, dropping the denominational ties from their name.

Pillar Church believed that to raise up leaders and serve Holland, they needed to address the division that was plaguing their church and tradition for more than a century. Thus, Pillar Church was reestablished in August 2012 with a vision for reconciliation that was accentuated by the reunification of two formerly severed traditions. Jonathan Gabhart described the reestablishment of Pillar, saying, "August of 2012, 'Pillar Christian Reformed Church' closed. This expression of the church as we knew it was no longer happening. The next Sunday we reopened and reestablished to a new way, around a new mission and vision. This allowed a sort of snap change that would otherwise be impossible." On August 26, 2012, the church held a liturgy of repentance. The congregation repented of its past divided history—a necessary step for moving forward as a reconciled church community.

Communal Impact

To get a sense of Pillar Church's impact on its worshiping community and on the broader community of Holland, I interviewed a focus group of congregants, asking them questions about Pillar's identity in worship and about Pillar's public witness.

---

10. Chris DeVos served in this capacity until 2015 and then left for Western Seminary to help revitalize churches across the US. He then served with the Colossian Forum before returning to Pillar Church in 2020 as the executive pastor.

When asked to describe their communal identity, one woman brought up the word "shifting." By this she meant that the community is a collective of varying, but related, theological perspectives. While Pillar comes from a strong Reformed tradition, it is welcoming to people from different church backgrounds. Another important theme that came up was that Pillar has strong ties to its physical location. One man said, "Some of [Pillar's] identity is shaped by its location. There are strong ties with the seminary and strong ties with Hope College downtown, and I think the Pillar community sees itself in the middle of Holland, providing services and lunches for college students, and taking advantage of the lawn's being a space not only for our church gatherings but for the community as well. In the summer, hosting events on the lawn and really hoping it's an invitational place . . . the attitude of bringing people in from the city is a big part of its identity."

The Pillar congregants view their church as a welcoming, accommodating, and outreaching community.

I asked the congregants how they define their worship ministry, and a common theme was that Pillar did a great job of approaching its historic Reformed tradition in fresh and relatable ways. One woman called Pillar's liturgy Spirit-led. She said, "I've had people come here, and they just literally sense the presence of the Spirit. It isn't so much the words in the liturgy or what's happening, but there's a presence that I believe draws people in."

There's something authentic and relational about the church's liturgy that helps congregants sense the Spirit in their midst. Another woman talked about how Pillar follows the Narrative Lectionary, and this unites Pillar's congregants spiritually with people from all over the world as they read through the same Scriptures, pray the same prayers, and reflect on the same messages. Yet this liturgy is presented in fresh and new ways.

Another woman said, "There's a format, there's confession, there's a call to worship, there are all these things that play out every single week. And yet, as far as I'm concerned, it feels so very organic. . . . It feels very natural and relational . . . it is a combination. You can see the structure that's been built into it, which provides that continuity for every person, but then there is also this familial sense that's comforting and relaxed."

A few of the congregants agreed that the worship creates a non-anxious environment that is grounded, uncoerced, and peaceful. This is partially attributed to the leadership of pastors Jon and Jonathan, and partially to the church's commitment to reconciliation. Here the church reconciles the formal and the informal—historic liturgical structures with present relevance.

When I asked the congregants how they were involved in the community, they all mentioned that they are "a church for the city," and that this sentiment is regularly proclaimed and reinforced in worship. For instance, every church service ends its benediction with the charge to enter every sector of public life to claim it for Christ. The congregants are to bring their faith to work, and conversely, bring their work with them to worship.[11] This means they are supposed to bring their whole selves to worship, not leaving what happens outside of the church at the threshold of the sanctuary. Being a witness in the world is both being Christ in the workplace and entering worship as someone from the public sector. One woman said, "Everything we do in the city . . . when we bless and serve, is a matter of ministry. There's really nothing secular. Everything matters. We are sent out with our benediction, 'May you all go out into every sector and be Christ, and if you can, speak Christ if it's appropriate.' So I think there's a great encouragement, empowerment, and belief that our presence [in the city] is sanctified."

One congregant mentioned how this looks different for every congregant depending on where they are in their lives. Some of

---

11. Kaemingk and Willson's book *Work and Worship: Reconnecting Our Labor and Liturgy* came up several times in these interviews as an important text that does a good job of defining Pillar's understanding of church and society.

the older church members are no longer working, so they are finding ways to serve the city through volunteer work.

The congregants also recited the church's vision known as Pillar's "Four *R*'s": reconciling divisions, raising up leaders, redeeming the city, and renewing the church. There was a sense that the congregants were deeply connected to the purpose and vision of the church. Instead of small groups, the church sponsors "city groups" that gather together to see what they can do as a group to help the city. Their service work varies from mucking out horse barns to bringing treats to policemen. There's an effort to impact the city, even in small ways, knowing that through their collective efforts, they are transforming lives, spreading love, and leaving a lasting legacy of compassion and hope.

An area of growth that both Jon and Jonathan brought up was diversity in the church, especially as it pertains to growing diversity in Holland. Holland is predominantly white (65.2 percent) but has a substantial minority population as well. As of 2023, 23.3 percent of Holland's residents are Hispanic, 4.7 percent are Black or African American, 3.68 percent are multiracial, and 2.96 percent are Asian.[12] More than half the students in Holland's public schools are non-white and mainly Hispanic. Jon and Jonathan both feel that Pillar Church, if it is to be a church for the city, should reflect the city's demographics more closely. As such, they are looking for ways to promote greater diversity in Pillar's congregation. To this end, Jon notes that diversity has been one of Pillar's primary objectives in hiring, both in terms of race and gender.. Additionally, Jonathan said that some of the worship music that is led by the ensemble could be enhanced with Latin and Spanish inflections. He noted various indie folk groups that were doing similar things. The hope is to diversify in a way that is organic, welcoming, and reconciliatory.

12. "Holland, MI," Data USA, accessed April 27, 2025, https://datausa.io/profile/geo/holland-mi.

Aesthetic Impressions

As I begin to describe what I observed during my church visit, let me first frame how Pastors Jon and Jonathan conceptualize worship at Pillar Church. In Jon's view, worship means, in its broadest sense, offering one's whole life as an offering to God. This reiterates what was discussed above, that bringing your whole self to worship also involves bringing your everyday burdens along. Jonathan added, "One of our big red flags is any sort of sentiment that says, 'Leave whatever you have at the door because now we're going to worship.' Well, no, actually, we're pretty convinced that God wants us to bring our honest selves to worship." The best setting to address what happens in the marketplace is worship. When we worship together, we encounter God as a community, and we reflect on how God has provided for us in every facet of life.

Pillar performs a mix of traditional hymns with a pipe organ, hymns with a band ensemble, and contemporary worship songs with a band ensemble. This is not a version of blended worship, however. **Blended worship** *integrates elements from traditional worship with contemporary worship expressions.* The goal of blended worship is to cater to different demographics, but because the music styles are compromised, neither party enjoys a truly authentic stylistic expression of worship. Pillar, on the other hand, looks to "reconcile" worship styles by moving from traditional pipe organ seamlessly into other liturgical elements that lead to contemporary worship songs.

When choosing a repertoire, Jonathan looks at how the songs form the congregation and the community. He does not choose songs simply because they are popular but asks, "What are the ways that these words as an expression of worship are leading us deeper into Scripture and our prayer life with God?" He looks for songs that work well with where the congregation is at spiritually. Both Jon and Jonathan see congregational music as deeply formational, so they want to make sure that the songs they choose are relevant expressions of their Reformed tradition. As we'll see, Pillar's worship service does a great job of embodying what Jon and Jonathan have conceptualized.

My experience with Pillar Church started before I ever arrived on campus. As Pillar Church is located in the heart of downtown Holland, there are many little shops nearby. My plan was to grab a coffee before going to church, and it just so happened that there was a trendy coffee shop right across the street. As I approached the coffee shop, not only did I notice Pillar's elegant architecture across the street but I heard soft music playing. I peered over at the church and noticed white chairs arranged in rows on the lawn with portable speakers and a large TV set up on the steps of the exterior entrance (fig. 6.1). With a few dozen congregants perched on the lawn, Pillar live-streamed the 9:00 a.m. service outdoors for the community. The sanctuary did not appear to be near capacity, so this lawn service wasn't there to accommodate overflow. It was a beautiful day at about 70 degrees.

FIGURE 6.1

Pillar Church lawn service

Photo by Steven Félix-Jäger, June 18, 2023

The sunlight danced through the branches of nearby trees, and chirping birds joined the congregants in song. Perhaps the possibility of a communal indoor-outdoor experience was too good to pass up.

With a freshly brewed coffee in hand, I arrived at Pillar Church at 10:15 a.m., a few minutes before the 10:30 worship service. Clusters of congregants gathered near the entrance, and friendly conversations filled the air. There was a sense of familiarity and unity as individuals gathered in community. The congregants were dressed in smart casual attire, striking a balance between relaxation and presentability. This style allows individuals to comfortably engage in worship and fellowship while maintaining a sense of reverence. Women and girls wore dresses, skirts, or fitted pants paired with T-shirts, blouses, sweaters, or light jackets. Virtually all the men wore tucked-in collared shirts without ties, paired with slacks, khakis, or nice jeans. Some of the men wore light jackets, but only a few of the older men wore blazers.

When I entered the church, I didn't see ushers or a hospitality team welcoming congregants—the congregants all seemed to know one another well. The interior of the church matched the exterior's beauty. The combination of light wood panels and columns, vaulted wooden ceilings, and white and light gray walls created a harmonious and inviting atmosphere. The space was well lit, with ample natural light streaming through several large windows.

I first entered a small foyer and noticed the entrance to the sanctuary in front of me, and the entrance to a much larger meeting room to my right. This room was named the Gathering Space, and several groups of congregants were engaged in conversation (fig. 6.2). One wall was occupied by a small display of local artworks on easels. Below the Gathering Space was a level that had classrooms and areas for children.

FIGURE 6.2

The Gathering Space

Photo by Steven Félix-Jäger, June 18, 2023

The sanctuary was a large, vertically oriented room. It had wooden floors, wooden pews, and white walls with wooden wainscoting along the bottom of the walls. Six massive windows adorned the walls, which let in a lot of light. The sanctuary also had a large, wooden vaulted ceiling lined with six pendant lights and a strip of stage lights near the stage. The stage was also made of wood and was backed by organ pipes and a wooden cross. Announcements, song lyrics and notations were projected onto the white walls on either side of the pipes. On stage, from left to right, were a grand piano, a bass guitar, an acoustic guitar, three vocal mics with stands, an organ, and an acoustic drum set. Floor wedge monitors and music stands were spread across the stage as well. A Communion table with a loaf of bread and three goblets of grape juice sat at the front of the stage. The congregants filed into the sanctuary as the service started. The congregants were not racially diverse—they were about 95 percent white. Although there was children's programming downstairs, several children attended the service. I sat in the balcony to take in all aspects of the service.

As people were settling into the pews, the band approached the stage. The full band was present except for the drummer, but the ensemble was joined by a violist (fig. 6.3).

There were three vocalists—Pastor Jonathan and two female singers. One of the female singers coled several songs with Jonathan, and the third singer mainly harmonized, although she led one verse. Jonathan signaled to the sound crew, and the band seamlessly transitioned from recorded background music to live music. They jammed for a little while, and then Jonathan, functioning throughout the service as liturgist and worship leader, calmly greeted the congregation, saying, "Friends, the Lord be with you," to which they responded in unison, "And also with you." After a few more words from Jonathan, the band led an opening refrain of "Trinity Song" by Sandra McCracken.[13] The female leader led this song, which seemed to function as a call to worship. The congregants remained seated during the song. They were not bodily expressive but were very engaged in singing. Toward the end of "Trinity Song," the congregants were asked to stand. The congregants stood in reverence as only the pipe organ played. The three singers sang into the microphones and led the hymn "Spirit, Working in Creation" by John Richards.[14] The congregants seemed obligated to stand whenever they sang hymns, but not necessarily when they sang contemporary worship songs. There were no hymnals in the pews; all the lyrics and music were projected. The first song displayed only lyrics; the rest of the songs projected lead sheets with lyrics, as seen in a hymnal, but only the melody lines were notated (fig. 6.4).

13. "Trinity Song," words and music by Sandra McCracken, CCLI #7068847 © 2016 Integrity Worship Music, Paper News Publishing (administrated by Integrity Music).

14. "Spirit, Working in Creation," words and music by John Richards, CCLI #357068 © 1978 John Richards.

FIGURE 6.3

Pillar Church sanctuary

Photo by Steven Félix-Jäger, June 18, 2023

FIGURE 6.4

Song projection at Pillar Church

Photo by Steven Félix-Jäger, June 18, 2023

After the hymn, the congregants sat back down, and Jonathan led a communal prayer. He then began unpacking how we need the Lord's help when we're in trouble and in the midst of celebration. He mentioned the celebrations of Father's Day and Juneteenth but also the heartache that sometimes goes along with these holidays. Then the female leader led a prayer of confession, and the congregants remained seated as they sang the contemporary hymn "Father, Only in Your Power" by Zac Hicks.[15] The congregation sang along loudly, and not only were the singers on stage harmonizing but several of the congregants joined in harmony as well.

Jonathan then transitioned out of the song by reciting John 3:16 and offering some explanation of the verse's significance and how it brings us peace. Jonathan then invited us to respond by "sharing the peace of Christ we have with one another." This "passing the peace" was a time to greet surrounding congregants, enter into short, friendly conversation, and leave the other congregant with a blessing of peace. This time ended with the pipe organ playing "Doxology" by Thomas Ken.[16] The congregation quickly joined and then sang the refrain once through. Interestingly, this is the only song where some congregants, about five or six, raised their hands in worship. Once the refrain ended, Jonathan invited the congregation to be seated, gave some explanation of peacekeeping, and then transitioned smoothly to community announcements. Jonathan ended this time by inviting the congregants to stand and sing the hymn "No, Not One" by George Hugg and Johnson Oatman Jr.[17] After the song, he invited the congregation to be seated as the speaker came up.

Jon Brown was preaching somewhere else that day, so the guest

---

15. "Father, Only in Your Power," words and music by Zac Hicks and Bruce Benedict © 2013 Unbudding Fig Music (ASCAP), Cardiphonia Music.

16. "Doxology," words and music by Thomas Ken, 1674, CCLI #6115489, public domain.

17. "No, Not One," words by Johnson Oatman Jr., music by George Hugg, 1895, CCLI #101898, public domain.

preacher was Jon's father, Tim Brown. Pastor Tim was the former pastor at Christ Memorial Church (also in Holland) from 1983 to 1995. After his tenure at Christ Memorial, Tim served as professor of preaching, and later president, of Western Theological Seminary until 2020. Because it was Father's Day, it seemed appropriate to have Jon's father preach in his place. Tim preached on Luke 15:11–32—the parable of the prodigal son—and showed how the father of the story represents Christ.[18] The biblical story demonstrates Jesus' compassion for us and shows us that Christ will wait for us to repent and return to him. It was a short but powerful sermon with great illustrations and biblical background.

After the sermon, Jonathan came back up and invited the congregation to the table for Communion. Jonathan explained how Communion would go and then invited the other servers up. The church did Communion by intinction—the congregants came up row by row to receive the elements, and the band played quietly in the background. After a little while, they led the song "The Day of the Lord (Psalm 37)" by Wendell Kimbrough[19] and then sang the refrain of "No, Not One" until all the congregants had a chance to go forward and take Communion. Jonathan ended the Communion time with a prayer. Afterward Jonathan invited the congregation to stand once more to sing the hymn "Jesus Shall Reign Where'er the Sun" by Isaac Watts.[20]

To end the service, Pastor Tim came back to give a benediction, one that is recited every week at Pillar: "You are about to enter every sector of public life to claim it for Christ, so let your transparency with Jesus be evident, and let your Bible be bold print so all can read. And may the grace of our Lord Jesus, and

18. Watch the full service here: Pillar Church, Holland, Michigan, 10:30 a.m., June 18, 2023, www.youtube.com/watch?v=r7Jp8FgqmAU.

19. "The Day of the Lord (Psalm 37)," words and music by Wendell Kimbrough, CCLI #7100081 © 2017 Wendell Kimbrough (administrated by Wendell Kimbrough).

20. "Jesus Shall Reign Where'er the Sun," words and music by Isaac Watts, 1719, CCLI #1039017 © 1982 The Jubilate Group (administrated by Hope Publishing Company).

the love of God, and the fellowship of the Holy Spirit be with us all. Go in peace."[21] The congregation was dismissed and everyone filed out of the church.

The service very clearly followed the fourfold pattern of worship. The gathering had a formal call to worship, prayers, hymns and contemporary songs, announcements, and a greeting by passing the peace. The word incorporated Scripture readings, reflections, and a sermon. The table response was Communion by intinction, which is Pillar's weekly response to worship. And the sending was a charge to enter every sector of public life.

Some songs, like "Father, Only in Your Power" and "Doxology," functioned as transitional parts of the service. The former served as part of the call to worship, and the latter transitioned the service out of passing the peace. Other songs served the flow of the service but did not directly reflect the contents of the sermon. Overall, the aesthetic choices that were made throughout the worship service seem to support the church's confessed identity as a church for the city that encourages reconciliation.

BIBLICAL, AESTHETIC, THEOLOGICAL, AND PASTORAL JUDGMENTS IN PILLAR'S WORSHIP

Having acquired a deeper understanding of Pillar Church's narrative, we can now assess how its worship fits within its framework biblically, aesthetically, theologically, and pastorally. Here we will analyze a particular Reformed church's worship tradition against the context of its Reformed values. Pillar's aim to be a church for the city is supported by a Reformed understanding of church and social engagement. In particular Pillar approaches outreach based on Calvinistic perspectives on public engagement. In terms of governance, Calvin advocated for the separation of church and state,

21. According to Pastor Jon, this benediction derives from the work of missionary and theologian Leslie Newbigin. See Leslie Newbigin, *The Gospel in a Pluralist Society* (Grand Rapids: Eerdmans, 1989), 232–33.

but he encouraged the church to indirectly influence government. Through his two kingdoms theology, Calvin argued that the church has prophetic authority when it limits its proclamation to that of Christ, rather than ideological agendas. The church can and should speak on public matters, but only insofar as it prophetically brings the gospel to bear on social issues.[22] In this context, we will examine four things: Is Pillar's worship biblically faithful given its context? Are the worship practices of the church in keeping with its doxology? What effect do Pillar's theological beliefs have on its worship practices? What role does musical worship play in caring for congregants?

Biblical Judgment

As mentioned above, Pillar Church uses the **Narrative Lectionary**, *a set of Scripture readings for worship that many Reformed churches use to guide their congregational worship and preaching*. It follows a four-year cycle and each year focuses on one of the four Gospels. The readings progress through the Bible chronologically to give worshipers a comprehensive view of the biblical narrative. For Jon one of the benefits of a liturgy is that it retells salvation history every time worshipers gather together. Thus, through repetition and habituation, liturgies form people in the ways of Christ. One of the weaknesses of a liturgy is that it may lead to a traditionalism where ritual is practiced for its own sake and not as a means to draw close to God. To mitigate this concern, Pillar Church practices what is called a **creative liturgical** approach to worship that *balances tradition and innovation, emphasizes participation and inclusivity, and is committed to both historical depth and contemporary relevance.*[23] Jonathan describes this approach as utilizing "a really historic Christian form of worship as it pertains to an order of worship and liturgy, but done in

22. Matthew Tuininga, *Calvin's Political Theology and the Public Engagement of the Church: Christ's Two Kingdoms* (Cambridge: Cambridge University Press, 2017), 377.

23. Jonathan cited borrowing this concept from theologian John Witvliet.

a way that is a little bit more contextual to the time and place that we are in. It creates space for people that have deep faith and have been Christians their whole lives, and also space for people who are just learning about Christianity or are not Christian at all, or have doubts. It provides room for all those different places to find an entryway into worship."

This is practically played out when the elements of worship are offered in a relaxed, conversational manner.

Jon and Jonathan recite Scripture and the formal elements of the liturgy from a place of "interior realization." Long Scripture passages are dramatically recited from memory, and other worship elements are known so well by the liturgists that they express them as if they were talking candidly to a friend. Jon said the reason they take this approach is because they want to "celebrate and honor the gift of the liturgy that's been handed to us down from centuries but offer it in a way that's comprehensible, accessible, and available to all." If first-time guests came to the worship service, they wouldn't know a liturgy was being followed. With this approach, not only is Pillar's worship biblically faithful but it comes to life through a creative contemporary retelling.

Aesthetic Judgment

To assess aesthetic fit, we must ask if Pillar's worship music is authentically suited to its community. As a Reformed church, is Pillar's worship music faithful to its liturgical tradition? Does Pillar's worship resonate with its members? As a historic church with a rich history, Pillar should embrace the traditionalism that has defined it for many years. Yet because Pillar has such a strong emphasis on reconciliation and public witness, it has a desire to bring together people with differing backgrounds and tastes. Because Pillar is located in downtown Holland and right next to a major Christian college, it tends to have a generationally diverse congregation. So to stay in keeping with its historical roots while exploring fresh, new expressions of worship, Pillar seeks to reconcile musical styles that naturally integrate well. To this end, Jonathan interweaves traditional hymns led by vocalists and a pipe organ, with hymns and contemporary songs led by vocalists and a band.

The ensemble performs an indie-folk style that is, according to Jonathan, "amenable to Americana." **Americana** is *a subgenre of rock that draws from older American musical styles such as folk, blues, country, bluegrass, and Southern Gospel.* It typically utilizes acoustic instruments such as guitars, violins, and banjos. If the songs utilize percussion, the drums are sparse and dynamic. The songs are typically led by timeless melodies and rich vocal harmonies. For Jonathan Americana easily integrates with older hymns for at least three reasons: (1) it leaves a lot of space for vocals to come to the front, which leads to greater congregational engagement; (2) its song forms are structurally similar to hymns; and (3) the instrumentation is nonaggressive and beautiful. Thus, Pillar has found a way to bring complementary sounds together so that neither genre loses its authenticity. This way of doing music touches everyone, young and old, newcomers and those who are experienced in the faith.

The performed songs evoked responses of reflection, confession, and adoration. Since the Reformed tradition utilizes worship songs and congregational prayers to encourage certain postures of worship, each song was coupled with a prayer or ministerial explanation of how the worshiper should be postured. In contrast to Pentecostal churches that perform a few songs for a long time, Reformed churches tend to perform a greater number of songs for a shorter time. Each song has a function and leads to other elements of worship like congregational prayers of repentance or reflections on a Scripture. Pillar performed seven worship songs and hymns, seamlessly moving from style to style. "Trinity Song" is a contemporary song that was led by the band ensemble as part of a call to worship. "Spirit, Working in Creation" is a hymn that was led by vocalists and the pipe organ. "Father, Only in Your Power" is a contemporary hymn led by the band ensemble. "Doxology" is a hymn that was played through once to transition out of passing the peace. "No, Not One" is a hymn that was performed by the band ensemble. "The Day of the Lord (Psalm 37)" is a contemporary worship song led by the band ensemble during Communion. Finally, "Jesus Shall Reign Where'er the Sun" is a hymn that was led by vocalists and the pipe organ before the benediction. Altogether the songs created a reflective mood that people were able to enter into.

The pace of the service was quick. No liturgical element lingered for very long, but the delivery of every element was relaxed and calming. While the song performances were not overly dynamic, they fostered strong congregational responses. As a reconciliation between styles in the context of Reformed worship, these songs fit the aesthetic mood of the service very well. The songs functioned more as prayers than as thematic setups of the sermon, and in this way the songs worked perfectly to fulfill every element of the service with aesthetic excellence.

Theological Judgment

As discussed in chapter 1, Reformed worship yearns to offer a biblically and theologically balanced gospel narrative in every worship service by following the creation-fall-redemption-consummation motif. Pillar's song selection clearly followed this pattern. "Trinity Song," as the title suggests, discusses the holy communion between the Father, Son, and Spirit. This song also calls worshipers to join in communion with God:

> Come with Your peace, with Your invitation;
> Bind us together in holy love.[24]

This song perfectly functioned as a calming and beautiful call to worship to begin the service. Then, "Spirit, Working in Creation" began the balanced gospel narrative emphasizing the Spirit's

---

24. "Trinity Song."

role in creation. Next, "Father, Only in Your Power" moved the narrative to the fall. This song takes a Trinitarian approach to proclaim our need for God's deliverance from sin and destruction. Pillar performs "Doxology" every service as a transitional piece. This well-known hymn is a short, confessional, hymn of praise that ends with the Trinitarian formula: "Praise Father, Son, and Holy Ghost. Amen."[25] Although it broke a bit from the creation-fall-redemption-consummation motif, it still established primary theological beliefs about God.

Next, "No, Not One" picked up with the balanced gospel narrative focusing on redemption through the "lowly" Jesus. This song shows that our Savior is relatable because he is also our friend. Then, the contemporary hymn "The Day of the Lord (Psalm 37)," was performed. This song has an eschatological focus on how all things will be restored when Christ returns:

> Everything that is broken will soon be restored.
> It's not long till the Day of the Lord![26]

This song was performed during Communion, which recontextualizes the Lord's Table as an eschatological foretaste of what is to come. Finally, the hymn "Jesus Shall Reign Where'er the Sun" ended the service, also expressing the consummation part of the gospel story.

Not only did the service demonstrate the creation-fall-redemption-consummation motif but Jonathan said he also checks to see if in a span of six weeks, the music thoroughly approaches a full range of theological themes. If anything substantial is missing, he's sure to modify the song selection for the following week. In addition to the creation-fall-redemption-consummation motif, this week happened to have a strong

25. "Doxology."
26. "The Day of the Lord (Psalm 37)."

Trinitarian theme. "Trinity Song," "Father, Only in Your Power," and "Doxology" all had explicit Trinitarian language in the lyrics, and the rest of the songs focused either on the Spirit or the Son. While the Trinity is valued as a doctrine at Pillar, Jonathan said the theme was not intentionally chosen but organically emerged during the song selection process.

Although the performed songs did not emphasize the church's commitment to be a church for the city, other elements of the service, such as the benediction, did. Nevertheless, the songs did an excellent job of authentically expressing the church's Reformed theological tradition.

Pastoral Judgment

The chosen songs promoted an attitude of humility, repentance, and peacefulness. Pillar successfully reconciled traditional and contemporary worship styles in a way that was authentic yet inclusive, causing every church member to be fully engaged in worship without hesitancy. The congregants displayed a great deal of trust in Jonathan and the worship team, believing that they would guide them well and help them center their hearts and minds on God. Congregants seemingly left the service spiritually refreshed and inspired to serve their community.

While the sung words were significantly formative, they were not understood in isolation. Prayers, Scripture readings, and every aspect of the creative liturgy worked together to help deepen the congregants' relationships with God and one another. Pillar's service was very structured, which did not leave room for spontaneous responses to any of the elements of worship. This has a lot to do with Pillar's tradition as a Reformed church. Although God can move in dramatic ways in any church context, Pillar's service does not create a space for intense, individually transformative spiritual experiences like one might see at a church with deep revivalist roots. Rather, Pillar's gatherings are communally oriented and then outwardly focused to serve the community.

Thus, the service's main pastoral function is to reaffirm the gospel narrative in a way that it becomes deeply internalized, affecting every part of the worshiper's life.

CONCLUSION

To conclude this case study, let us consider one more identifying marker of Pillar Church: the copper rooster. The columns at the front of the church are capped by a triangular pediment, and on top of that is a steeple that supports a copper rooster. As Pillar's website explains, in 1856 the church founders crowned the building with a weather vane in the form of a tin rooster. Through the years the rooster has come to symbolize two things: (1) it reflects Peter's denial of Christ and subsequent reinstatement as a faithful follower, which serves as an analogy for Pillar's division and subsequent reconciliation, and (2) the rooster heralds the morning sun, which serves as an analogy for Pillar's public witness.[27]

At Pillar each element of worship serves two primary functions: establishing the worshiper's posture in front of God and reinforcing the gospel narrative in the hearts and minds of the worshipers. Thus, the songs' meanings are shaped not only by their lyrics but also by their place in the liturgical celebration. Pillar's musical worship is an excellent reflection of the church's identity as a church for the city because it reinforces the gospel narrative and then sends out the congregants to be faithful witnesses in the community. The humble, noncoercive, and comforting leadership style allows congregants to feel accepted and welcomed at Pillar.

I would recommend three areas of growth for Pillar Church: (1) The church should consider forming a hospitality team to welcome new faces on Sunday mornings. I was not greeted by anyone during my observation, which seemed unusual since Pillar is so communally focused. Having a team welcome newcomers would

27. "About Us," Pillar, accessed July 1, 2023, https://pillarchurch.com/about/.

help the church bridge the gap between long-standing members and new arrivals. (2) Pillar would benefit from doing more outreach to the growing Hispanic population. People from newer, culturally diverse communities might have difficulty entering and feeling welcomed by a historic church; therefore, in an effort to strengthen its communal hospitality, Pillar should aim to draw in people from the Hispanic community. (3) As mentioned in the communal impact section above, Pillar's band ensemble songs would benefit from incorporating Latin and Afro-Caribbean musical elements. These influences work well with Pillar's indie-folk Americana style and can help the growing Hispanic community feel seen and welcomed.

This chapter mapped Pillar Church's narrative framework to understand the ecclesial and social context of its worship music. Among the factors considered in the analysis were the church's tradition, history, social impact, and aesthetic impressions. Following that, I analyzed Pillar's worship on biblical, aesthetic, theological, and pastoral grounds. The findings revealed an exemplary Reformed church that lives up to its identity as a church for the city.

STUDY QUESTIONS

1. Does Pillar Church's focus on serving the city inspire you in your ministry? How can your worship ministry serve its community?
2. Do you find the "creative liturgical" approach to worship worthwhile? Why or why not?
3. What's the difference between "blended worship" and Pillar's "reconciled" approach for worship?
4. What can congregations learn from Pillar Church's powerful story of communal and denominational reconciliation?
5. How can congregations benefit from a noncoercive and comforting leadership style?

KEY TERMS

Americana: a subgenre of rock that draws from older American musical styles such as folk, blues, country, bluegrass, and Southern Gospel.

Blended worship: a worship style that integrates elements from traditional worship with contemporary worship expressions.

Christian Reformed Church (CRC): a historic Reformed denomination that formed in the mid-nineteenth century after splitting from the Reformed Church in America.

Congregational churches: Calvinist churches that stem from the Calvinist Puritans who left England and headed to North America to flee religious persecution from the Church of England.

Creative liturgical: an approach to worship that balances tradition and innovation, emphasizes participation and inclusivity, and is committed to both historical depth and contemporary relevance.

Institutes of the Christian Religion (1536): a foundational text by John Calvin that exposits a broadly Augustinian view of grace and election and a covenantal view of Christian living.

Narrative Lectionary: a set of Scripture readings for worship that many Reformed churches use to guide their congregational worship and preaching.

Presbyterian churches: Calvinist churches that began in Scotland under Scottish pastor John Knox, one of Calvin's students.

Reformed Church in America (RCA): the oldest Reformed denomination in the US with roots tracing back to the early Dutch settlers of the seventeenth century.

Reformed churches: the principal Calvinist churches of continental Europe, and were particularly popular in the Netherlands.

TULIP: an acrostic that is often used to summarize the main theological tenets of Calvinism. The letters stand for total depravity, unconditional election, limited atonement, irresistible grace, and the perseverance of the saints.

CHAPTER 7

Evaluating Pentecostal Worship

Life Church, Lancaster, California

In 1979 a church member named John gave a prophetic word about Lancaster Foursquare Church (now Life Church): *Lancaster Foursquare would be a house of healing.* Congregants understood this word to encompass not only physical healing but mental, emotional, and spiritual healing as well. According to Tim Lee, lead pastor of the church's current iteration, this prophetic word frames how Life Church understands itself today. He said, "That word was given in 1979, and I'd say it is probably the most significant identity marker from the historic church that we continue to walk in today. We get a lot of people who need healing from many things like church hurt or broken marriages. It runs the gamut of people who have not just physical needs but emotional, mental, and spiritual needs as well." Through worship, Life Church hopes to create a safe space for people to experience God and see what God has in store for them, whether healing, encouragement, or rapprochement.

This chapter explores how congregational worship is utilized to shepherd a fruitful Pentecostal community, and how Life Church in particular utilizes worship to foster its identity as a house of healing. As in chapter 6, this chapter attempts to understand the church's social and ecclesial context by mapping its narrative framework. This entails looking at the church's tradition, history, communal impact, and aesthetic impressions. Having done that, we'll be able to judge Life Church's worship on biblical, aesthetic, theological, and pastoral grounds against its narrative framework. This will help us determine what Life Church's worship means in its narrative-hermeneutical context, giving us the framework to make commendations and recommendations moving forward.

UNDERSTANDING: Mapping the Narrative Framework of Life Church

Like the previous chapter, this chapter is informed by a mix of primary and scholarly sources along with ethnographical research that was conducted in May and June 2023. My research assistant and I visited and observed a Sunday morning service. We also conducted a focus group interview with seven church members, asking questions about the community and church identity. We later conducted a series of interviews: an interview with lead pastor Tim Lee about the history of the church, a pastoral interview with Pastors Tim and Sharon Lee about worship and the life of the church, and an interview with the worship leader, Pastor Danny Saltzman, about the church's worship practices. Between the observation, interviews, and external sources, this section maps Life Church's narrative framework. Thus, the rest of this section will consider, respectively, the church's tradition, history, communal impact, and aesthetic impressions.

Tradition

Life Church is part of the Western District of the Foursquare Church, which is also known as the International Church of the Foursquare Gospel. **The Foursquare Church** is *a Pentecostal* *denomination that originated in the early twentieth century in the United States.* Its founder, Canadian-born evangelist Aimee Semple McPherson, played a significant role in the establishment and development of the denomination. After years of itinerant evangelism, McPherson settled in Los Angeles in 1921. Shortly thereafter, in 1923, McPherson opened the historic Angelus Temple, the world's first Foursquare church, in the Echo Park district of Los Angeles. That same year, McPherson opened Foursquare's first educational institution, the Echo Park Evangelistic and Missionary Training Institute (known today as Life Pacific University), and Foursquare churches began being planted across California.[1] By 1927 Foursquare had successfully established 105 churches and fully incorporated as a denomination.[2]

Although the Foursquare Church made many ministerial innovations early on under the leadership of McPherson,[3] Sam Rockwell pinpoints five "Domains of Expertise" that encapsulate what sets Foursquare apart as a Pentecostal denomination in the US today. The Domains of Expertise are drawn from, and build upon, the Foursquare Global Distinctives—six foundational principles that were codified by the Foursquare Global Council in 2012.[4]

---

1. "History," The Foursquare Church, accessed June 12, 2023, www.foursquare.org/about/history/.

2. Nathaniel Van Cleave, *The Vine and the Branches: A History of the International Church of the Foursquare Gospel* (Los Angeles: Foursquare Media, 2014), 31.

3. For instance, Angelus Temple was one of the first megachurches in history. In 1928 Angelus Temple opened its commissary, which fed 1.5 million Americans during the Great Depression. McPherson was the first woman to own a major radio station and was one of the first evangelists, male or female, on the radio in general. She incorporated dramatic skits and the arts in worship, attracting celebrities like Charlie Chaplin and Jean Harlow. See Daniel Mark Epstein, *Sister Aimee: The Life of Aimee Semple McPherson* (New York: Houghton Mifflin Harcourt, 1993).

4. The global distinctives are kingdom partnerships, sound doctrine, empowering leadership, family relationships, spirit empowerment, and shared mission. See "Global Distinctives Announced by Foursquare Global Council," Foursquare, June 20, 2012, https://resources.foursquare.org/global-distinctives-announced-by-foursquare-global-council/.

The first domain is Integrated Mission and refers to Foursquare's goal to blend the objectives of evangelism, social service, and justice.[5] As well as focusing on evangelism and church planting, Foursquare aims to facilitate and contribute to global missions and ministry to the poor, oppressed, and disenfranchised in the community. The second domain, Women in Senior Leadership, refers to Foursquare's goal to see women advance in all areas of human endeavor, which includes senior church leadership.[6] Rockwell points out that although McPherson benefited from the egalitarian nature of early Pentecostalism, "Momentum toward gender equality in the Pentecostal Movement is always undercut and diminished when Pentecostals attempt alliances with fundamentalists and conservative evangelicals."[7] As such, championing the cause for women in ministry is a distinctive that separates Foursquare from many other Pentecostal and Evangelical denominations in the US. The third domain, Pentecostal Ethos, refers to Foursquare's holistic, pneumatocentric spirituality. **Pentecostal ethos** indicates *a way of being that embraces tongues-speech, physical healing, and miracles, along with expressive worship, prayer, and exhortation*.[8] The fourth domain, Indigenous Empowerment, refers to Foursquare's focus on "including members and cultivating leadership across genders, ethnicities, and nations."[9] This domain refers to the pastor's autonomy on how he or she chooses to lead a local church. Indigenous empowerment also looks to embolden leaders from varying cultures to lead in culturally relevant ways. This is essential for avoiding the colonial impulse to Westernize majority-

5. Sam Rockwell, "Our Unique Foursquare Identity and Opportunity," in *Identity Keystones: What Makes Us Foursquare*, ed. Sam Rockwell (Los Angeles: The Foursquare Church, 2017), 27.

6. Rockwell, "Our Unique Foursquare Identity and Opportunity," 29.

7. Rockwell, "Our Unique Foursquare Identity and Opportunity," 29–30.

8. Rockwell, "Our Unique Foursquare Identity and Opportunity," 31–35.

9. Rockwell, "Our Unique Foursquare Identity and Opportunity," 35.

world churches through global missions. Finally, the fifth domain, Moderation/Middle-of-the-Road Policy, refers to an approach to ministry that isn't overly formal or overly fanaticized.[10] This domain derives from McPherson's own conviction to avoid "extremes, fanaticism, unseemly manifestations, backbiting, [and] murmurings,"[11] and to be viewed as balanced or moderate within the larger realm of Pentecostalism.[12] These five domains encapsulate what Foursquare churches in the US, including Life Church, aspire to be like.

History

Life Church has seen many iterations in its nearly one hundred years of existence. The church was planted in 1928 by Elsworth Johnson. The original church meetings were held at a different location near the center of Lancaster, just off Lancaster Boulevard. Johnson pastored the church for about a year and then handed it off to Jeanette Boerner, who assumed pastoral duties for the next four years. In 1931 Boerner married Edward O'Donnell, changing her name to Jeanette Boerner O'Donnell.[13] That same year, still during Boerner O'Donnell's tenure, a charter was signed by Aimee Semple McPherson to officially welcome the church into Foursquare. The church was a small, tight-knit community until the 1950s when the church began to grow under the leadership of LaVern Goodell. The church continued to see growth through Dennis Easter's tenure as pastor from 1975 to 1982, which coincided with the latter parts of the Jesus Movement. From its inception until now, Lancaster Foursquare Church has

10. Rockwell, "Our Unique Foursquare Identity and Opportunity," 38.

11. Aimee Semple McPherson, "Declaration of Faith," 9, accessed April 27, 2025, https://storage.snappages.site/WMTFC3/assets/files/Foursquare_Declaration_of_Faith.pdf

12. Rockwell, "Our Unique Foursquare Identity and Opportunity," 38–39.

13. "Jeanette K. Boerner O'Donnell," Boerner Family History in Pictures, accessed June 13, 2023, https://boernerfamily.wordpress.com/jeanette-k-boerner-odonnell/.

seen twelve different senior pastors and has fluctuated in size from small to midsize.[14]

The church moved to Challenger Way in the mid-1990s under the leadership of Jan Spencer. Spencer, the church's longest tenured lead pastor, served for thirty-two years, until 2015. Although the church's legal name has been Lancaster Foursquare Church throughout its history, the church's slogan name during Spencer's tenure was Living Way Church.

FIGURE 7.1

Life Church exterior

Photo by Steven Félix-Jäger, May 21, 2023

Tim Lee and Sharon Baird met at Living Way Church during Spencer's tenure. They eventually got married there and even served on staff as pastors for five years. Then, after brief stints ministering in Avondale, Arizona, and Palmdale, California, Tim and Sharon returned to Lancaster in 2011 to plant a church called

---

14. The specific pastoral tenures are as follows: Elsworth Johnson (1928–29), Jeanette Boerner O'Donnell (1929–33), Raymond McNally (1933–38), Charles Freeman (1939), Ralph Barber (1940–41), Francis Coffey (1942–43), Raymond McNally (1944–49), LaVern Goodell (1950–75), Dennis Easter (1975–82), Jerry Howell (1982–84), Jan Spencer (1985–2015), and Tim Lee (2015–present).

Life Church. With Spencer's retirement looming, Spencer and the Lees discussed merging their churches and having Tim and Sharon assume pastoral leadership.

In 2015 the churches merged, keeping Lancaster Foursquare Church's legal name but adopting Life Church as the slogan name. Tim and Sharon describe the merge as a series of restarts for the church. First, the merger itself was a restart as the old church and the new church created something new. Following a few years of steady attendance and membership growth, the COVID-19 pandemic brought about another restart in 2020. Throughout a tumultuous season of closures, social distancing, and mask mandates, the church's attendance of about three hundred shrank to roughly one hundred. Rather than a structural restart, the Lees describe this era as a *cultural* restart. Some of the church members got caught up in partisan politics and ended up leaving the church. While there wasn't a full-blown church split, there was enough cultural change to mark a new era. As mentioned in the introduction to this chapter, Life Church understands healing to include every aspect of a person's life. After 2020 the sort of healing that was needed was social and communal healing. In subsequent years, the Lees led the remaining congregants out of those trying times back to health.

Moving forward, Life Church seeks to continue making disciples, fostering holistic healing, and blessing the surrounding community. To this end, the church has established five clearly defined goals for 2023 and beyond: (1) foster unified multigenerational ministries, (2) establish discipleship pathways among congregants, (3) expand leadership structures, (4) extend stronger community engagement, and (5) develop a fresh culture of creativity.[15]

15. "Assemble 2023," Life Church, accessed June 13, 2023, https://avlife.church/assemble.

Communal Impact

To discuss communal impact, we asked a focus group of congregants questions about the church community's internal functions and identity in worship as well as the church community's external engagements with the public.

When asked to describe their communal identity, one common theme emerged: freedom in the Spirit. One congregant said that freedom comes from an ecclesial focus on the Holy Spirit and that in such an environment one can "experience freedom in the Spirit to worship God freely like David did." In her interview, Pastor Sharon mentioned that freedom in worship is frequently emphasized at Life Church. She said, "Half of our church would know the phrase 'free people worship.' This freedom comes from what Jesus has done for us. That's how we live our lives—we're free people, and so we worship. That's been a phrase that we've really used often here." This notion of freedom in the Spirit not only was brought up frequently in the interviews but also, as we'll see, was ubiquitous throughout the church service observation.

One woman mentioned that she grew up in a strict Baptist church that tightly regulated what was allowed in worship. Life Church's open and expressive culture allowed her to open up and worship God in the way she always felt she should. She said, "I had a bit of an internal battle when I first started coming here because I had grown to dislike what I thought was unacceptable about myself. But here I was able to put the real me out on the table and say, 'That's not a bad thing.' That made a huge difference for me because, for the first time, I felt like I was actually allowed to exist in worship." She felt that her former church's restrictions on expressiveness in worship were an indictment on her as a person.

Individual and communal healing was another prevalent theme that was brought up by the focus group. One congregant mentioned that Life Church is a place for healing and restoration.

He said, "I think that for me, and I know several others, this place has been a community and a family where a whole lot of heartbreak has been righted. People that have had poor experiences with the church have been able to restore faith in it here." This congregant's sentiments affirm the 1979 prophetic word that the church would be a house of healing. Pastor Tim sees worship as leading to healing through repentance and prayer:

> Because we're intentional about worship, we believe congregational worship leads to things like repentance and prayer. If we were to ask our congregation where they feel most nourished in their week, I feel pretty confident that most of the people would mention a specific time during Sunday worship. We're intentional about the church's response to worship, so it's not just "sing three songs and then get to the talk." What we're trying to do every week is give somebody an opportunity to think about what's happening right now—whether that's through the words of the songs, the sermon, other times of ministry, and so on.

Tim sees every aspect of the worship service as constituting worship—not just the musical portion of the service. Many elements of worship are intertwined and underscored by musical expression, which creates a dynamic atmosphere for response.

When asked about the church's external engagements with the public, the congregants brought up that the church displays a friendly and welcoming disposition to the public. One congregant said, "I think we contribute to the community in a sense that we love everybody in this valley, in our city, and we do what we can to help, like offer marriage support, prayer breakfasts, and things like that. We're pretty well accepted in that. And we want to be active in the community. We don't want to just be 'that group over there.'" Some congregants mentioned how Pastor Tim makes efforts to connect with other local pastors so the surrounding churches can support one another. This was especially true during the COVID season, when the Valley Ministerial Association came together to support one another and the community with humanitarian efforts.

The congregants also mentioned a desire to find ways to serve the poor and disenfranchised in the community. Lancaster is one of the northernmost cities in Los Angeles County, and it is the final Metrolink station that begins with Los Angeles's Union Station. Since the station is at the end of the line, a large number of homeless people from Los Angeles end up in Lancaster. In fact, Lancaster's homeless population increased by 44 percent in 2020 alone.[16] Life Church sees itself as an integral part of its broader community with a mission to serve and aid those around them. As such the church aspires to find ways to support and resource individuals as they transition out of homelessness. Being a house of healing is both an internal and external aspiration.

Aesthetic Impressions

Before I describe what I observed during my church visit, I would like to frame how Pastors Tim and Danny conceptually view worship at Life Church. As mentioned, Tim sees the gathered expression of praise and worship as something more robust than just "three songs and a TED talk." Rather, the whole worship experience is about encountering God in community and growing together in discipleship. Since each element of worship supports this cause, music plays a pivotal role in fostering the community's praise and worship. For Danny relationality is key to fostering a rich environment of worship: "I am never one to play a few songs

16. Julie Drake, "Homeless Population Increases by 44 percent," *Antelope Valley Press*, June 30, 2020, www.avpress.com/news/local_news/homeless-population-increases-by-44/article_fbc7d65e-ba79-11ea-ad99-bf5f8067bc49.html#:~:text=LANCASTER percent20 percentE2 percent80 percent94 percent20The percent20Antelope percent 20Valley's percent20homeless,largest percent20increase percent20in percent20four percent20years.

and be done. I am also less for highly produced styles of worship, where the goal is to simply perform songs excellently and allow congregants to worship. I think worship is corporate, between the people in the congregation and the people on stage. All of us together are offering our worship to God." Church services at Life Church are communal gatherings where congregants expect to encounter God together in worship, which results in healings, breakthroughs, and spiritual nourishment.

Musical worship helps congregants enter into an environment of encounter that was already available. Under pastoral guidance, music helps congregants let go of distraction and focus their hearts and inner intentions on Jesus. Musical worship, specifically, helps congregants be sensitive to hearing God. Tim said, "It's almost as if [musical] worship has the function of prayer. I might be singing the songs, and then the prophetic happens. Prophetic ministry doesn't happen that much in our church outside of moments of praise and worship." As we'll see throughout the observation below, musical worship is cohesively integrated with prayer, prophetic response, testimony, and virtually every liturgical element. Conceptually and aesthetically, music works to create an environment of spiritual encounter.

I arrived at Life Church at about 9:45 a.m. before the 10:00 worship service. To get to the worship center, I passed through a courtyard. The courtyard was not particularly large or ornate but was well kept, reflecting a humble charm. The walls of the worship center and other administrative buildings enveloped the courtyard, creating a cozy enclosure. The sounds of chatter grew louder as I approached the entrance to the worship center, and I was met by a couple of friendly greeters at the building's entrance.

I stepped into a small church foyer that led into the sanctuary. To my left, I noticed a large built-in baptismal that seemed to be out of commission—this appeared to be a dated holdover from a previous iteration of the church. Next to it stood a small coffee bar stocked with donuts and coffee drinks for purchase.

Teenage baristas stood behind the counter, ready to make coffee or chat with fellow congregants. Adjacent to the coffee bar was a merchandise booth displaying T-shirts and brochures in front of a television that was scrolling church announcements. Both sides of the foyer extended out with hallways that had accessible bathrooms and various closed rooms.

The foyer itself was compact but thoughtfully designed. The walls were painted dark gray with a white drop ceiling and tan faux-tile flooring. The walls were not adorned with pictures or stencils, but the space was occupied by freestanding wooden walls that displayed photos and information. Soft lighting illuminated the space, creating a calm and welcoming environment. People milled about, engaging in conversation and connecting with one another.

After I met up with my research assistant, we entered the sanctuary. As in the foyer, relaxed preservice conversation floated through the air. People gathered in small clusters, engaging in conversations that ranged from catching up on personal news to discussing community events and church activities. After a few moments, we were greeted by Pastor Tim and a few lay leaders. As minutes passed, the gathering area filled up, the lights dimmed, and the service was ready to start.

The design of the sanctuary reflected a clean and uncluttered aesthetic, allowing the focus to remain on the worship experience itself. The walls were unadorned and painted in a light, neutral tan. The space felt intimate yet spacious enough to accommodate a congregation of about 275 people, although about 150 congregants were present. The square room was set up with a stage catty-corner in the back corner of the room (fig. 7.2). The seating arrangement was flexible, with comfortable chairs surrounding the stage rather than traditional pews. The chairs were arranged in three sections, creating a curve around the stage. This seemed to promote a sense of inclusivity that encouraged interaction among the worshipers.

FIGURE 7.2

Life Church sanctuary

Photo by Steven Félix-Jäger, May 21, 2023

The stage was a simple, carpeted elevated area backed by a gray, wooden wall feature. At the center of the stage was an illuminated cross, and above that hung the screen that projected song lyrics and sermon points. Three PA speakers were hung on either side of the stage, and wedge monitors were spread across the floor of the stage. The acoustic drum set was tucked away behind a half wall where one might typically find a baptismal. Soft, diffused lighting illuminated the stage, setting a tranquil and contemplative mood. Unlike some contemporary Pentecostal churches in the US, there were no moving lights, fog machines, or LED walls.

The overall aesthetic of the space was minimalistic, comforting, and inviting. The congregants and pastoral staff were all dressed casually, and there was a relaxed atmosphere of familial joy. The congregation appeared to be mostly white (about 70 percent), with a strong minority of Hispanics and African Americans. While church staff members were present, everyone integrated so well that it was often difficult to distinguish between congregants, volunteers, and pastoral staff. There were a few disabled congregants present who were fully engaged in the service and embraced by the community. There were some young families holding babies, and children and youth remained in the service until they were dismissed after the musical worship.

The worship team was made up of a bassist, acoustic guitarist, keys player, drummer, five vocalists, and the worship leader, who also played electric guitar. Pastor Danny greeted the congregation with enthusiasm, inviting the congregants to stand up and join in song. The team started playing "No One" by Elevation Worship and Chandler Moore.[17] The singers on the worship team encouraged the congregation to clap. Even though the congregation was not overly animated, they were very responsive and engaged. After "No One," Danny played soft electric guitar while offering a quick transitional prayer. The next song performed was "Tremble" by Mosaic MSC.[18] One of the female singers led this song, with the other vocalists popping in and out of the arrangement with spot harmonies. This song transitioned the service into a more contemplative state—everyone in the congregation was singing along, many people were swaying to the music, some people raised their hands, and a few people sang spontaneously, offering countermelodies to the sung bridge and choruses of the song. One nearby worshiper was audibly praying in tongues. Toward the end of "Tremble," Marcus, a lay leader, led the congregation in a responsive ministry time. He encouraged congregants to proclaim victory in Christ over fear, hurt, and pain. He asked

17. "No One," words and music by Chandler Moore, Chris Brown, Chris Tomlin, Jason Ingram, and Steven Furtick, CCLI #7188354 © 2022 For Humans Publishing, Maverick City Publishing, Capitol CMG Paragon, S.D.G. Publishing, Be Essential Songs, Music by Elevation Worship Publishing, My Magnolia Music (administrated by Capitol CMG Publishing, Essential Music Publishing LLC).

18. "Tremble," words and music by Andrés Figueroa, Hank Bentley, Mariah McManus, and Mia Fieldes, CCLI #7065049 © 2016 All Essential Music, Be Essential Songs, Bentley Street Songs, Mosaic LA Music, Mosaic MSC Music, and Tempo Music Investments (administrated by Essential Music Publishing LLC).

the congregants to raise their hands in response, entering into a posture of surrender to Christ.

After this time of ministry, the worship team went into a third song, "Fall Afresh," by Kari Jobe.[19] They started softly with the chorus, creating a lot of space for continued intercessory prayer. Many people throughout the sanctuary were praying quietly, some of the older congregants were sitting but still completely engaged in worship. There appeared to be an unspoken endorsement for worshipers to respond in worship however they felt was appropriate. Danny began praying, and there was some spontaneous clapping and verbal responses to the prayer.

Danny quickly transitioned into the fourth song—the anthem-like "Graves into Gardens" by Elevation Worship.[20] While expressive response was always present, the energy in the room really picked up during this song. The band members moved more demonstrably while playing, and the whole congregation clapped in a pattern they appeared to know well. Toward the end of the song, Pastor Marc, an associate pastor, came up to lead the congregation through another time of intentional ministry while the band kept vamping in the background. Marc was funny and lighthearted in his approach but quickly led to another message about victory over sin and death. He focused particularly on the resurrection of Christ and how there is life and abundance in Christ through the resurrection. The congregation clapped and cheered throughout Marc's exhortations. Then Marc called up Michael, one of Life Church's sound engineers, to give a quick testimony and prophetic word. Michael quoted 1 Corinthians

19. "Fall Afresh," words and music by Henry Seeley, Kari Jobe, and Sarah Reeves, CCLI #7078780 © 2017 Kari Jobe Carnes Music, Ninetysix Publishing, TBCO Music, Worship Together Music, Curb Congregation Songs, Dreaming in Color Publishing (administered by Capitol CMG Publishing, Curb Music Publishing).

20. "Graves into Gardens," words and music by Brandon Lake, Chris Brown, Steven Furtick, and Tiffany Hudson, CCLI #7138219 © 2019 Brandon Lake Music, Maverick City Publishing Worldwide, Music by Elevation Worship Publishing (administered by Bethel Music Publishing, Essential Music Publishing LLC).

15:54, exclaiming that because death was swallowed up in victory, we all have victory over fear, anxiety, and depression. After Michael's testimony, Marc said, "Let's lift up an anthem of praise," and the band played a reprieve of "Graves into Gardens." Next Marc gave announcements and discussed how tithes were taken at Life Church, then dismissed the youth and children to their respective services.

It was at this point that Pastor Tim came up and offered a warm welcome. He welcomed visitors and recapped what sermon series they were on.[21] He discussed how his sermon topic followed the previous three messages. He then preached a thirty-five minute sermon on Ephesians 4:25.[22] The church had been walking through the book of Ephesians, and Tim's topic landed on "truthfulness." Tim's sermon was exegetically astute, insightful, and practical. He pulled examples from life, culture, and even neuroscience. At the end of the sermon, Tim had the congregation respond with a moment of prayerful silence so they could repent from untruthfulness in their lives. He said he did not want to leave the meeting without giving his church family the proper space to respond and make things right with God. He then pulled everyone back and gave the congregants "homework"—a series of practical steps for the congregants to consider throughout the week (fig. 7.3).

The pianist came up and quietly played in the background, and Tim prayed a blessing over the congregation before dismissing them. It was only a partial dismissal, however, because right outside of the foyer they would be doing after-service baptisms.

---

21. Although a bit tangential, it's interesting to note that in his welcome, Pastor Tim mentioned that women in ministry are very valued at Life Church, which is indicative of the Foursquare denomination, and that he copastors with his wife, Sharon. He also mentioned that Life Church intentionally had three women preach over the previous three weeks.

22. Watch the full sermon here: Tim Lee, "Ephesians 4:25," accessed June 9, 2023, www.youtube.com/watch?v=UBPyGlx820U&t=1534s.

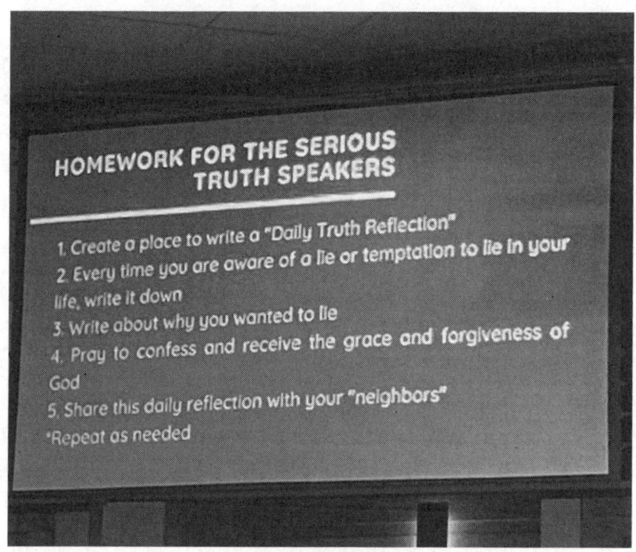

FIGURE 7.3

Life Church sermon slide

Photo by Steven Félix-Jäger, May 21, 2023

FIGURE 7.4

Life Church baptism

Photo by Sharon Lee, May 21,2023. Used with permission.

A small tub was set up as a baptismal in the church courtyard, and several of the pastors and lay leaders guided three congregants, one by one, into the baptismal space to receive baptism by full immersion (fig. 7.4). Many members of the church remained for the baptisms, which were joyful and celebratory. After the baptisms, Tim gave an informal dismissal. Many church members lingered a bit but eventually left the church premises.

This service followed the fourfold pattern of worship in an informal way. The gathering had greetings, announcements, prayers, congregational singing, and a time for fellowship. The word incorporated preaching, testimonials, Scripture readings, and extended ministry times. The table and alternate responses utilized water baptisms, a response of silence in reflection, and various prayerful responses throughout the service. Finally, the sending had both a prayer of benediction and a charge of "homework" for the congregants to be mindful of throughout the week. Unlike the other traditions, the fourfold pattern at Life Church was highly informal and integrative, and many worship elements overlapped with others.

BIBLICAL, AESTHETIC, THEOLOGICAL, AND PASTORAL JUDGMENTS IN LIFE CHURCH'S WORSHIP

Now that we have a solid grasp of Life Church's narrative framework, we can judge the biblical, aesthetic, theological, and pastoral fit of its worship against its own narrative. Here we will assess the worship tradition of a particular Pentecostal church against the values of its Pentecostal tradition. The idea that Life Church strives to be a "house of healing" can only adequately make sense in their Pentecostal context. Other traditions might have varying views on what healing means in the church today, and some cessationist traditions would go so far as to say that physical healing does not occur in the present day. Thus, it would be totally fruitless to judge Life's worship practice against the rubrics of a cessationist worship tradition. So we will look contextually at four things: Is the worship biblically faithful in its contextual expression? Does the doxology match its worship practices? Do the beliefs influence its worship practices? And how are congregants cared for through the musical worship? These topics concern biblical, aesthetic, theological, and pastoral judgments, respectively.

Biblical Judgment

The songs chosen for the service were thematically consistent with one another, but they were not necessarily chosen to support the week's sermon topic or biblical passage. While Tim provides Danny and the worship team general sermon themes and Scriptures, sometimes the worship songs reflect the themes and Scriptures, but often they reflect whatever is going on spiritually with the church community. Danny put it this way: "Sometimes we'll choose songs that we feel connect well with what we're learning about. Sometimes we're picking songs just because they're current and popular, and our congregants might listen to and sing them at home. I'm also peripherally connected to where I feel God is leading us in certain moments. . . . There are a lot of different factors that go into choosing songs. It could be just a topic or a theme that I feel like God is leading us toward, or it might be a topic or theme that I feel is connecting with the messages we're learning about." The song selection during my visit better reflected the church's overall identity as a house of healing than the particular sermon theme of truthfulness.

The songs were all centered around a biblical theme: "No One" is about Exodus 20:3, the first commandment, which prohibits idolatry; "Fall Afresh" is about Ephesians 5:27 and talks about the church being made a pure bride without blemish; "Graves into Gardens" is about Ezekiel 37, where Ezekiel sees a valley of dry bones given life and forming into a mighty army;

and "Tremble" is about Psalm 97:4, where the earth reacts with trembling because of the coming of the Lord. Other than "No One," the songs do not quote the verses outright but are based on the passages' themes. This portrays a personal internalization of the biblical themes—a commitment that demonstrates that the Bible is directly applicable to today's world.

Aesthetic Judgment

When assessing the aesthetic fit of Life's worship music, we first must ask if its genre of music authentically fits its community. From its inception, the Pentecostal tradition has valued fresh and spontaneous expressions of musical worship. Pentecostals take the psalmist's instruction to "sing to the LORD a new song; sing to the LORD, all the earth" (Ps. 96:1) as a mandate. Hence, Pentecostals tend to perform contemporary worship songs from many of the major Pentecostal or Charismatic worship collectives that are presently releasing music (e.g., Hillsong UNITED, Bethel Music, Maverick City Music, Elevation Worship, Isla Vista Worship, Mosaic MSC, UPPERROOM). Additionally, many Pentecostal churches strive to write their own worship music—something Tim and Danny expressed interest in doing. When older praise choruses or hymns are done in Pentecostal worship, they are usually tagged onto other songs or done as part of a medley of songs. A **tag** in worship is *a short song or section of a song that is added to the middle or end of a song.* It's not unusual, for instance, to hear "It Is Well," "How Great Thou Art," "Blessed Assurance," "Great Is Thy Faithfulness," or "Nothing but the Blood" tagged onto the end or middle of a contemporary worship song. Pentecostals often tag older contemporary worship songs as well, such as "Breathe," "Here I Am to Worship," "Shout to the Lord," "Alpha and Omega," or "Let It Rain." These tags help to connect the historical church with the contemporary church, but they are typically performed in a modern style and within a contemporary context.

As discussed in the latter part of chapter 2, Pentecostals want music to help create space for moments of spontaneous prayer and intercession. As such, the music should be open and simple enough to accommodate impromptu ministerial moments. Life Church clearly fits this context of worship. The performed songs, "No One," "Fall Afresh," "Graves into Gardens," and "Tremble" were all released by major Pentecostal or Charismatic worship collectives or artists, and were all written within the past seven years. Although Life didn't perform any tags, they frequently revisited refrains of these songs, leaving a lot of space for impromptu ministry.

The performed songs evoked responses of devotion and triumph. "No One," reflects on God's holiness as it responds to Exodus 20:3: "There will be no other god before You." The bridge of the song goes on to proclaim God's power and uniqueness:

> Who else can lead us, lead us to freedom?
> No one, no one, no one.[23]

"Fall Afresh" is also devotional but invites worshipers to turn their hearts to God's presence in reverence:

> Let this be a house
> Where You long to stay[24]

Finally, both "Graves into Gardens" and "Tremble" have themes of God triumphing and declaring victory over shame, hurt, and death. For instance, the bridge of "Graves into Gardens" expresses how God redeems, turning bad things into good situations. Similarly, "Tremble" describes Christ's sovereign power over evil:

---

23. "No One."
24. "Fall Afresh."

Jesus, Jesus, You make the darkness tremble.
Jesus, Jesus, You silence fear.[25]

It is in Christ that we are victorious. These songs all convey a message of presence and power—believers can find healing from hurt and deliverance from sin and death when they dwell in the presence of the sovereign God who reigns victorious over all.

The song performances were all dynamic with slow builds and powerful resolutions. They allowed worshipers to dwell for a while in a prayerful, contemplative space but also grew toward big, celebratory shouts of victory. Since Life Church is heavily focused on healing and spiritual breakthrough, these songs completely fit the aesthetic mood of the service. The songs worked perfectly to facilitate an extemporaneous and informal order of worship that emphasized spontaneity. The songs were performed mostly by volunteers, and although the music was not complex, they did an excellent job of navigating musical dynamics and following the emotional swings present throughout the service. In other words, the worship team was very sensitive to where the congregants were at spiritually and emotionally, and they did a great job of utilizing structure and dynamics to help people draw near to God.

Theological Judgment

In the context of Life Church's narrative framework, all of the performed songs made theological sense. Life is a Pentecostal church that sees itself as a house of healing, and all the songs carried messages of healing, deliverance, victory, and presence. While these themes were not the main topic of Tim's sermon, the sermon was preached in a way that supported the church's overall identity of healing and freedom in the Spirit and a biblical commitment to an eschatological reading of Luke-Acts. Tim spoke about confession as a necessary first step of healing and even made the point

25. "Tremble."

that "knowing the truth sets people free." Overall, the way the service was conducted and the choices that were made seem to support the church's confessed theological identity.

Each of the songs fit the broader eschatological context of already and not yet. Healing, victory, and deliverance are presently available as foretastes of what is to come. This is especially true with "Graves into Gardens," which says that the God of the mountain is also the God of the valley. Andrew, the Pentecostal pastor from Virginia we met in chapter 3, says that the already and not yet is the time between times. He says, "The present reality, therefore, has mountaintops and valleys, triumphs and laments." "Fall Afresh" and "Tremble" both bear strong eschatological themes while reflecting on God's powerful presence. In this eschatological framework, victory and healing are seen as present glimpses of the total victory and healing that are available at the eschaton. Although the language used is broad and not particularly sectarian, this eschatological framework goes beyond the mere proclamation of Christ's return, representing, thus, a secondary belief that situates the songs in a Pentecostal theological tradition. The performed songs authentically extended the church's narrative framework while acting as catalysts for divine encounter.

Pastoral Judgment

Life Church's chosen songs all worked very well to create the space to relationally know and be known by God. The set moved from intimate expressions of devotion to clamorous shouts of praise. The way the songs were performed created a dynamic space for Danny and the worship team to discern where the Spirit was moving. This sensitivity to the Spirit was expressed in a mixed structural spontaneity—they would play the songs with their normal structures but spend a lot of time vamping on bridges or choruses to allow space for impromptu ministry. It was in these moments of spontaneous vamping that Marcus and Marc came up to minister.

Congregants were being formed both by the sung words of the worship songs and by the intercession that took place during the songs. Thus, religious meaning was transmitted through the espoused theology of the song lyrics and by the way the songs were performed and received by the congregation. Music also underscored most of the service elements. The music stopped only when Tim began to preach. The ubiquity of music throughout the service served the congregants' general state of expectancy—there was a sense that God could move in the hearts of the congregants at any time. The continual music also helped worship elements flow together in a way that made the whole service feel like an experiential pursuit. Hence, the worship music was crucially important for Life Church's pastoral ministry.

CONCLUSION

A worship song's function at Life Church transcends mere enjoyment—it facilitates divine encounter. This does not mean worship songs carry inherent, mediatory power—Pentecostals believe Christ and the Spirit are the only mediators. People are reconciled to God through Jesus' death and resurrection, and experience God's presence through the Spirit, who mediates a direct relationship between people and God. Yet worship songs help facilitate a space where God is encountered. God is not called down to join worshipers at church, but rather music helps worshipers turn their hearts toward God, who has already called out to them. God is already present and beckoning all to turn to Christ, so worship is a person's response to God's divine revelation. Worship music helps make worshipers aware of the divine presence already there.

While lyrics do portray didactic enrichment, and each element of worship helps situate the worshiper's posture in front of God, the primary function of worship music at Life Church is faciliatory. Therefore, the songs' meanings are constructed by the espoused theology present in the lyrics, and, significantly, by how the songs are received aesthetically and pastorally. Life Church demonstrated an excellent grasp of their own identity as a house of healing and utilized worship music in a way that reinforced their identity. Life's leaders were friendly, humble, and noncoercive, which allowed congregants the freedom to respond to God however they wanted. The worship music was also dynamic, and a full range of emotional expression was possible throughout the service. Life Church displayed perfectly an enacted theology of encounter that is indicative of Pentecostal worship.

I would recommend three areas of growth for Life Church: (1) The worship team should consider utilizing tags of hymns and older praise choruses more frequently. Life Church is made up of a great diversity of ages, so tapping into older songs might help some congregants connect their past and present spiritual encounters. (2) As the church grows, the musical worship can also grow in musical and technical excellence. While the music and sound can be improved, that doesn't mean it was poorly done. Aside from Danny, the worship team and sound crew were led by volunteers, who, while doing an admirable job given their parameters and resources, would benefit from more training in sound and musical proficiency. (3) As was mentioned in the communal impact section above, Life Church would do well to find more ways to facilitate public outreach. A stronger effort to help mitigate some of Lancaster's biggest issues could help establish Life Church as a house of healing for the city.

By mapping Life Church's narrative framework, this chapter sought to understand the social and ecclesial context for its worship music. The analysis included examining the church's tradition, history, social impact, and aesthetic impressions. Then I evaluated Life Church's worship on biblical, aesthetic, theological, and pastoral grounds. What I found was an exceptional Pentecostal church that lives up to its identity as a house of healing.

STUDY QUESTIONS

1. Do you believe Life Church lives up to its slogan of being a house of healing? Why or why not?
2. Did the worship at Life Church authentically display a Pentecostal ethos?
3. What can you take away from Life Church's ability to integrate moments of structure and spontaneity throughout the service?
4. Do you think Life Church would have benefited from choosing songs that explicitly referenced the sermon theme, or was it appropriate to choose songs that reinforced the church's general biblical and theological commitments?
5. Do you feel Life Church adequately created a charged atmosphere for worshipers to encounter God? Why or why not?

KEY TERMS

The Foursquare Church: also known as the International Church of the Foursquare Gospel, a Pentecostal denomination that originated in the early twentieth century in the United States.

Pentecostal ethos: a way of being that embraces tongues-speech, physical healing, and miracles, along with expressive worship, prayer, and exhortation.

Tag: a short song or section of a song that is added to the middle or end of a song.

CHAPTER 8

Evaluating Black Gospel Worship

St. John AME Church, Fairburn, Georgia

During our visit to St. John AME Church's worship service, something interesting happened. Toward the beginning of this special "International Sunday" service, a church member performed a praise dance (fig. 8.1). A **praise dance** is *a liturgical form of expressive movement that is performed as a special act of worship in a worship service*. Dressed in traditional African attire, the congregant danced to a recording of Phil and Victor Thompson's "Jesus, Lamb of God."[1] The dance was a free-flowing, liturgical dance that told a story—each motion was imbued with symbolic meaning. About halfway through the dance, the streamed song was abruptly, and unintentionally, interrupted by a commercial for gun insurance. The dancer smiled and began gesturing with his hands, and after a short pause the band began to play an unrehearsed rhythm on the djembe and drums. The choreographed praise dance suddenly turned into a spontaneous dance that

1. "Jesus, Lamb of God," words and music by Geoffrey Golden, Jasmine Rae, Mark Alan Schoolmeesters, and Phil Thompson, © 2024 PhilThompsonWorship (administrated by Integrity Music).

evoked a West African cadence. The atmosphere was now charged with energy as the congregants vocalized support and admiration. When the song died down, the dancer walked back down the center aisle of the sanctuary to cheers and a standing ovation.

FIGURE 8.1

"Praise dance" at St. John AME Church

Livestream film-still, June 30, 2024. Used with permission.

As I witnessed this beautiful act of worship, not only was I impressed by the dancer's quick, impromptu recovery but I couldn't help but notice that this whole sequence seemed poetic. St. John is an African Methodist Episcopal (AME) church right outside of Atlanta, Georgia. On June 17, 2015, almost exactly nine years prior, a white twenty-one-year old man attended a Bible study at Emanuel AME Church in Charleston, South Carolina, and shot and killed nine churchgoers.[2] Similarly, in 2003 a woman with mental illness shot and killed the pastor and two churchgoers during a service at Turner Monumental AME

2. Debbie Elliott, "Five Years After Charleston Church Massacre, What Have We Learned?" NPR, June 17, 2020, www.npr.org/2020/06/17/878828088/5-years-after-charleston-church-massacre-what-have-we-learned.

Church in Atlanta.[3] As noted above, the dancer's contemporary worship song was interrupted by a commercial about gun insurance, which creates an interesting parallel to the tragic episodes of gun violence that took place at nearby AME churches some years prior. Rather than continuing the contemporary Gospel song that was interrupted, the band and dancer performed a new song—a song of resilience. This episode could be seen as a metaphor of the resilience that Black Gospel worshipers have always needed. After the dance, the pastor proclaimed, "Praise God, hallelujah. Now *that's* how you know. That's all I'm gonna say; that's how you know." Without expressing anything directly, the congregants seemed to feel the weight of this episode.

This chapter looks at the worship of St. John AME Church, a healthy Black Gospel church, and how, in particular, music fosters communal identity. Once again, we'll look at the church's tradition, history, communal impact, and aesthetic impressions to establish a context for judging St. John's worship practices on biblical, aesthetic, theological, and pastoral grounds. Using this method, we'll see what worship means in St. John's narrative-hermeneutical context. Hence, we'll be able to use this framework to faithfully assess St. John's worship practices and make commendations and recommendations for consideration.

UNDERSTANDING: Mapping the Narrative Framework of St. John AME Church

This chapter, like the preceding two, draws on a combination of primary scholarly sources as well as ethnographic research that was conducted in June and July 2024. My research assistant and I attended and observed a Sunday morning service at St. John. Later that day, we held a focus group interview with five church

3. Jeffrey Gettleman, "Pastor and Two Others Are Killed in Shooting at Atlanta Church," *New York Times*, October 6, 2003, www.nytimes.com/2003/10/06/us/pastor-and-2-others-are-killed-in-shooting-at-atlanta-church.html.

members, inquiring about the community and church identity. We also conducted an interview with lead pastor Rev. Dr. Greta Fowler about worship and the life of the church, and an interview with the minister of music, Rev. Edward Menifee II,[4] who is affectionately nicknamed "Chief," about the church's worship practices. Through an analysis of observation, interviews, and external sources, this section elucidates St. John's narrative framework. The following sections delve into the church's tradition, history, communal impact, and aesthetic impressions.

Tradition

The Black Gospel worship tradition is rooted in what Henry Louis Gates Jr. calls the "Black church."[5] While there is no monolithic Black church, Gates uses this term "as a way to acknowledge the importance of institutions of organized religion to African Americans over time."[6] Esau McCaulley uses the more precise term **Black ecclesial tradition** as *the unique theological, spiritual, and cultural expressions of Christianity that have developed within African American communities.* As mentioned in chapter 3, this tradition extends a Black ecclesial theology that uses a biblical hermeneutic rooted in the Black lived experience (Black ecclesial interpretation).[7]

While there is a wide range of theological positions throughout the Black ecclesial tradition, McCaulley says the Black church generally holds to orthodox theological beliefs—those primary beliefs held by all Christians throughout history. This is evidenced by the statements of faith of three of the larger Black

---

4. Having been trained at Candler Theological Seminary, Menifee also serves as a recording artist and itinerant music minster to other churches in the greater Atlanta area. His ministry involves scholarship, chaplaincy, preaching, pastoral care, and counseling.

5. Henry Louis Gates Jr., *The Black Church: This Is Our Story, This Is Our Song* (New York: Penguin, 2022), 1.

6. Gates, *The Black Church*, 1.

7. Esau McCaulley, *Reading While Black: African American Biblical Interpretation as an Exercise of Hope* (Downers Grove, IL: IVP Academic, 2020), 5–6.

church denominations: the Church of God in Christ (COGIC), the National Baptist Convention (NBC), and the African Methodist Episcopal (AME) Church.[8] Yet even while there is much diversity in the Black ecclesial tradition, it approaches worship, teaching, theology, communal activism, and cultural identity in ways that are distinct from non-Black worshiping traditions.

This chapter focuses on the **African Methodist Episcopal (AME) Church**. The AME Church is *a historical Black Protestant denomination founded by Richard Allen in Philadelphia, Pennsylvania, in 1816*. Significantly, it is the first independent Protestant denomination founded by Black people. The AME Church was established as a response to the discriminatory treatment of Black congregants at St. George's Methodist Episcopal Church in Philadelphia.[9] Richard Allen, a former slave who purchased his own freedom in 1783, became the AME's first bishop and was a leading figure in the church's formation and expansion.[10] While the AME Church is based primarily in the US, it has expanded its reach globally to include congregations in Africa, the Caribbean, and other parts of the world. Today the AME Church has more than two million members and six thousand churches globally.[11]

As part of the Methodist tradition, the AME Church adheres to a Wesleyan-Arminian theology that focuses on freewill and personal holiness. Like other Methodists, the AME Church has an episcopalian polity that is governed by bishops.[12] Socially, the AME Church focuses on education, economic development, and political advocacy in African American communities. Jason

8. McCaulley, *Reading While Black*, 5.

9. Dennis Dickerson, "Our History," AME Church, accessed July 13, 2024, www.ame-church.com/our-church/our-history/.

10. Tony Evans, *A Survey of the Black Church in America: Exploring Its History, Ministry, and Unique Strengths* (Chicago: Moody, 2023), 30.

11. Evans, *A Survey of the Black Church in America*, 30.

12. "Church Structure," AME Church, accessed July 13, 2024, www.ame-church.com/our-church/our-structure/.

Evans has argued that the AME's worship cultivates the identity and praxis of African Methodists as a "liberating and reconciling people."[13] As such, the themes of justice and unity frequent AME worship. While the church follows a liturgical worship style, worship services are typically lively and participatory, interweaving prayer, music, and exhortation.

History

St. John formed as an independent Methodist church sometime between 1840 and 1860 but incorporated into the AME denomination in 1880 under the leadership of Rev. Jordan Jay. When it came time to establish a permanent house of worship, the church suffered many setbacks. The church purchased its first site in 1907, but it was destroyed in 1918 by a major storm. For many years, the congregants worshiped wherever they could until they raised enough money to build a new sanctuary. But in 1937 strong winds made the poorly constructed church dangerous for worship. In 1938 the church was rebuilt under the leadership of Rev. C. C. Blake, and St. John found a permanent house of worship until 1991. Finally, in 1991, under the leadership of Rev. Isaiah Juran Waddy, St. John purchased 7.8 acres of land just outside of Atlanta in the city of Fairburn and began building the church that would be dedicated in 1992 and remains St. John's permanent house of worship until the present.[14] Today the city of Fairburn has roughly seventeen thousand residents. Demographically, Fairburn is predominately Black (82.59 percent) with a median age of 33.5 years.[15]

The years following St. John's move to Fairburn consisted of a succession of administrations that brought various levels of

---

13. Jason Evans, "The Identity, Liturgy, and Praxis of the African Methodist Episcopal Church," St. Paul AME Church, Des Moines, accessed July 14, 2024, www.stpauldesmoines.org/essay.

14. "Our History," St. John AME Church, accessed July 5, 2024, www.stjohnfairburn.com/church-history/.

15. "Fairburn Population," World Population Review, accessed April 27, 2025, https://worldpopulationreview.com/us-cities/georgia/fairburn#demographics.

health and growth to the church. After Reverend Waddy's tenure as pastor from 1986 to 1993, the denomination appointed Rev. Dr. Keith Lawrence to serve as pastor. Under Reverend Lawrence's leadership from 1993 to 2004, the church grew, began holding multiple services, and acquired additional properties. Then in 2004 Rev. B. A. Hart was appointed to serve St. John. Under Reverend Hart's tenure (2004–17), St. John was able to secure financial stability, improve the sanctuary and the landscaping, and launch several ministries and community outreach programs. In 2017 Rev. Charles Ramsey Jr. was appointed as pastor, and during his tenure (2017–23) St. John adopted the theme "A place of divine possibilities." Reverend Ramsey led St. John through difficult times that included a polarizing US presidency, social unrest stemming from police brutality and racial injustice, and lockdowns and restrictions because of the COVID-19 pandemic. Yet during this time St. John developed a social media presence that included streaming and was able to serve the Fairburn community by organizing food giveaways, testing and vaccine centers, and social justice programs.[16] As in many other churches during that time, the pandemic also streamlined how the worship services would function. While the order of service was more complex before COVID-19, it was simplified during the pandemic to accommodate streaming and social distancing. Church services went from more than two hours long to about an hour and fifteen minutes.

In 2023 the AME appointed St. John's first female pastor, Rev. Dr. Greta Fowler. After serving at two different AME churches in Thomson and Adairsville, Georgia, respectively, Reverend Fowler was promoted by her bishop to serve at St. John. Reverend Fowler's vision for the church is for them to heal from past hurts and then to reach out and make their presence more felt in the community. Hence, she brought a new motto to St. John: "Building beyond the

16. "Our History," St. John AME Church.

wall." "Building" here must first consist of an internal building—a renovation—before it can step out beyond the church walls. St. John remains a healthy and flourishing church today.

Communal Impact

To get a sense of St. John's communal impact, we interviewed a focus group of congregants and asked questions about their identity as a worshiping community. We also asked questions about how the church functions internally and as a public witness.

When asked to describe their communal identity, one congregant quickly brought up that when a new pastor comes aboard, the pastor establishes a motto that helps shape the identity of the church. The last few mottos were all socially oriented, and the current motto, "Building beyond the wall," follows suit. This means St. John feels called to do more work outside of the church walls and to live into their identity of being a *connectional church*. In the AME denomination, a **connectional church** refers to *a denominational structure that emphasizes the interconnectedness and mutual support among its churches and leadership*. Along with helping foster an accountable governing system, the AME's connectional system allows churches to share resources for educational and missional programs. One congregant brought up that being a connectional church entails spreading God's love outside the church walls. The church participates in many outreach endeavors through their twelve active church ministries, which include the church school, the Commission on Christian Education, the media ministry, the Virginia Henderson Harris Lay Organization, the Edith White Ming Women's Missionary Society, the board of stewards, the board of trustees, the stewardess board, the doorkeepers and greeters ministry, the youth ministries, the men's fellowship, and the Richard Allen Youth Council.[17]

---

17. "About Us," St. John AME Church, accessed July 6, 2024, www.stjohnfairburn.com/ministries/.

The congregants said that being a church that reaches out means being nonjudgmental and welcoming. People are encouraged to join St. John's community because of the congregants' witness of God's love. One congregant said, "If I say that I love God and that he has blessed me, how am I going to tell that to other people outside of this building? . . . We have to be that arm of God that reaches out." Being a church that reaches out also means encouraging people and helping them rekindle their faith if they have been disconnected from God and the community. Many people experienced displacement because of COVID, so the church seeks to help bring people back into St. John's worshiping community.

A welcoming spirit was very evident during the worship service as Reverend Fowler and the congregants interacted with joy and laughter throughout the whole service. One congregant said her joy comes from an overflow of the Spirit she experiences in worship. The music is used congregationally as another way to minister to the people. The music isn't there just to set up the sermon, but the words and musical expressions can minister to the people as well. Another congregant said worship for St. John is all-encompassing—many people can get involved. The AME Church, they said, emphasizes education and fellowship, which emerges as a holistic, lived worship experience. Considering all that has been stated, we might say St. John views itself as a welcoming, community-oriented congregation of Spirit-filled and socially conscious worshipers.

Aesthetic Impressions

Before I describe what we observed during our church visit, I would like to frame how Reverend Fowler and Chief view worship at St. John. According to Reverend Fowler, broadly speaking, worship is viewed as a "corporate love letter" to God. Everything that happens in the worship service is meant to bring honor and adoration to God. Organizationally, St. John follows an order of worship called a "worship outline." A **worship outline** provides *a structured format for conducting a worship service.* It consists of various elements, such as a call to worship, an opening hymn, a doxology, a Scripture reading, tithes and offerings, a pastoral prayer, the sermon, and more. The term "worship leader" essentially means "liturgist" and refers to the person who drives the order of worship. Chief is the minister of music—he leads vocally, plays the organ, and directs both the band and the choirs. Chief leads a band that consists of three instruments—organ, electric guitar, and drums. The band stays the same from week to week, but every week a different group in the church is responsible for providing the worship outline, putting together a choir, and leading the worship service. The church alternates between the clergy, men, women, youth, and young adults to lead the worship service. Reverend Fowler typically preaches but doesn't always lead the worship.

Reverend Fowler said that worship music fosters the congregation's spiritual growth and nourishment. It helps unite all the components of worship so they all can speak in some way to the hearts and minds of all who are present. While the sermon and the music get a lot of attention, every act of worship is significant in ministry and should be given appropriate attentiveness. Prayers and fellowship, for instance, foster communal solidarity. Music, for Chief, helps create a culture of response. Music helps combine the elements of worship, undergirding what is happening in the pulpit and lessening the opportunity for dead space. In other words, music helps drive the service.

At St. John, Chief focuses on three things when he chooses songs. First, he makes sure the songs are of interest to the members, especially to those who serve in the choir. Chief is sensitive to present songs that feel authentic to St. John's worshiping community. Second, he chooses songs that not only work with the elements of worship but also will be received well by the congregants. Finally, he chooses songs based on the level of difficulty. St. John's choirs are comprised of volunteers, so Chief does not want to choose music that is too intricate or difficult to grasp. Hence, he chooses Gospel songs that are relatively easy to learn and perform but are still interesting. This helps maximize congregational engagement. Now that we understand how St. John's leadership views worship, let's consider our church visit.

To get to St. John, we drove through some beautifully wooded suburbs of Fairburn. Tall pine trees and stately oaks formed a canopy overhead, and buildings poked through periodic openings between the trees. We passed by charming homes with well-kept lawns, their colors popping against the wooded, green backdrop. We arrived at the church, a gray building with a white façade and steeple nestled amid the trees (fig. 8.2).

FIGURE 8.2

St. John AME Church exterior

Photo by Steven Félix-Jäger, June 30,2024

We were greeted at the door, and ushers pointed the way to the sanctuary. Once in the sanctuary, several church members greeted us as we found our way to our seats. About eighty people were present in worship. The sanctuary is small and clean with white painted walls and recessed lights in a drop ceiling (fig. 8.3). On stage, behind the lectern, were about twenty cushioned chairs set up for a choir. In front of the lectern was a wooden Communion table and a wooden altar with knee pads. The band was set up on the left side of the room and consisted of a drummer, an electric guitarist, and an organist. The church members were exceptionally expressive and jovial throughout the service. Worship felt like a celebratory family gathering.

FIGURE 8.3

St. John AME Church sanctuary

Photo by Steven Félix-Jäger, June 30, 2024

Our observation landed on a special day: "International Sunday."[18] This Sunday was designed to celebrate diverse cultures from across the diaspora. The **global Black diaspora** consists of *people of African descent across continents*. International Sunday was meant to foster a sense of shared heritage and solidarity, rallying around the different customs and regional experiences of St. John's congregants. As the service began, the band played an African beat on the djembe. Chief functioned as the band leader and music

18. Watch the full service here: St. John AME Church Fairburn, Georgia, "E Pluribus Unum Acs 2:1–12 NIV, June 30, 2024," www.youtube.com/watch?v=NzzPlsXosiw&t=604s.

director, and periodically switched to the djembe when the song called for it. Soon after, a jubilant procession led by Reverend Fowler entered the sanctuary. A line of congregants dressed in traditional attire carried various national flags and walked down the middle aisle of the sanctuary before settling on stage.

Reverend Fowler served as both the preacher and the worship leader. After the processional, she greeted the congregants and transitioned to a Gospel rendition of Thomas Ken's "Doxology."[19] Following the "Doxology" was a call to worship that gave thanks for the unity and diversity of those present from the African diaspora, honored those who worked toward the liberation of oppressed Black people, and prayed for justice. Reverend Fowler said repeatedly that this service was a time of celebration and praise. St. John's worship is very communally oriented, utilizing several congregants to perform various worship elements throughout the service. One member led a prayer, another read the Scripture passage, several members gave announcements, and several gave testimonial "cultural talks." After the first corporate prayer, the band played a calypso beat and sang "Kumbaya, My Lord." Another member subsequently came up and read the Scripture passage, Lamentations 3:21–33.

The service then transitioned to a part of the service called "worship through song." The team played an upbeat jazz fusion, Gospel rendition of "Shabach" while five women from the young adult group sang the melody in unison. Then Reverend Fowler invited up two of the young adult leaders to give the welcome. The leaders asked all the first-time guests (which included us) to stand and receive a gift. Then the band led a song titled "Welcome Song"—an original Gospel song that played during a prolonged meet and greet (fig. 8.4). Here everyone moved around the sanctuary, greeting one another with smiles, hugs, and brief

19. Thomas Ken, "Praise God, from Whom All Blessings Flow (Doxology)," in *African Methodist Episcopal Church Hymnal* (Nashville: African Methodist Episcopal Church, 2000), no. 647.

conversation. The lyrics of the song encouraged welcoming interaction. One line, "Welcome to St. John, we're glad you're here," repeated. The refrain also gave literal instruction: "Hug somebody, tell them that you love them, put your arms around them, show them that you care."

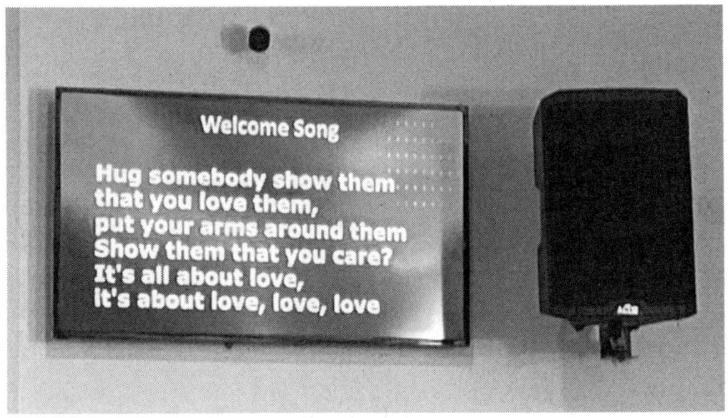

FIGURE 8.4

Picture of "Welcome Song" slide

Photo by Steven Félix-Jäger, June 30, 2024

Afterward a congregant came up and gave a "cultural talk"—a testimonial talk about her Nigerian and Dominican heritage and upbringing. This doesn't typically happen every Sunday but was a special added element for the International Sunday service. Reverend Fowler then introduced another congregant to do the special "praise dance" mentioned above, which was also a special worship element for the service. After that Reverend Fowler prayed over a time of giving. Congregants walked up and placed their offerings in baskets, and the band played Fred Hammond's "We're Blessed."[20] After the offering, Reverend Fowler led the congregation in the short hymn "All Things

20. "We're Blessed," words and music by Fred Hammond and Tommie Walker, CCLI #1672979 © 1995 K&F Music, New Spring, Universal Music–Z Songs (administered by Brentwood-Benson Music Publishing, Inc., Universal Music Publishing Group).

Come of Thee,"[21] which functioned as a congregational prayer. Two families then came up and gave cultural talks about their Jamaican background. Afterward Reverend Fowler gave some announcements, directed the audience to view video announcements, and invited two members to give more announcements. Then, to round out the first part of the service, the worship team and young adult singers led the South African hymn "Siyahamba,"[22] which was based off a traditional Zulu folk song. After the song, Reverend Fowler led a prayer to precede the sermon but spontaneously called for a reprise of "Siyahamba." All of these elements took the first hour of the service.

Reverend Fowler then transitioned to the sermon by expressively reading Acts 2:1–12, the sermon's scriptural focus. She titled the sermon "*E Pluribus Unum,*" which means "out of many, one." Because this Sunday took place a few days before Independence Day, Reverend Fowler was able to make the connection that the US is one nation that was made up of many immigrants coming together. She also demonstrated how diasporic communities came together during their International Sunday service. These points were woven together to demonstrate how the disciples came together at Pentecost to receive power and form a church out of many tribes and tongues. At Pentecost, she said, *e pluribus unum* was on full display. When the Spirit fell upon the Galileans, God's language exceeded their expectations. In the same way, when we are filled with the Spirit, God will cause us to speak in ways that cross cultures, denominations, nationalities, creed, color, and gender. God will cause us to speak in a tongue we don't know to people we don't know, and they will understand what we're trying to say. So reaching others beyond our locales requires total reliance on the Holy Spirit. God has a language that speaks to all. On our own accord, we talk about the wrong things, like politics

21. Ludwig van Beethoven, "All Things Come of Thee," in *African Methodist Episcopal Church Hymnal* (Nashville: African Methodist Episcopal Church, 2000), no. 644.
22. Andries Van Tonder, "Siyahamba," public domain.

and divisive social issues. Instead, we should declare the wonders of God, like the disciples did at Pentecost. The reason God's language transcended beyond the disciples is because they weren't talking about just anything, they were talking about God and Christ's sacrifice. Throughout the sermon, the congregants were extremely responsive, and the organ also punctuated main points.

While many Pentecostals focus on Acts 2 as a normative text for theological ideas like Spirit baptism and empowerment, Reverend Fowler focused on the unity through diversity that happened when the Spirit was poured out on all flesh. Reverend Fowler challenged the congregants and said it's not too late to have a witness like the one at Pentecost. She ended with an altar call for salvation, prayer, and membership. During the altar call, the band played Bill and Gloria Gaither's "Because He Lives,"[23] and people came up for prayer. Then they brought up a congregant who was wishing to join the church. She gave a short testimony about why she wanted to join the church, and a small group of congregants came up to lay hands on her and pray while the band reprised "Welcome Song." After this Reverend Fowler gave a few final instructions and invited the church to a "taste of cultures" potluck that contained food from the many cultures present at the church.

This service was incredibly uplifting, demonstrating both joy and resilience. Although Reverend Fowler followed a clear liturgical structure, the transitions were funny, lighthearted, and relational. The congregants were very engaged, and everything felt very welcoming. The service clearly followed the fourfold pattern of worship through a liturgy, commonly referred to as a "worship outline" in the AME Church. The gathering had a processional, a praise dance, a time of greeting, announcements, prayers, congregational singing, special songs, and a time for fellowship. The word incorporated preaching, Scripture readings, testimonies, and

23. "Because He Lives," words and music by Gloria Gaither and William Gaither, CCLI #16880 © 1971 Hanna Street Music (administered by Gaither Copyright Management).

extended ministry times. The table and alternate responses utilized an altar call as well as various opportunities to respond extemporaneously throughout the service. Finally, the sending had a prayer, a time of recognition of clergy, and communal instructions for after the service. The fourfold pattern was formal but extremely integrative, and many worship elements were backed with music.

BIBLICAL, AESTHETIC, THEOLOGICAL, AND PASTORAL JUDGMENTS IN ST. JOHN'S WORSHIP

With a full grasp of St. John's narrative framework, we can assess the biblical, aesthetic, theological, and pastoral fit of St. John's congregational worship against its own narrative standards of judgment. Thus, we will contrast this particular Black Gospel church against the values of the Black Gospel tradition as defined throughout this book. Hence, we will not judge St. John against Reformed, Pentecostal, Evangelical, or Charismatic Catholic standards but will only consider standards of evaluation that authentically engage St. John's narrative framework. Furthermore, since St. John views itself as a welcoming, community-oriented congregation of Spirit-filled and socially conscious worshipers, we can see if the church's worship practices align with the sort of community St. John aspires to be. We will assess four things: Is St. John's contextual expression of worship biblically faithful? Do the worship practices match what is proclaimed? Are St. John's theological beliefs evident through their worship practices? And how is musical worship used to minister to the congregants?

Biblical Judgment

The AME Church uses *The Book of Worship*, a publication of the AME Church Commission on Worship and Liturgy.[24] AME's ***Book of Worship*** provides *a comprehensive guide for*

24. Roderick D. Belin, *The Book of Worship of the African Methodist Episcopal Church: Digital Edition* (Nashville: AME Sunday School Union, 2018).

worship at AME churches, including orders of service for the entire liturgical calendar. For International Sunday, St. John used an outline that had a reading out of Lamentations 3:21–33 (NIV):

> Yet this I call to mind
>   and therefore I have hope:
>
> Because of the LORD's great love we are not consumed,
>   for his compassions never fail.
> They are new every morning;
>   great is your faithfulness.
> I say to myself, "The LORD is my portion;
>   therefore I will wait for him."
>
> The LORD is good to those whose hope is in him,
>   to the one who seeks him;
> it is good to wait quietly
>   for the salvation of the LORD.
> It is good for a man to bear the yoke
>   while he is young.
>
> Let him sit alone in silence,
>   for the LORD has laid it on him.
> Let him bury his face in the dust—
>   there may yet be hope.
> Let him offer his cheek to one who would strike him,
>   and let him be filled with disgrace.
>
> For no one is cast off
>   by the Lord forever.
> Though he brings grief, he will show compassion,
>   so great is his unfailing love.
> For he does not willingly bring affliction
>   or grief to anyone.

What's interesting about this Scripture reading is that St. John read the whole passage in context. Churches often read verses 22–23, which talk about faithfulness and God's compassion, but the second half of this extended passage is a lament. A **lament** is *a type of poetic expression in the Bible that is often directed toward God, conveying sorrow, mourning, or grief as a plea for help or justice.* Verse 32 talks about seeing God's compassion in the midst of grief. The Bible is full of laments, and while many churches ignore these passages, the AME Church reads and embodies them again and again in a liturgical setting. Such a reading evokes both the sorrows of Black oppression and expresses the AME's commitment to justice.

Altogether St. John played eight songs throughout the worship service. Because the songs played specific ministerial roles in the liturgy, they did not align specifically with the sermon's biblical theme of Pentecost. Yet because it was International Sunday, a strong theme of unity and heritage ran all the way through the songs. By doing a mix of hymns, Gospel songs, and traditional songs, St. John's worship was globally inspired and multigenerational. While some of the songs implied biblical passages, they did not explicitly evoke scriptural passages. The sermon focused on Acts 2:1–12, and while many Pentecostals like to highlight spiritual empowerment as the church is formed, Reverend Fowler highlighted the theme of "unity" as three thousand people from many different cultures formed the church that day. This approach to the text highlights AME's identity as "liberating and reconciling people." True to the identity of the AME Church at large, St. John's worship was biblically faithful and focused on justice and unity.

Aesthetic Judgment

St. John's worship music authentically suited its community. The AME Church seeks to foster unity among Black Christians throughout the African diaspora, which was emphasized to an even greater extent during International Sunday. The service included cultural talks from various countries and cultures around the world, and parts of some of the songs were sung in different languages. While the music hovered around a contemporary Gospel style, it incorporated jazz fusion, calypso, reggae, and traditional African rhythms. The song choices were stylistically varied, which portrayed a sensitivity to the many generations that were present at the service. There was a mix of hymns ("Doxology" and "All Things Come of Thee"), traditional African-inspired songs ("Shabach" and "Siyahamba"), a traditional African American folk song ("Kumbaya, My Lord"), and Gospel songs—both contemporary ("We're Blessed" and "Welcome Song") and traditional ("Because He Lives"). Chief skillfully wove the service elements together through music, fostering a unified and joyfully expressive worship experience.

The pace of the service was quick, and the transitions between elements were lighthearted and festive. On many occasions, Reverend Fowler laughed or jovially mentioned a congregant by name. Congregants smiled and laughed throughout the service, and they greeted one another with warm hugs and joyous banter during the "Welcome Song." While the electric guitarist and drummer seemed to concentrate intently on the music, Chief often wore a smile as he directed the congregants through the turns of the songs. The overall mood of the service was jubilation and thanksgiving, and every facet of the service emulated unity and encouragement.

Theological Judgment

At St. John we saw a clear example of McCaulley's description of Black ecclesial theology being generally orthodox in expression but rooted in the Black church experience. Every worship element highlighted something about the triune God and the life of the church. But there were several instances when liturgical elements said something about the social and political lives of Black people around the world. The call to worship, for instance, stated the following:

Leader: We praise you, O God, for the richness of cultures borne from Africa,

People: From the rhythms of the drums to the poetry of the soul, we celebrate.

Leader: We remember the resilience of those who crossed oceans in bondage,

People: Their spirit enduring, their faith unbroken, their stories told.

Leader: We honor the leaders and visionaries who forged paths of liberation;

People: From Harriet Tubman to Nelson Mandela, their courage lights our way.

Leader: We give thanks for the diversity of gifts and talents across nations,

People: Creativity, wisdom, and strength woven into our heritage.

Leader: We pray for justice and equality to reign in every land,

People: That all may thrive and flourish, united in harmony.

Leader: We commit ourselves to honoring our ancestors' legacy,

People: Embracing our identity with pride, rooted in faith and hope.

All: Blessed are you, Creator of all peoples, who calls us to unity in diversity. Amen.[25]

As can be seen, the congregants affirmed a unified sense of pride for Black people throughout the African diaspora as calls for justice and equality shaped petitions for harmony and flourishing. Thus, St. John's theological expression is affirmed through the lens of the lived Black experience.

---

25. This call to worship was developed by one of the congregants through AI.

This theological approach in worship is also significant for the church's public witness. Chief said it well: "Being able to worship across ethnic lines is important for the church, but what's important is the essence of being honest, being honest about what everyone's dealing with in their walks with Christ. Like if someone is sharing about police brutality, or discrimination, if churches are willing to confront these things as part of the congregation's particular experience, it will enable us to be more sensitive and sympathetic to where we are in our witness."

While people of other races and ethnicities are always welcome to worship alongside members of the Black church community, we must recognize that it is a specific shared social experience that unites Black worshipers. Hence, unity across racial lines can be fostered through love and empathy, even while Black worshipers share an exclusive solidarity based on the Black experience.

Pastoral Judgment

The performed songs played many ministerial roles throughout the worship service. They were interwoven with many liturgical elements, including prayers, Scripture readings, and testimonies. But these songs not only underscored the flow of the service, they also played ministerial roles through their lyrical themes and the point in the service at which they were sung.

Both "Doxology" and "Shabach" are about praise and adoration and were performed toward the beginning of the service. Hence, the gathering of the service was filled with praise. "Welcome Song" is about love and solidarity and its offering created a space for congregants to embrace one another and foster community. "Kumbaya, My Lord" is about presence, and functioned as an invitation to experience the Spirit. "We're Blessed" and "All Things Come of Thee" were performed during the tithes and offerings, and deal with blessing and declaration. The Zulu lyrics of "Siyahamba" are "Siyahamb' ekukhanyen' kwenkhos'," which translates to "We are marching in the light of truth."

This is a celebratory song that ties together the pertinent themes of community, empowerment, freedom, and resilience. Finally, "Because He Lives" was performed after the sermon and during the altar call. Thematically, the song concerns faith and assurance, so it was sung as an encouragement for the congregants before they went back out into the community. The worship service's main pastoral function was to gather as a community, worship God through praise and adoration, and reaffirm the community as a liberating and reconciling people.

CONCLUSION

Worship at St. John is dynamic, multifaceted, and, as one congregant stated, all-encompassing. Everyone in the congregation was fully involved in the service we observed, both onstage and offstage. A variety of creative worship elements expressed a range of spiritual postures, from joy to lament, to thanksgiving, to reverence. Prayers and Scripture passages didn't gloss over life's difficulties but addressed them head-on. Yet no matter how difficult things were to talk about, the community always responded with hope. There was truly a communal sense that joy can always be found in the midst of sorrow.

The service demonstrated a lively energy, even with a formal liturgical structure. While there was a deep sense of historical and global unity between Black worshipers, my research assistant and I still felt very welcome. By the end of the service, we felt loved, accepted, and encouraged. This wonderful service evinced a beautiful, resilient community.

After considering the many commendations for St. John, I would recommend three areas of growth that emerged from the interviews and observation: (1) The church might try to further integrate the various groups who plan the worship. Reverend Fowler mentioned that when the different groups are in charge, they sometimes feel that they have to plan and execute every part of the service. Reverend Fowler would prefer a more intergenerational integration between the groups, so even if one group plans worship, they can call on anyone from the congregation to enact the worship elements. (2) As the church continues to grow, it should consider hiring a dedicated choir director to work alongside Chief. As the minister of music, Chief has to direct the music, lead the songs, and direct the choirs. Chief does a great job of multitasking and giving cues from the microphone in musical ways but would love to work alongside a trusted choir director to share some of those responsibilities. The choirs vary from week to week, so between the music and the choirs, there's a lot to rehearse. (3) St. John should work to dial in the sound for both the live service and the streaming. Since the groups change from week to week, the sound changes drastically. It would be great if the PA team developed a way to label and set general standards for the sounds and then to attend rehearsals. This could go a long way in fostering consistency.

This chapter looked at St. John AME Church's narrative framework to see how its musical worship functions in context. We looked at the church's tradition, history, social impact, and aesthetic impressions before analyzing its worship on biblical, aesthetic, theological, and pastoral grounds. What we found was a vibrant Black Gospel worshiping community that lives up to its identity as a liberating and reconciling people who are welcoming, community-oriented, Spirit-filled, and socially conscious.

STUDY QUESTIONS

1. What can you glean from St. John's expressions of joy in worship?
2. What was your reaction to the way St. John engaged social issues while remaining rooted in Scripture?
3. In what ways did St. John create flow between the various worship elements?

4. How can your church celebrate and engage the global church?
5. Do you prefer liturgical worship outlines or free church orders of worship? What strengths or potential weaknesses do you see in each approach?

KEY TERMS

African Methodist Episcopal Church: a historical Black Protestant denomination founded by Richard Allen in Philadelphia, Pennsylvania, in 1816.

Black ecclesial tradition: the unique theological, spiritual, and cultural expressions of Christianity that have developed within African American communities.

***Book of Worship* (AME):** a comprehensive guide for worship at AME churches, including orders of service for the entire liturgical calendar.

Connectional church: a denominational structure that emphasizes the interconnectedness and mutual support among its churches and leadership.

Global Black diaspora: people of African descent across continents.

Lament: a type of poetic expression in the Bible that is often directed toward God, conveying sorrow, mourning, or grief as a plea for help or justice.

Praise dance: a liturgical form of expressive movement that is performed as a special act of worship in a worship service.

Worship outline: an order of worship that provides a structured format for conducting a worship service.

CHAPTER 9

Evaluating Evangelical Worship

Park Avenue Baptist Church, Titusville, Florida

In the mid-1970s, Peter Lord, founder and then senior pastor of Park Avenue Baptist Church (PABC) of Titusville, Florida, had a vision to establish a twenty-four-hours-a-day prayer chain on the church campus. Members of the church were invited to sign up for time slots so that someone was always on campus praying for church members and for the broader community. At the time, the church was a little strapped for resources, so Peter bought and cleared out an old school bus. He furnished the bus with chairs and gave the congregants a Rolodex of church member names so people could be prayed for by name. Eventually the church raised enough money to build a permanent twenty-four-hours-a-day prayer chapel. They decided to build it on the highest elevation point of the campus to symbolically gesture toward the primacy of prayer at PABC.

Although there's no longer a sign-up sheet, the prayer chapel is still regularly used for prayer and worship and is open to the church community at any hour, day or night. The chapel's interior was recently remodeled with new flooring, comfortable seating, and prayer boards (fig. 9.1). The interior is filled with Bibles, prayer cards, and pamphlets, and elevated on the back wall of the room is a stained glass cross—a testament to PABC's faith and devotion to Christ. At certain times of the day, filtered light streams through the cruciform window and the cross comes alive with vibrant colors.

FIGURE 9.1

Park Avenue Baptist Church prayer chapel interior

Photo by Steven Félix-Jäger, July 16, 2023

The story of PABC's prayer chapel perfectly demonstrates the way congregants view the church: community-oriented, biblically based, Christ-centered, and Spirit-led. While many Southern Baptist churches would identify themselves as community oriented, biblically based, and Christ-centered, they don't always define themselves as being **Spirit-led**—*being guided, directed, or influenced by the Holy Spirit.* Understanding this distinction, the pastors and congregants of PABC commonly refer to themselves as "**Bapticostal,**" *a Baptist church with charismatic sensibilities.* As such, PABC is a Baptist church that strives to be both biblically strong and Spirit-led.

The purpose of this chapter is to explore how congregational worship can support a healthy Evangelical community and how PABC specifically uses worship to bolster its identity as a Spirit-led Evangelical church. Thus, this chapter presents a narrative framework that attempts to capture the church's social and ecclesial context. As part of this process, we'll assess the church's tradition, history, social impact, and aesthetic impressions. Only after we've sufficiently understood PABC's narrative framework will we be able to evaluate its worship on biblical, aesthetic, theological, and pastoral grounds. As in previous chapters, we'll be able to understand what the worship means within PABC's narrative-hermeneutical context, which allows us to make informed commendations and recommendations for the future.

UNDERSTANDING: Mapping the Narrative Framework of Park Avenue Baptist Church

The content of this chapter is drawn from a mix of scholarly and primary sources, formal observations, and personal interviews conducted in May and July 2023. Following preliminary meetings in May with some of the church's staff, my research assistant and I visited and observed the 9:15 Sunday morning service. Additionally, we conducted several interviews, including an interview with director of family ministries, Richie Lord, alongside long-standing church member Evelyn,[1] about the history of PABC; an interview with Braiden Wood, director of worship and creative arts, regarding the church's worship practices; an interview with senior pastor Steve Yuke about worship and church

---

1. Because Evelyn is not on staff at PABC, we will avoid using her last name to maintain a degree of anonymity.

life; and an interview with a focus group of five church members regarding community and church identity. These sources are used to analyze the church's tradition, history, social impact, and aesthetic impressions.

Tradition

In broad terms, the **Evangelical tradition** is *an expression of Protestant Christianity that emphasizes biblical authority, personal faith in Jesus, and individual conversion*. American Evangelicalism was strongly influenced by both the First and Second Great Awakenings of the eighteenth and nineteenth centuries, respectively.[2] A fundamental aspect of these revivals was stressing the importance of being "born again." The term "born again" refers to a regenerative conversion experience that is personally experienced by a believer.[3] It refers to a soteriological individualism that opposes a more communal understanding of salvation often found in Catholicism or some mainline Protestant traditions. As a transdenominational coalition, Evangelicalism includes a seemingly endless number of denominations that consider themselves Evangelical. Yet the National Association of Evangelicals lists forty denominations in its database.[4] Perhaps the best known

---

2. Thomas Kidd, *Who Is an Evangelical? The History of a Movement in Crisis* (New Haven, CT: Yale University Press, 2019), 20.

3. Kidd, *Who Is an Evangelical?* 91.

4. "NAE Denominations and Networks," National Association of Evangelicals, accessed July 21, 2023, https://nae.org/full-list-of-nae-denominations/. The list includes Advent Christian General Conference, Aspire Network, Assemblies of God, The Brethren Church, Brethren in Christ Church, Christian and Missionary Alliance, Christian Reformed Church in North America, Church of God (Anderson), Church of God (Cleveland, Tennessee), Church of God of Prophecy, Church of the Nazarene, Conservative Congregational Christian Conference, Converge Worldwide, ECO: A Covenant Order of Evangelical Presbyterians, Elim Fellowship, The Evangelical Church, Evangelical Congregational Church, Evangelical Free Church of America, Evangelical Friends Church International, Evangelical Presbyterian Church, Every Nation Churches, Fellowship of Evangelical Churches, The Foursquare Church, Free Methodist Church USA, Grace Communion International, International Pentecostal Church of Christ, International Pentecostal Holiness Church, Missionary Church, Inc., North American Baptist Conference, Open Bible Churches, Pentecostal Free Will Baptist Church, Primitive Methodist

Evangelical denomination in the US is the **Southern Baptist Convention (SBC)**.

PABC is part of the SBC, the *largest Protestant denomination in the US and the largest Baptist denomination in the world.* Baptists emigrated from Great Britain to the American colonies as early as the seventeenth century.[5] The first Baptist churches in the South appeared in South Carolina (c. 1696), Virginia (1715), and North Carolina (1727).[6] While Northern American Baptist churches still resembled the Baptist churches of England, Southern churches began to emulate a distinctively different character that reflected the emerging culture of the Southern colonies.[7]

The SBC was born in 1845 when Northern Baptists restricted Southerners from serving as missionaries because they were slave owners. The Southerners maintained that the Bible allowed for chattel slavery, so they split and formed the SBC.[8] Thus, the primary catalyst for the SBC's formation was the belief that Southerners needed a separate, distinct organization to protect and promote their sociopolitical views and values, which included the continuation of slavery. While the SBC gradually moved to a more open stance on race, the SBC formally apologized for its pro-slavery past during its 1995 convention and adopted a resolution condemning white supremacy in its 2017 meeting.[9] In 2018

Church USA, Royalhouse Chapel International, The Salvation Army, Seventh Day Baptist General Conference of the USA and Canada, Transformation Ministries, United Brethren in Christ, US Conference of the Mennonite Brethren Churches, Vineyard USA, and The Wesleyan Church.

5. Robert Baker, *The Southern Baptist Convention and Its People: 1607–1972* (Nashville: Broadman, 1974), 15.

6. Baker, *The Southern Baptist Convention and Its People*, 28.

7. Baker, *The Southern Baptist Convention and Its People*, 28.

8. Diane Winston, "The Southern Baptist Story," in *Southern Baptists Observed: Multiple Perspectives on a Changing Denomination*, ed. Nancy Tatom Ammerman (Knoxville: University of Tennessee Press, 1993), 12.

9. Tom Gjelten, "Southern Baptist Seminary Confronts History of Slaveholding and 'Deep Racism,'" NPR, December 13, 2018, www.npr.org/2018/12/13/676333342/southern-baptist-seminary-confronts-history-of-slaveholding-and-deep-racism.

the Southern Baptist Theological Seminary, the SBC's flagship institution of higher education, released a seventy-one-page report on racism and slavery's role in the SBC's origins and growth.[10] Though much work still needs to be done in the SBC, it is at least confronting its past in order to promote a reconciled present.[11]

Today, with millions of members and thousands of affiliated churches, the SBC remains one of the largest Protestant denominations in the US. It refers to itself as "a body of like-minded local churches cooperating together to reach the world with the Good News of Jesus Christ."[12] The SBC is not a "creedal" denomination that requires its members to embrace a standardized set of beliefs, but it is a "confessional" affiliation that adheres to ***The Baptist Faith and Message****—a "confessional consensus" of beliefs that all Southern Baptists adhere to.*[13]

Although there are more than two hundred Southern Baptist megachurches in the US, the vast majority of their churches are small, with congregations of fewer than two hundred people. The SBC avoids centralization, so each church is its own autonomous entity that exists in a broad affiliation. SBC's website puts it this way: "Southern Baptists are as varied and diverse as the cities, towns, neighborhoods, and rural communities where they

---

10. Gjelten, "Southern Baptist Seminary Confronts History."

11. Today one of the SBC's biggest challenges is church attrition because of its complementarian stance on women and ordination. In 2023 the SBC voted to disfellowship the Lake Forest, California, megachurch Saddleback Church for having a female teaching pastor on staff (see Kate Shellnutt, "Southern Baptist Convention Disfellowships Saddleback Church," *Christianity Today*, February 21, 2023, www.christianitytoday.com/news/2023/february/saddleback-church-southern-baptist-sbc-disfellowship-female.html. Later that same year, North Carolina megachurch Elevation Church voluntarily left the SBC because of its stance on female pastors (see Bob Smietana, "Steven Furtick's Elevation Church Leaves the SBC," *Christianity Today*, July 3, 2023, www.christianitytoday.com/news/2023/july/elevation-church-steven-furtick-leave-southern-baptist-sbc-.html.

12. "About the SBC," SBC, accessed July 21, 2023, www.sbc.net/about/.

13. "About the SBC." The concepts of a "creed" and a "confessional consensus" are, more or less, identical, but the SBC is careful with its terminology to avoid any sense of strong centralization. This disposition seems to stem back to the denomination's colonial roots.

live. Each Southern Baptist church is autonomous and unique; only when viewed together can one grasp the diversity that is the Southern Baptist Convention."[14] Because of its diversity, no two Southern Baptist churches are exactly alike. It is SBC's broadness and decentralization that allows PABC to exist as a unique, Spirit-filled, Bapticostal church. Organizationally, PABC has established accountability measures that go beyond typical Southern Baptist structures: In addition to deacons, PABC selects a group of elders to consult and help make decisions with the senior pastor and staff, and they have "apostles" that come and offer spiritual guidance and consultation. These apostles live in other parts of the country, advise PABC's leadership, and periodically come and preach at the church to offer spiritual guidance to the congregation. This accountability structure constitutes a unique arrangement that is unlike any other Southern Baptist church.

History

PABC began in 1969 as an offshoot of First Baptist Church, Downtown (now First Baptist Church of Titusville). The founding pastor of PABC was Jamaican-born Peter Lord (1929–2021), whose forebears came to Jamaica as missionaries from England. Peter came to the US in 1946 at the age of sixteen to attend college at Bob Jones University. There he met Johnnie Belle Sapp, who became his wife in 1951. After college Peter attended New Orleans Baptist Theological Seminary and then served as a pastor at several churches around Florida.[15]

In the mid-1960s Peter served at Haverhill Baptist Church (now Haverhill Community Church) in West Palm Beach. During this time, First Baptist Church, Downtown, was searching for a new senior pastor. In 1966 the search committee from

14. "About the SBC."

15. "Peter Lord," Obituary, accessed July 14, 2023, www.northbrevardfuneralhome.com/tributes/Peter-Lord.

First Baptist happened to be visiting Haverhill Baptist Church. Peter preached, and a man named Bill Flanders filled in that Sunday as the minister of music. Both Peter and Bill were subsequently asked to serve at First Baptist—after some initial reluctance, they eventually agreed.

Shortly after Peter and Bill's arrival, First Baptist experienced rapid growth, which caused the church to look for a new location to expand. The church bought property on Park Avenue in hopes of building a new campus where the congregation could relocate. They began construction, but when it was time to move in 1969, a large constituency of church members wanted to stay at the downtown location. So for a while Peter preached at both churches every Sunday—he first preached at the Park Avenue site and then drove downtown to preach at the original site. This arrangement was similar to what happens at multisite churches today that are led by the same pastor. After about a year, the church decided this arrangement was not sustainable, so they split the church into two separate congregations, and PABC was officially incorporated in 1970 with Peter Lord as the senior pastor.

Peter served as senior pastor from 1969 until his retirement in 1996. After a period of transition, Marty Schafer served as senior pastor from 1998 to 2000, and was then succeeded by Peter's son, Richard Lord, who served from 2000 to 2018. After a long and successful tenure, Richard retired and handed over the pastorate to Steve Yuke, who has served as senior pastor since 2018. Park Avenue has tremendous influence throughout Titusville, launching ministries along the Space Coast, including The Grove Church, which is led by former PABC youth pastor Brad Russell.[16] Today PABC is growing and continues to look at how it can serve North Brevard and be a positive presence in the community.

16. Flora Reigada, "Church Will Celebrate Milestone Anniversary," *Viera Voice*, May 1, 2029, updated November 9, 2020, www.vieravoice.com/church-will-celebrate-milestone-anniversary/article_6cba7c88-7b00-5919-9e66-871d12c9a7d5.html.

Communal Impact

As part of this study, we surveyed a focus group of churchgoers about PABC's internal functions and identity in worship, and about its external interactions with the community. In their view, PABC is like a multigenerational family. One woman reported that her entire family attends PABC, from as young as her six-year-old son to as old as her grandmother in her nineties. PABC is also one of the most welcoming and communal churches in the area. One woman said she felt a familial embrace from the church community the moment she walked through its doors sixteen years prior.

One man said there was a strong presence of the Holy Spirit that rested on PABC, like a "covering" that extended out into the community. He said, "Friends of mine have come into this town and said they felt the presence of God . . . like there's a covering over it. I've been a member off and on here for more than fifty years, and I always felt like there's been a spiritual covering that seems to emanate from here." This point indicates two things: (1) the congregants believe PABC has a strong, positive spiritual influence in the community, and (2) PABC practices a Charismatic form of Evangelicalism that congregants understand to be Spirit-led.

Titusville is a small Space Coast city of fewer than fifty thousand people. The city is not very racially diverse: 77.1 percent of the city is white, 12.7 percent is Black or African American, 7.2 percent is Hispanic or Latino, and 3 percent is mixed race or another race. Most people are considered lower middle class, and 12.8 percent are considered impoverished.[17] PABC is a relatively large church for such a small city—it has sixteen hundred members, with a thousand to eleven hundred congregants attending church every Sunday. That equates to roughly one out of every

---

17. "Quick Facts: Titusville City, Florida," United Stated Census Bureau, accessed July 24, 2023, www.census.gov/quickfacts/fact/table/titusvillecityflorida/PST045222.

twenty-five residents attending PABC regularly. The church's demographics reflect the demographics of the city—predominately white with a minority of Black and Hispanic congregants.

PABC is extremely active in Titusville. A focus group member responded affably to the question of how PABC congregants are involved in the community: "It's almost like, how aren't they?" The congregants went on to describe how the church engages with the community as a whole, including outreach to impoverished people, divorce care, single mom ministries, widow ministries, and a large recreation ministry led by the church's own director of recreation. Youth ministry leaders regularly visit local middle and high schools, providing meals for teens, and the church also has a private school named Park Avenue Christian Academy, with more than five hundred K–8 students.

PABC has great influence in Titusville because of the many community programs it provides, as well as its spiritual openness. Pastor Steve commented,

> I would say Park Avenue carries a tremendous amount of respect in town. Our mayor and city council, the police force, the fire department, the county commissioners—they all respect Park Avenue. The church has developed that kind of a heritage and is spoken of in high esteem. And I think one of the reasons for that is the different ministries that go out—we reach out to the community like crazy. . . . Our credibility's been earned through community outreach but also through our openness to spiritual things. We're not legalistic, we're not *really* Baptist, and we're not Pentecostal—you can just come here and be a part of the family of God.

In Steve's view, this openness to the Spirit dates back to the church's founding by Peter Lord. Despite being part of the SBC, PABC has always resisted labels that were too restrictive. After all, PABC has been calling itself Bapticostal (one of the few labels they endorse) since the 1970s. Having been brought up in the Charismatic movement, Pastor Steve helps carry PABC's Bapticostal designation forward. According to Steve, this Bapticostal dynamic can be interpreted in terms of honor: "There's no question, Baptists honor the Word, but they're mixed on the Spirit. It's not that they would say they outright dishonor the Spirit but they often don't fully accept the workings of the Spirit. For Pentecostals there's no question they honor the Spirit, but on the Word? I can see there's a bit of dishonoring. . . . But if you can come to that balance where there's a marriage between Word and Spirit—that's where the hand of God is."

For Steve a dynamic and healthy church honors both the Word and the Spirit. In all the interviews, PABC was consistently described as a creative, Spirit-led force for good in Titúsville.

Aesthetic Impressions

Before I describe what I observed during my church visit, I would like to frame how the focus group and pastors Steve and Braiden conceptually view worship at PABC. I noticed a mix between Evangelical and Pentecostal understandings of the role of musical worship in the service. Some from the focus group saw one of musical worship's major functions as supporting the sermon. They viewed both the music and sermon as equally important but saw worship as preparing hearts and minds for the reception of the Word. One woman said, "The point of [musical] worship is to usher in the Holy Spirit. We help create the environment for people to experience the presence of the Holy Spirit, to soften people's hearts to receive what the pastor, or whoever's bringing the Word, is preaching. We help prepare people so God can work in those hearts for change to happen." Unlike other Evangelical churches, the sermon, while still very important, is not central to PABC's Sunday morning service. To support this point, Steve described the role of worship by appealing to the biblical imagery of the temple's inner sanctuary:

> I do not believe that the [musical] worship is the precursor to the Word. It's in worship where people can encounter God directly. That's my hope of what would happen every Sunday. I'm very big on the "holy of holies." So you come through the outer court experience, you enter into the inner sanctuary, and then there's the place of the holy of holies. It's my hope that some people can get to the holy of holies. . . . I think a lot of people get to the inner sanctuary on Sunday mornings. The holy of holies is another step spiritually into the presence of God. That's my hope.

For Steve musical worship creates the atmosphere for worshipers to deeply enter into the presence of God.

Steve understands that worshipers on Sunday morning do not always get to a place of such spiritual depth. He likens the Sunday morning service to a family meal—it often feels like an obligation, but the conversation and food are still very rich and communally oriented. Sunday night services, or other worship nights, could be likened to date nights where relationships can be explored more deeply. True to PABC's Bapticostal identity, Steve sees the church's worship as balancing between a "presentation of truth" and an experiential encounter with God. He said, "There can be experiential things that happen on Sunday mornings, but it tilts more toward the presentation of truth and the togetherness of the people of God. In your nighttime services, and however that unfolds, it tilts more toward the experiential side." This understanding of worship seems to blend an Evangelical theology of worship as biblical expression with a Pentecostal theology of worship as encounter.

PABC takes a typical, contemporary approach to worship design. Braiden meets with the service planning team, which is comprised of him, Steve, and the director of media and marketing. Together they try to align songs thematically with the sermon series, Scripture passages used in the service, or with whatever the congregation is going through spiritually. They strive to create cohesion between the songs and the other elements of worship in the service.

Since PABC is a multigenerational congregation with a strong historical lineage, Braiden sees himself as a bridge that can help everyone in the congregation be effectively drawn into worship. For song selection, Braiden prefers songs that he calls "vertical" rather than "horizontal." By "**vertical worship songs**," he means "*songs that are more lyrically focused on praising God and talking about God's character directly, or songs that are sung directly to God.*" He said, "Other songs, which are still legitimate worship songs, have their place but might be more focused on personal relationships. These songs might talk about my personal life or how broken I was. We try to stay more in the vein of 'I exalt thee,' or 'God you're worthy,' or 'You deserve it all.'" The service planning team rates songs on a scale from one to five, with five being the most vertical and one the most horizontal. While lower rated songs are done from time to time depending on the function of the song in the service (like when a testimonial song is done as a special), the service planning team tends to prefer higher rated songs for regular congregational singing. All in all, for PABC music works conceptually and aesthetically to bridge an environment of biblical expression with that of spiritual encounter.

My research assistant and I arrived at PABC at about 9:00 a.m. ahead of the 9:15 worship service. As we approached the church, we were immediately struck by the sight of its unique and impressive architecture (fig. 9.2). The church is circular and flat, but the roof shoots up, piercing the sky. The expansive roof looks like a pointed wizard's hat topped by a cross. Apparently the church's design was drawn up by Peter Lord while he was still at First Baptist. Since Titusville is located at the heart of the Space Coast across the river from the Kennedy Space Center, Peter wanted the church to emulate a rocket's plume and the cross to mimic a rocket that is lifting out of Titusville and toward the heavens.[18]

18. No formal records of how the church's design was conceived of exist, and conflicting stories are told by congregants and staff members.

FIGURE 9.2

Park Avenue Baptist Church sanctuary exterior

Photo by Steven Félix-Jäger, July 16, 2023

FIGURE 9.3

Park Avenue Baptist Church prayer chapel exterior

Photo by Steven Félix-Jäger, July 16, 2023

Needless to say, the church building is striking. Behind the sanctuary stand two other buildings: To the left is a school, and to the right is a conference center. The prayer chapel sits atop a hill on the far right side of the campus (fig. 9.3). As mentioned in the introduction to this chapter, the goal was to construct the prayer chapel on the most elevated part of the campus.

As we approached the front entrance, we were greeted by friendly ushers who welcomed us with warm smiles. Stepping through the doors, we were instantly enveloped by a friendly and peaceful atmosphere. The interior of the sanctuary was arguably more impressive than the exterior (fig. 9.4). The wooden, vaulted ceiling pointed up to the heavens. Three large, intricately designed stained glass windows hovered above the stage. Directly above the stage was a truss that supported lights and speakers, and to the sides of the stage hung two sizable projector screens. The stage had a façade that looked like the entrance to an ancient Jewish temple.[19] The temple doors were printed on a transparent screen that covered the drum room. Surrounding the stage was comfortable, theater-style seating. A countdown video was running on the screens, and three minutes before the start of the service, a well-produced, preservice announcement video played.

The congregation was mostly white with only a few Black and Hispanic families present. A good diversity of generations was represented, although most of the congregants at this service seemed to be middle-aged or older.[20] The congregants were dressed semicasually—most of the men wore untucked, collared shirts with jeans, and the women wore dresses, skirts, or pants with nice blouses. As service time approached, the volume of conversation quickly decreased, and people settled into their seats.

At the start of the service, the church was greeted by Jonathan, the director of student ministry. Dressed casually in a T-shirt

19. PABC likes to creatively indulge in set designs that line up with sermon themes.

20. We stayed for the beginning of the 11:00 a.m. service and noted that the congregation in that service was noticeably younger and slightly more racially diverse.

and jeans, he spoke about the connect cards, announced other upcoming events, and did a short recap of some of the community outreaches the youth ministry took part in. Jonathan then asked everyone to do a meet and greet with surrounding congregants as the band and choir transitioned to the stage. A twenty-one-member choir filled out the left side of the stage, and a full band filled out the right side. The band was made up of a drummer, bassist, keyboard player, and two electric guitarists. Standing with the band was a woman who was signing the words of the songs in American Sign Language. Braiden was leading with an acoustic guitar and was accompanied by two female vocalists. They occupied the center of the stage.

FIGURE 9.4

Park Avenue Baptist Church sanctuary interior

Photo by Steven Félix-Jäger, July 16, 2023

Braiden welcomed the congregation as the band vamped behind him, and the crowd responded with excitement. Braiden then said a quick prayer while the lights dimmed throughout the sanctuary. The first song the team performed was "Alleluia" by Jesus Culture.[21] This song is about adopting the right posture in front of God, and it functioned as a call to worship in the service. After "Alleluia," the band vamped and seamlessly transitioned into "Awake My Soul" by Hillsong.[22] Braiden said a few transitional words, and the team began to sing the verse together. Although this song is more upbeat than "Alleluia," Braiden and his team displayed a comfortable, calming demeanor from the stage.

As the song ended, the band immediately went into the holiness hymn "Blessed Assurance" by Fanny Crosby and Phoebe Palmer Knapp.[23] The team performed this song in 6/8 and added a nonverbal vocal refrain between choruses. This was drawn from Jeremy Riddle's arrangement of the "Blessed Assurance" in Worship Circle Hymns.[24] Toward the end of the song, the choir continued the vocalized refrain while Braiden sang ad libs. The song ended with some prayerful, spontaneous singing as the band effortlessly transitioned into Hillsong's "New Wine,"[25] led by one of the female singers. The congregants were very engaged throughout each of these songs. Just about everyone was singing, most bodies were swaying, and many hands were raised

---

21. "Alleluia," words and music by Chris Quilala, Ian McIntosh, Jeffrey Kunde, and Jeremy Riddle, CCLI #6514578 © 2012 Capitol CMG Genesis, Jesus Culture Music, Bethel Music Publishing (administrated by Bethel Music Publishing, Capitol CMG Publishing).

22. "Awake My Soul," words and music by Brooke Ligertwood, CCLI #7134998 © 2019 Hillsong Music Publishing Australia (administrated by Capitol CMG Publishing).

23. "Blessed Assurance," words and music by Fanny Crosby and Phoebe Palmer Knapp, CCLI #22324, public domain.

24. See "Blessed Assurance—Jeremy Riddle | Worship Circle Hymns," accessed July 22, 2023, www.youtube.com/watch?v=7SSJicZO6_g.

25. "New Wine," words and music by Brooke Ligertwood, CCLI #7102397 © 2017 Hillsong Music Publishing Australia (administrated by Capitol CMG Publishing).

at different points during the worship set. At the end of "New Wine," Braiden closed out the worship set with a congregational prayer and invited everyone to be seated.

Immediately after Braiden's prayer, a highly produced video bumper for the sermon series played on the screens. This video allowed the worship team and choir to transition off the stage and for Pastor Steve to approach the stage. Steve was dressed semicasually in jeans, T-shirt, and a blazer. He offered a humorous welcome, gave some quick announcements, and began preaching. Steve preached for about forty-five minutes, offering some contextual background for the book of Esther, explaining the story, showing the overall biblical narrative that leads to Christ, and applying the story to the congregants' everyday lives.[26]

At the end of the sermon, Steve called up Braiden, the band, and the singers to respond to the sermon by leading "Tremble" by Mosaic MSC.[27] After the song, Steve came back up and offered a bit of ministry time, rearticulating some of the main points of the sermon and leading to a time of prayer. During the prayer, Steve transitioned into a call for salvation. With everyone's eyes closed, Steve asked anyone who felt the Lord calling them to commit their lives to Christ to raise their hands. Six people responded, so Steve asked everyone in the congregation to join in unison and repeat a prayer of salvation. This act shows that while salvation is personal between God and the individual, it's also communal as the body of Christ welcomes the new believer into the family. Following the prayer, the congregation cheered and Steve gave next steps for the new believers to meet people and pray with church leaders. Congregants were then invited to come

---

26. Watch the full service here: Steve Yuke, "Esther: The Unexpected at the Right Time," accessed July 22, 2023, www.youtube.com/watch?v=isaUUNcHT1g.

27. "Tremble," words and music by Andrés Figueroa, Hank Bentley, Mariah McManus, and Mia Fieldes, CCLI #7065049 © 2016 All Essential Music, Be Essential Songs, Bentley Street Songs, Mosaic LA Music, Mosaic MSC Music, and Tempo Music Investments (administrated by Essential Music Publishing LLC).

up to the stage after the service if they had something going on in their lives that they needed prayer for. The prayer team would remain up front. After a short charge to love God and love others, the congregation was dismissed.

PABC seemed to implicitly follow the fourfold order of worship. Greetings, announcements, prayers, congregational singing, and fellowship were all part of the gathering. The word incorporated preaching and Scripture readings and an extended ministry time after the sermon. The table came as alternate responses that utilized short ministry times at the end of songs, prayer, and a call for salvation. Finally, the sending had a closing song, a charge to love God and others, and an invitation for additional prayer if needed. Despite being thematically consistent, the songs chosen for the service did not necessarily support the sermon topic of the week. The songs, however, were all "vertical," with themes of direct adoration to God, so they fit well with PABC's overall vision for worship.

BIBLICAL, AESTHETIC, THEOLOGICAL, AND PASTORAL JUDGMENTS IN PABC'S WORSHIP

With a solid understanding of PABC's narrative framework, we can now assess against its own narrative whether its worship is biblically, aesthetically, theologically, and pastorally fitting. Here we will evaluate the worship tradition of a particular Evangelical church, PABC, in light of Evangelicalism's broader values. As mentioned above, "Evangelicalism" is an incredibly broad designation that refers to an interdenominational coalition of churches. As such, no one distinct style is universally adopted by Evangelical churches. Some Evangelicals perform traditional music led on a piano or pipe organ, others play contemporary worship led by a praise band. Many churches offer multiple services with varying styles, or they intermingle styles, creating blended worship services.

Most Evangelical churches would describe their musical worship as communally oriented, biblically based, and Christ-centered, but as mentioned in the introduction, PABC also embraces the pneumatocentric designation of being "Spirit-filled." The following assessment will look at how PABC displays and extends its identity as a Bapticostal church through its worship. Thus, we will examine four things contextually: Is PABC's worship biblically faithful? Does PABC's doxology match its worship practices? How are PABC's beliefs reflected in its worship practices? And in what way does PABC's musical worship provide pastoral care for its congregants? These topics concern, respectively, biblical, aesthetic, theological, and pastoral judgments.

Biblical Judgment

Scripture readings and explicit references to biblical passages didn't really come into play until the sermon. While the worship songs were based on biblical themes, they didn't link thematically with the sermon. Rather, the songs seemed to portray PABC's operant communal identity as an eschatologically oriented, Bapticostal community. I have written elsewhere that both Evangelicalism and Pentecostalism regularly describe worship in eschatological terms, albeit through slightly different frames of reference.[28] Pentecostals often describe worship as an inbreaking of the Spirit. They'll use a now-and-not-yet framework to understand the kingdom of God as already established through Christ's earthly ministry, but as yet to come in its fullness. So when the eschatological Spirit breaks into the present, worshipers have an experiential encounter with God—worshipers get glimpses of heaven, like snapshots or foretastes of what is to come. Evangelicals, on the other hand, often speak about corporate worship as joining in with the eternal worship that is found in

28. Steven Félix-Jäger, *Renewal Worship: A Theology of Pentecostal Doxology* (Downers Grove, IL: InterVarsity, 2022), 40–44.

the book of Revelation. Present-day worshipers join, cosmically, with every tribe and tongue in heavenly worship. All voices join together in the song that is being eternally sung in heaven.[29] As described further below, both of these sentiments can be found in PABC's song selection.

The Bible was heavily emphasized, however, in the sermon. Throughout 2023 PABC was engaged in a long sermon series titled "The Jesus Narrative: Through All 66 Books of the Bible." The church was going from Genesis to Revelation, demonstrating how the whole biblical narrative unfolds, and how Christ is central from beginning to end. This week's sermon was titled "Esther: The Unexpected at the Right Time" and worked through the book of Esther. Pastor Steve's sermon included a lengthy exposition of Esther's context, which even included a word study. The sermon was very didactically oriented, offering hermeneutical insight on how to read Scripture in light of redemption. The way the service was constructed seemed to agree with the insight of the congregant who said that worship is meant to soften people's hearts to the reception of the Word.

Aesthetic Judgment

Our first consideration when evaluating PABC's worship music is whether its genre of music is authentic to its community. As noted in chapter 2, Evangelicals often look to balance musical styles to satisfy the various generations of a congregation. This is evident at PABC in both its instrumentation and song selection. PABC has a full band setup that plays every week but also utilizes a twenty plus person choir and a small orchestra. In fact, the worship ministry has a three-week rotation whereby one week the band plays alone, the next week it plays with the choir, and the next week it plays with the orchestra. This allows for many church members to get involved in the worship ministry,

---

29. Félix-Jäger, *Renewal Worship*, 39–42.

and it brings a more diverse stylistic approach to contemporary worship. One could say PABC's worship is centered around a contemporary style, but it branches out into other directions to expand its parameters. This is also true for the songs that were performed. The team mostly performed contemporary songs by a few major Charismatic/Evangelical groups, namely, Jesus Culture, Hillsong, and Mosaic MSC. However, they also performed the hymn "Blessed Assurance," albeit in a contemporized style. This mixture of songs seemed to accommodate a congregation that generally prefers contemporary worship but appreciates songs from earlier generations.

For the size of the production, the sound was full but relatively soft, peaking out at around ninety-one decibels. Every instrument was clearly audible in the mix, but the vocals, while totally distinguishable, were softer than what might be typical in a contemporary worship mix. This allowed the vocals to be set back into the music, which seemingly encouraged a greater congregational response. While this lower volume seems to accommodate the sensitivity of an older congregation, there are communal benefits that accompany this aesthetic decision. From the crowd's perspective, congregants can hear not only Braiden, the singers, and the choir but also themselves and all the other congregants surrounding them. This creates a greater sense of community through the sung worship.

The song performances were all very well done. Although the worship team and choir were both presumably made up of volunteers, they displayed a high level of musical competence. The team played to a click with backing tracks, so there was not too much room for improvisation. This is done intentionally, however, since the Sunday morning worship service is a bit more inclusive as the "family meal." Braiden said that when they hold worship nights, they often just play with a click to leave space for spontaneous worship. Altogether the musical worship was very well done and intentionally focused. The worship style and noncoercive atmosphere was welcoming to worshipers from both Evangelical and Pentecostal backgrounds.

Theological Judgment

Theologically PABC demonstrates an Evangelical identity that embraces some Pentecostal commitments. For instance, PABC is Christocentric, missionally oriented, and evangelistically focused on personal conversion, and holds a high view of biblical authority. Yet even on this last point, Steve pointed out that other Baptist churches tend to put too much emphasis on Scripture, effectively deifying the Bible. These churches run the risk of supplanting the Spirit with the Bible. As Steve said, "When the Word of God is heavily emphasized in Baptist circles, the Trinity becomes more like 'God the Father, God the Son, and the Holy Bible.' . . . Now, they would not say it that way, but that's the impression that's kind of given off. And I think they get a bit hung up on that, because they would always say they acknowledge the Holy Spirit, but I don't know that they always invite the Holy Spirit in."

So while PABC holds a high view of the Bible, the church is careful not to neglect but rather promote the workings of the Spirit in the lives of believers. Both Steve and Braiden spoke about the importance of Spirit baptism and the present-day accessibility of spiritual gifts, and everyone who was interviewed talked about being Spirit-led in worship.

The selected songs' lyrics seem to support PABC's identity as a Bapticostal church. "Alleluia" is a vertical song that directs worship to God. It imagines the congregation joining in with heaven and singing out:

> Alleluia, lover of my soul,
> Alleluia, with all of heaven we are singing.[30]

---

30. "Alleluia."

"Awake My Soul" is addressed to the worshiper and to God, as the soul is called to awaken and "sing His praise aloud."[31] It imagines the eschatological sight of seeing the resurrected Christ dressed in white robes. Both of these songs lean toward an Evangelical eschatological understanding of worship.

The next three songs, conversely, demonstrate now-and-not-yet eschatological imagery. For instance, "Blessed Assurance" has a line that says, "O what a foretaste of glory divine."[32] The language of "foretaste" demonstrates an eschatological inbreaking. The team also performed "New Wine," a song that functions as a prayer in which the worshiper asks to be made a pure and holy offering before God. Even though this song is not overtly eschatological like the previous three, there is a line in the bridge that says,

> There is new freedom,
> The kingdom is here.[33]

So although the song was personal and devotional, it was still couched in a framework that understands earthly worship as an inbreaking of the kingdom of God.

Finally, "Tremble" was performed as a response and talks about Christ's power to overcome evil and darkness. It could also be understood through a now-and-not-yet framework as Christ's sacrifice already conquered death—even if the fullness of the effects are yet to come. Lyrically and musically through dynamics, this song functioned as a great setup for Steve's call for salvation. Altogether we see a mix of Evangelical and Pentecostal theological commitments and eschatological themes that are expressed from both traditions. Theologically, therefore, the worship music perfectly demonstrates PABC's Bapticostal identity.

---

31. "Awake My Soul."
32. "Blessed Assurance."
33. "New Wine."

Pastoral Judgment

The chosen songs all worked well together to create a cohesive, invitational space to freely worship God. The songs were performed successively without interruptions, which preserved the flow of worship. This allowed worshipers to go deeper as they sang along, responding to the words that were communally proclaimed. The congregation was also ready to engage in worship without much coaching, which demonstrates a culture of openness to expressive worship. Braiden proclaimed short encouragements, prayers, and vocalizations between songs, which helped the songs cohesively flow together.

Although the flow between service elements was smooth, each element of worship was a bit compartmentalized. The welcome and announcements led to the musical worship, which led to the sermon bumper, which led to the sermon, which led to a response song, which led to a prayer for salvation and dismissal. This is a typical Evangelical service structure, but since PABC is Bapticostal, it might have been helpful to integrate elements of worship more and to allow responses to occur during the songs. For instance, in the middle of the worship set, the band could vamp while someone gives a short testimony, or a relevant Scripture passage could be read and reflected on, or a period of extended ministry time could be established to allow congregants the space to pray for one another. The most integrated part of the service was at the end when Steve joined Braiden on stage after "Tremble." Here Braiden and the team vamped softly as Steve offered some pastoral reflection before leading into a prayer for salvation. This integrated approach to worship is common among Pentecostal churches, and doing it throughout the service might help worshipers enter the "holy of holies" without breaking the flow of the service. Adopting elements from this integrated approach would likely be well received because of PABC's spiritual openness in worship.

CONCLUSION

At PABC worship songs are expressive, communal proclamations of adoration to God. They are vertically oriented and performed to help people draw into deep relational encounters with God. The music supports the sermon but only in the sense that every worship element should support the others. As such, the sermon, while crucially important, is not central to PABC's worship. Although Sunday morning services lean toward a presentation of truth, the goal of worship is always to be drawn into God's presence and transformed into Christ's likeness. Thus, in PABC we see a fusion of Evangelical and Pentecostal commitments that views musical worship as Christ-centered and Spirit-led.

Although worship music at PABC features didactic enrichment, the primary purpose of its congregational music is to help congregants worship in Spirit and truth. Thus, songs' meanings are constructed by the espoused theology of the lyrics, as well as by their aesthetically and pastorally received meanings. As a communally oriented Bapticostal church, PABC demonstrates an excellent grasp of its identity and uses worship music in a way that reinforces it. A welcoming, humble, and noncoercive leadership style allows congregants to respond to God as they see fit. All in all, PABC displays a perfect blending of worship as biblical expression and an enacted theology of encounter.

I would recommend three areas of growth for PABC: (1) The worship service would benefit from a more dynamic introduction. The preservice video announcements were followed by more announcements before the band approached the stage during the meet and greet. If Braiden welcomed the church with the band vamping behind him, the congregation could immediately be drawn into the worship service. (2) The congregation would benefit from worship elements that were less compartmentalized. Integrating prayers, Scripture readings, testimonies, and response times into the musical worship could create a more dynamic flow between service elements, and worshipers would have more intentionally designed opportunities to respond in worship. When the worship is less compartmentalized, worshipers can find more varied ways to respond in worship throughout the service, which could help them enter into the holy of holies. (3) Although the leadership of PABC is doing an excellent job looking at ways to serve the greater Titusville community, PABC should continue efforts to reach out to minoritized groups. Because of Titusville's lack of racial diversity, greater efforts toward racial inclusion could help PABC create a powerful witness of ethnic and cultural mutuality.

The purpose of this chapter was to map PABC's narrative framework in order to understand its social and ecclesial context. Among the factors examined were the church's traditions, history, social impact, and aesthetic impressions. We then evaluated PABC's worship music contextually based on aesthetic, theological, and pastoral considerations. Our findings reveal an excellent Evangelical church that lives up to its identity as a communally oriented, biblically based, Christ-centered, and Spirit-led church.

STUDY QUESTIONS

1. PABC has long regarded itself a Bapticostal church. A trend in the global church is for churches, regardless of denomination, to adopt Charismatic sensibilities in worship. Have you witnessed this trend in your community?
2. PABC strives to be a spiritual blessing to its community. What can your worshiping community learn from PABC to become a spiritual blessing to your community?
3. Do you find it helpful to distinguish between the functions of a Sunday morning worship service (family meal) and a midweek worship night (date night)? Why or why not?
4. Does your church compartmentalize elements of the worship service like PABC? What are some ways you could integrate elements?
5. What are the benefits of having a dedicated space for prayer like PABC?

KEY TERMS

Bapticostal: a Baptist church with Charismatic sensibilities.

Baptist Faith and Message: a "confessional consensus" of beliefs that all Southern Baptists adhere to.

Evangelical tradition: an expression of Protestant Christianity that emphasizes biblical authority, personal faith in Jesus, and individual conversion.

Southern Baptist Convention (SBC): established in 1845, it's the largest Protestant denomination in the US and the largest Baptist denomination in the world.

Spirit-led: being guided, directed, or influenced by the Holy Spirit.

Vertical worship songs: songs that are more lyrically focused on praising God and talking about God's character directly, or songs that are sung directly to God.

CHAPTER 10

Evaluating Charismatic Catholic Worship

The Diocese of Colorado Springs, Colorado

Throughout the latter half of the 1980s, a group of Charismatic Catholics met regularly for prayer meetings in a small chapel inside Holy Apostles Catholic Church in Colorado Springs, Colorado. A **prayer meeting** in the Charismatic Renewal movement is *a communal gathering where participants come together to pray, worship, and experience the presence of the Holy Spirit in a dynamic and often spontaneous way.* By 1988 there were about fifteen regular attendees at these meetings.

The pastoral team gathered for prayer before the prayer meetings began. On one occasion while the pastoral team was praying for the upcoming service, one member of the team felt a deep stirring in his spirit and was given a prophetic word from God: "Are you ready to see me fill this room, fill this church, and fill this city with people whose hearts are turned toward me?" This question resonated deeply with the team, and they responded with an emphatic "Yes!" They expected to see a full chapel at the upcoming prayer meeting, but only the faithful group of fifteen showed up.

The group, however, held fast to the prophetic word, and

in the following months and years, they saw the word come to fruition. Soon after the word was given, the group held a Life in the Spirit Seminar at their parish, which was attended by more than a hundred people. After the seminar, the group grew rapidly to fifty regular attendees, and they had to move the meetings to the main sanctuary. Additionally, many Christian organizations, such as Focus on the Family, Every Home for Christ, and Save the Storks, moved their headquarters to Colorado Springs in the months and years that followed. Many people from the prayer meeting felt that this was a partial fulfillment of the prophecy that God would "fill the city" with people whose hearts are turned toward God.

The story above exemplifies how the Catholic Charismatic Renewal movement exists within the Roman Catholic Church and operates both within local parishes and outside the parish halls. This chapter explores how congregational worship music helps to foster the Charismatic Renewal in a Catholic diocese. In particular it maps the narrative framework of the Charismatic Renewal in the Diocese of Colorado Springs to understand its social and ecclesial context. This is done by considering the diocese's tradition, history, communal impact, and aesthetic impressions. After we have a solid grasp on the diocese's narrative framework, we can assess the biblical, aesthetic, theological, and pastoral value of Charismatic Renewal worship against its narrative framework and make commendations and recommendations about the worship practices.

UNDERSTANDING: Mapping the Narrative Framework of the Diocese of Colorado Springs

This chapter was informed by a mix of primary and scholarly sources, as well as ethnographic research conducted between June and August 2024. My research assistant and I traveled to Colorado Springs, and we observed a prayer meeting at Holy

Apostles Catholic Church[1] and a Sunday Mass at Our Lady of the Pines Catholic Church. We also conducted a series of interviews, including an interview with Deacon Chuck and Barb Matzker about the history of the Charismatic Renewal in Colorado Springs and about the worship ministries of the diocese; an interview with CeCe Beauchamp, the worship leader of the prayer meetings and a member of the pastoral team, about the diocese's worship practices; an interview with four parishioners who regularly attend the prayer meetings on how the Charismatic Renewal has affected their spiritual lives; and a lunch meeting with the pastoral team recapping the research project. Deacon Chuck and Barb also introduced us to several leaders throughout the diocese. The first part of this chapter utilizes these sources to analyze the church's tradition, history, social impact, and aesthetic impressions.

Tradition

While the Roman Catholic Church has a deep tradition that stems all the way back to Christ's own ministry, we will only trace the origins of the Charismatic Renewal within the Catholic Church. One pivotal event that made the Charismatic Renewal possible is the **Second Vatican Council**, also known as Vatican II. Vatican II was *a significant ecumenical council of the Catholic Church that took place from 1962 to 1965*. It was first convened by Pope John XXIII and later continued by Pope Paul VI. The purpose of Vatican II was to update church practices, making them more relevant for the modern world. The council promoted ecumenical dialogue between the Catholic Church and other Christian denominations, and it promoted the active participation of the laity at Mass. Significantly, Vatican II allowed for the use of vernacular languages instead of Latin

1. Because of travel issues, we arrived at Colorado Springs after the meeting concluded. We were, however, able to watch a full stream of the meeting and attend everything else in person.

during Mass.[2] The authorization of modern languages in Mass not only supported the participation of laity who were not trained in Latin but also paved the way for the usage of non-Latin songs in the Mass. These significant modifications introduced in Vatican II laid the groundwork for the Catholic Charismatic Renewal.

The Catholic Charismatic Renewal began in 1967 during a retreat at Duquesne University in Pittsburgh, Pennsylvania. In preparation for the retreat, the retreat planners had the students read the book of Acts and David Wilkerson's *The Cross and the Switchblade*.[3] Over the course of the weekend, some of the students began expressing worship in ways congruent to Pentecostal worship.[4] The students and faculty present began to experience the Holy Spirit and manifested charismatic gifts such as tongues and prophecy. This weekend became known as "the Duquesne Weekend" and marks a pivotal starting point for the Charismatic Renewal. After the Duquesne Weekend, a fresh Pentecostal-like spirituality spread to other Catholic communities, particularly through prayer groups and retreats. Major universities such as the University of Notre Dame and Michigan State University became important hubs of the movement.[5] By the early 1970s, the Charismatic Renewal had gained significant momentum, with thousands of Catholics participating in Charismatic prayer groups, conferences, and renewal events around the world.[6]

Another important thing that happened in the early days of the Charismatic Renewal was the creation of covenant communities. A **covenant community** is *a form of intentional community where members commit to living out their faith together in a*

2. See article 36 of *Sacrosanctum Concilium*, December 4, 1963, www.vatican.va/archive/hist_councils/ii_vatican_council/documents/vat-ii_const_19631204_sacrosanctum-concilium_en.html.

3. David Wilkerson, *The Cross and the Switchblade* (New York: Jove, 1962).

4. William Kangas, "Worship in the Charismatic Renewal: A Case Study in the Word of God Community" (PhD diss., Catholic University of America, 2022), 57–58.

5. Kangas, "Worship in the Charismatic Renewal," 59–60.

6. Kangas, "Worship in the Charismatic Renewal," 66.

structured, communal way. One of the earliest and most influential covenant communities was the Word of God Community in Ann Arbor, Michigan.[7] In 1981 Bishop Kenneth Povish worked alongside leaders of the Word of God Community to initiate what was then referred to as the Catholic Fellowship of the Word of God.[8] Throughout the next several years, this fellowship saw a few different iterations and eventually became a parish of the Diocese of Lansing named Christ the King Catholic Church.[9] Christ the King remains as one of the most influential hubs of Charismatic Catholicism in the world today.

In 2019, at the request of Pope Francis, the Roman Catholic Church created the Catholic Charismatic Renewal International Service (CHARIS), a single international service that fosters the worldwide Charismatic Renewal movement.[10] CHARIS's mission is threefold: to share baptism in the Holy Spirit with everyone in the Catholic Church, to serve the unity of the body of Christ, and to serve the poor and those in greatest need.[11] Its mission is, therefore, centered on spiritual renewal, ecumenism, and service. Significantly, CHARIS was instituted by the Vatican, marking a shift from the Charismatic Renewal's status as a fringe movement at the outskirts of Catholicism, to a supported global movement within the Catholic Church.

History

In December 1985, Father Paul Wicker,[12] pastor of Holy Apostles Catholic Church in Colorado Springs, Colorado, talked

7. Kangas, "Worship in the Charismatic Renewal," 17.

8. "A Detailed History of Christ the King," Christ the King Catholic Church, accessed August 17, 2024, https://ctkcc.net/about-us/a-detailed-history-of-christ-the-king/.

9. "A Detailed History of Christ the King."

10. "About CHARIS," CHARIS, accessed August 17, 2024, www.charis.international/en/about-charis/.

11. "Our Mission," CHARIS, accessed August 17, 2024, www.charis.international/en/mission/.

12. Father Paul Wicker was a beloved pastor who served Holy Apostles for more than thirty-five years. He passed away on May 31, 2021.

to Chuck Matzker at the parish Christmas dinner. Father Paul knew that even though Chuck was not yet an ordained deacon, he was already working on the diocesan Charismatic Renewal Board. Father Paul invited Chuck and his wife, Barbara ("Barb"), to meet with him and envision what a "renewed parish" might look like. Chuck and Barb shared that they saw a renewed parish as consisting of parishioners working in the gifts (charisms) of the Holy Spirit. *The Catholic Spiritual Gifts Inventory* defines a **charism** as *a special ability given to Christians by the Holy Spirit to enable them to be a channel of God's love and presence in the world.*[13] Both ordinary charisms (e.g., teaching, administration, service, encouragement) and extraordinary charisms (e.g., healing, prophecy, tongues, miracles) are to be used in service to build up the church.

Father Wicker introduced Chuck and Barb to another couple, Tom and Linda Gilbert. Tom and Linda were previously involved with the Charismatic Renewal in Virginia, and they were hoping to see a prayer group form at Holy Apostles. Father Paul asked the two couples to join him and the director of religious education for the parish to form a core group that would help facilitate the Charismatic Renewal at Holy Apostles. Together they served the people of Holy Apostles by providing a place where all parishioners could learn to function in the spiritual gifts God has given them.

Their work began by hosting a **Life in the Spirit Seminar** (LISS) in the parish. A LISS is *a multi-week or weekend program conducted by Catholics to help parishioners grow in their relationship with the Holy Spirit.* The seminar typically consists of a series of teachings, discussions, and prayer sessions that guide participants through key teaching about the Holy Spirit and spiritual gifts. The first LISS was held in May 1986, and more than seventy people attended. A prophetic word that was uttered at the closing

13. Sherry Weddell, *The Catholic Spiritual Gifts Inventory*, 3rd ed. (Colorado Springs, CO: Siena Institute Press, 1997), 6.

Mass of the seminar was: "I have planted the seeds in the hearts, do not worry, I have planted the seeds, I will nurture them; I will give the growth."[14]

By the summer of 1987, Tom, Father Paul, and the director of religious education all stepped down from the core group because of other responsibilities. A new leadership group was formed that included Chuck, Barb, Linda, and three of the attendees from the LISS. In that year, Chuck and Barb went to a weeklong National Leaders' Institute Conference at Franciscan University in Steubenville, Ohio. Franciscan University was an educational hub for the Charismatic Renewal Movement as many Charismatic Catholics, both in the US and globally, were educated or had formative experiences at the university. At this conference, Chuck and Barb learned about the Catholic vision for leaders in the Charismatic Renewal and how to facilitate the work of renewal in a parish.

Ever since, the group has held regular prayer meetings, hosted LISSs and gift and spiritual growth workshops. Chuck became a deacon and was appointed as the bishop's liaison to the Charismatic Renewal by Bishop Hanifen. This appointment was later extended by Bishop Sheridan, and by the current bishop, Bishop Golka. The Charismatic Renewal ministries are still led by Deacon Chuck and Barb, along with a small pastoral team from various parishes throughout the diocese. While the group started as a parish ministry with a diocesan outreach, it became a diocesan mission with a parish home. The group's mission is summed up well on their website: "Our ministry is to help to bring to the all [*sic*] in the Church the grace of 'baptism in the Holy Spirit,' and to renew the wonders and powers of a 'New Pentecost' in our time."[15]

14. This prophetic word was recounted by Barb Matzker.

15. "Our Ministry," Catholic Charismatic Renewal Services, accessed August 16, 2024, www.newpentecost.net/.

Communal Impact

Thinking about the communal impact of a Catholic diocese is a little different than that of a single Protestant church. While Protestant churches often develop unique ministries to serve their greater communities, a Catholic diocese carries out a number of ministries to regionally serve the mission of the whole Catholic Church. Catholic Charities of Central Colorado is the social service arm of the Diocese of Colorado Springs.[16] Catholic Charities offers many social services, such as food services, employment and life skills services, immigration services, rent and utility services, health services, and more. As part of their food services, for instance, they offer daily hot meals at Marian House Kitchen. They also offer groceries and hygiene products at the Marketplace Pantry.[17] Furthermore, the Diocese of Colorado Springs offers pastoral care to Catholics living in long-term care facilities and conducts liturgical and sacramental services for incarcerated people through their prison and jail ministries.

When we interviewed the focus group of parishioners involved in the Charismatic Renewal throughout the Diocese of Colorado Springs, one congregant said that the prayer meetings helped soften his heart toward what God was doing in the community. The congregant said he is more willing to get involved with some of the social services, like volunteering for the soup kitchen. He said he volunteers for things less out of a sense of duty and more from a sense of being led by the Spirit. He also feels the Spirit nudging him from time to time to talk to people about his faith. Another congregant said being in tune with the Spirit helps him see people with more compassion. While before he didn't always see the need to help others, now he frequently sees the Spirit leading him to help people.

---

16. "About Us," Catholic Charities of Central Colorado, accessed August 16, 2024, www.ccharitiescc.org/about-us/.

17. "Food and Nutrition Services," Catholic Charities of Central Colorado, accessed August 16, 2024, www.ccharitiescc.org/get-help/food-and-nutrition-services/.

While the Charismatic Renewal movement has enhanced the parishioners' social efforts for the broader Colorado Springs community, the group also cited many ways the prayer meetings have affected them internally in their spiritual lives. They all said that Scripture came alive to them as they were subsumed into life in the Spirit. The Spirit enables them to read the Bible in fresh and new ways. They pray for one another more frequently and operate in their spiritual giftings regularly. They feel like the Spirit transforms them and gives them spiritual boldness. The Spirit breaks barriers between divergent people groups and leads them toward unity with others. In all, life in the Spirit is a life of joy as Spirit-filled worshipers experience the love of God in abundance. Worship in the Charismatic Renewal facilitates a sensitivity to what the Spirit is doing in the parishioners' lives and in the world around them.

Aesthetic Impressions

Unlike the previous chapters that observed only one service, this chapter observes both a Thursday night prayer meeting and a Sunday Mass. By observing both of these worship services, we'll be able to compare and contrast the two services and see how people are ministered to at a prayer meeting and at a traditional Mass that utilizes a contemporary liturgy. This contrast will reveal some of the ways the ministry of the Charismatic Catholics has shaped different aspects of church life throughout the Diocese of Colorado Springs. The prayer meeting took place at Holy Apostles Catholic Church in Colorado Springs, and the Mass took place at Our Lady of the Pines Catholic Church in Black Forest, a community located in the northeastern part of Colorado Springs.

For the past few years, Holy Apostles' prayer meetings have been held at Mary's House, a small stand-alone building next door to the church, but still on the church property (fig. 10.1).

FIGURE 10.1

Exteriors of Holy Apostles Catholic Church (left) and Mary's House (right)

Photo by Steven Félix-Jäger, August 2, 2024

During our visit, however, the meeting was held in Wicker Hall, a large multipurpose parish hall located downstairs of Holy Apostles (fig. 10.2). The service began promptly at 6:30 p.m., and in attendance were about forty people from throughout the diocese. They were casually dressed and mostly racially white. While there was a full age range present, most of the worshipers were older. A small worship team set up on the left corner of the room was led by worship leader CeCe Beauchamp. CeCe sang and played the acoustic guitar and was accompanied by a keyboardist and a drummer who played an electric drum kit. CeCe, the keyboardist, and three other singers led the songs, often singing in unison but periodically breaking out into parts. While the environment was calm and friendly, a sense of expectation for divine encounter circulated among the worshipers.

At the start of the meeting, the worship team played the upbeat praise song "Louder,"[18] which ended with a short time of

18. "Louder," words and music by Jason Ingram, Jonas Myrin, and Matt Redman,

FIGURE 10.2

Prayer meeting at Holy Apostles

Photo by Deacon Chuck Matzker, August 1, 2024. Used with permission.

spontaneous prayer over the vamping band. Every song ended this way, which led to fluid transitions between songs, prayers, and prophetic words. CeCe then introduced the next song, "Rise, O People, Called to Worship,"[19] which was written by a Charismatic Catholic in Ann Arbor, Michigan. After the song, CeCe led a short prayer and transitioned to playing "Amazing Grace (My Chains Are Gone)."[20] Then Barb came up to a free-standing microphone opposite the band and offered a brief reflection on the previous Mass's Scripture reading. Then Deacon Chuck encouraged the worshipers to come up and share if God gave them any Scriptures, prophetic words, or images. Immediately

---

CCLI #7043171 © 2015 Rising Springs Music; Vamos Publishing; worshiptogether.com songs (administered by Capitol CMG Publishing).

19. "Rise, O People, Called to Worship," words and music by Ed Conlin © 2004 Ed Conlin.

20. "Amazing Grace (My Chains Are Gone)," words and music by Chris Tomlin, John Newton, and Louie Giglio, CCLI #4768151 © 2006 Atlas Mountain Songs; Said And Done Music; sixsteps Music; Thankyou Music; worshiptogether.com songs, So Essential Tunes (administered by Capitol CMG Publishing and Essential Music Publishing LLC).

worshipers came up one by one to share something with the group. First, a woman came up with a confirmation of what she thought the Mass's Scripture reading was saying. She said the verse meant some things would be "messy." Another woman came up and read Psalm 48:11, feeling that the Lord put it on her heart. Another woman came up and shared an image that she received from the Lord. She said they were approaching turbulent times in the world, so they need faith the size of a mustard seed to speak out and demonstrate Christ to the world. A fourth woman came up with the phrase "O taste and see" and agreed that things would be getting messy in the world, so we should remain steadfast.

After this time of sharing, the worship team led "Way Maker,"[21] which ended with spontaneous singing and prayer. Deacon Chuck came up to pray and asked that the congregants be receptive to what the Holy Spirit was doing in their midst. This led to another series of reflections and prophetic words. A woman came up and shared a verse from Psalm 23 and offered a bit of a reflection. Another woman came up with a reflection on some of the lyrics that were sung throughout the night. Another woman came up and recited a Bible verse. Then Barb came up and reflected on Way Maker, sharing that while she was worshiping she saw an image of the bleeding woman who touched Jesus' robe (Matt. 9:20–22). Just as the woman believed she would be healed by touching Jesus' tassel, so should we sit in silence a bit and strive to touch Jesus' tassel for ourselves. This word led to a reprisal of "Way Maker."

After the worship team performed "Way Maker" again, Deacon Chuck came up with a short prophetic word, stating that Jesus was saying, "My people, give me your hearts." At this point, a man came forward and gave a word in tongues. The **gift of tongues**, or *glossolalia*, is *a spiritual gift that refers to the supernatural ability to speak in an unknown language, often as a*

21. "Way Maker," words and music by Osinachi Kalu Okoro Egbu, CCLI #7115744 © 2016 Integrity Music (administered by Integrity Music).

response to the Holy Spirit's presence and activity. If the tongues message is spoken to a whole worshiping community, as was the case here, then the biblical expectation is that someone would be able to utilize the gift of discernment to interpret what God is saying through the gift (1 Cor. 14:27). Deacon Chuck came forward and prayed for an interpretation of the tongues. As a response, one man came forward with a Scripture passage. Then CeCe said that the sense she got from the tongues was that we are to display "faithfulness on the journey." Another woman said she heard the tongues proclaim, "Be aware, be alert, these are troubled times ahead." Then another woman spoke up and said, "God's majesty is with us." After these interpretations, Deacon Chuck came back up and encouraged the people to move boldly. This led a man to reflect on the lyrics of "Way Maker," citing John 1:4.

Then the worship team played "O Come to the Altar,"[22] which was followed by a time of spontaneous prayer. While people worshiped expressively throughout the prayer meeting, more and more hands were raised and people began to sing with more enthusiasm. This was especially the case when the group began to sing "Revelation Song."[23] During this song, one of the singers called the prayer team up to meet with anyone who wanted prayer. The congregants began singing loudly and exuberantly with shouts of joy. During the song, a woman came up and read Revelation 5, and the crowd began to cheer and pray spontaneously. People continued praying while the band vamped, and then the worship team went back into the song. After this the band played "We Fall Down,"[24] which was followed by another

22. "O Come to the Altar," words and music by Chris Brown, Mack Brock, Steven Furtick, and Wade Joye, CCLI #7051511 © 2015 Music by Elevation Worship Publishing (administered by Essential Music Publishing LLC).

23. "Revelation Song," words and music by Jennie Lee Riddle, CCLI #4447960 © 2004 Gateway Create Publishing (administered by Integrity Music).

24. "We Fall Down," words and music by Chris Tomlin, CCLI #2437367 © 1998 Rising Springs Music; Vamos Publishing; worshiptogether.com songs (administered by Capitol CMG Publishing).

time of spontaneous prayer. Deacon Chuck came up to pray and offer a benediction. To close out the service, CeCe gave two brief announcements before leading "Shout to the Lord."[25] When the song ended, the congregants stayed around chatting for a while before departing from the parish hall.

As is evident, the prayer meeting was focused on prayer and worship, and congregants were encouraged to operate in their spiritual giftings. There was no sermon or prepared message. Although some elements were planned (such as the songs that would be sung), the service flowed spontaneously, weaving in and out of prayers, reflections, and songs. Leaders such as CeCe, Deacon Chuck, and Barb helped to guide and encourage people to step out in boldness, but the service flow was intentionally unscripted. It was a time of gathering where worshipers would sing and pray together and seek the movement of the Holy Spirit. This is quite different from the Mass, which follows a set liturgical structure with specific prayers, readings, and rituals prescribed by the global church. Although the structure and atmosphere differ greatly between the prayer meeting and the Mass, both are integral parts of Charismatic Catholic worship.

As mentioned, we went to a different parish for Mass. Although Holy Apostles hosts the prayer meetings, Deacon Chuck and Barb invited us to attend Our Lady of the Pines because it is a good example of the influence of the Charismatic Renewal movement throughout the Diocese of Colorado Springs. In fact, the director of liturgical music, Bart McDonough, served as the main worship leader at Holy Apostles' prayer meetings for about a year prior to his post at Our Lady of the Pines. Thus, one of the main signs of the Charismatic Renewal movement's influence at Our Lady of the Pines is that the church utilizes a contemporary worship team to lead the music. They still hold to

---

25. "Shout to the Lord," words and music by Darlene Zschech, CCLI #1406918 © 1993 Wondrous Worship (administered by Reservoir Media Management, Inc.).

the liturgical structure of a typical Mass but perform music that is easily accessible to a contemporary audience. Although the Mass serves a liturgy that already exists, there are general principles in church documents on the type of music that can be used. Within these guidelines, there is latitude for parishes to offer their own unique expression of worship music. Our Lady of the Pines uses both traditional and contemporary music.

We arrived at Our Lady of the Pines at 10:00 a.m., thirty minutes before Mass started, to meet Deacon Chuck, Barb, and a few members of the pastoral team (fig. 10.3).

FIGURE 10.3

Our Lady of the Pines exterior

Photo by Steven Félix-Jäger, August 4, 2024

When we arrived, a group of people were praying the rosary in the sanctuary, so we waited in the vestibule for a bit before entering the sanctuary. We sat down at the back of the sanctuary a few minutes before the service started (fig. 10.4). Semicasually dressed parishioners began to trickle in, making the sign of the cross with holy water from the font at the entrance. Many genuflected, bending one knee to the ground. The sanctuary slowly filled with a quiet hum of activity, though the reverence remained unbroken. Some took their seats immediately, eyes closed in private prayer, while others knelt and bowed their heads. The sanctuary filled up entirely, with people sitting along the back walls and some even sitting in an overflow area in the vestibule. About five hundred parishioners were present—people of all ages. The congregation appeared to be about 80 percent white and 20 percent persons of color (predominately Hispanic and Asian).

FIGURE 10.4

Sunday Mass at Our Lady of the Pines

Photo by Steven Félix-Jäger, August 4, 2024

As the service was about to begin, altar servers, lectors, and other ministers moved through the sanctuary, making final preparations for the Mass.

Mass began with a performance of Curtis Stephan's "Bread of Angels"[26]—a contemporary Catholic worship song that blends traditional Latin with contemporary English, making it a popular

26. "Bread of Angels," English text adaptation and music by Curtis Stephan © 2002. Published by OCP.

choice for modern liturgies. The worship team was led by Bart, who played the piano. The rest of the team consisted of an acoustic guitar player, a drummer playing an electric drum kit, and a cellist. There were three singers—one male and two female—and the male singer was also the guitarist. The rest of the Mass followed the typical flow of a Catholic Mass that begins with the Liturgy of the Word and ends with the Liturgy of the Eucharist. Silent transitions between the elements of worship fostered a sense of reverence throughout the Mass. The main difference between this service and a typical Mass is that here all the music consisted of either contemporary worship songs or hymns that were performed in a contemporary style.

After "Bread of Angels" the team performed "In This Place"[27] while the priest, altar servers, and other ministers entered the sanctuary in a procession. Following the procession, the priest greeted the congregation and led a prayer of confession. Then we sang "Glory to God,"[28] which culminated with another prayer from the priest. At this point, we heard a series of Bible readings, one from the Old Testament, one from the New Testament, and one from the Gospels. A male congregant came up and offered the first reading from Exodus 16:2–4, 12–15. Then a young woman came up and led "Responsorial Psalm."[29] Then a female congregant came up and offered the second reading from Ephesians 4:17, 20–24, which was followed by a Gospel acclamation with the song "Alleluia."[30] Finally, an ordained deacon came up and offered the third reading from John 6:24–35. After the Bible readings, Father Matt Kane came up and offered a short homily about pursuing Jesus for his own sake and not because we want

27. "In This Place," text by Victoria Thomson, music by Trevor Thomson © 1996. Published by Spirit and Song®, a division of OCP.

28. "Glory to God," text © 2010, ICEL, music by Joshua Blakesley and Leland "Grae" McCullough IV © 2012. Published by OCP.

29. "Responsorial Psalm," music by Owen Alstott © 1977, 1990 by OCP.

30. "Alleluia," music by Joshua Blakesley and Leland "Grae" McCullough IV © 2012, 2016. Published by OCP.

something in return. A **homily** is *a short sermon or reflection given by the priest during the Mass, following the reading of the Gospel.* The homily was followed by a moment of silent reflection, which ended with the congregation standing to recite the Nicene Creed. We then ended the Liturgy of the Word with a time of prayer for the church and the world, where particular groups were named and prayed for, and the congregants responded to each petition with "Lord, hear our prayer."

We then entered into the Liturgy of the Eucharist, the second major part of the Mass, with an offering. As the offering plates were passed around the church, the worship team played "I Am the Bread of Life."[31] Meanwhile the deacon prepared the elements of the Eucharist. Father Matt then received the bread and wine and began the eucharistic prayer, which led to the congregation singing "Holy."[32] Father Matt then recited the words of Jesus at the Last Supper to consecrate the elements of the Eucharist. **Consecration** refers to *the moment when the bread and wine are transubstantiated into the real body and blood of Christ.* After the consecration, we sang "We Proclaim Your Death"[33] as the memorial acclamation. Father Matt then prayed intercessions for the church, the faithful, and even the deceased in Christ. This prayer ended with us singing "Amen"[34] as an affirmation of the prayer.

After this Father Matt led the congregation in praying the Lord's Prayer, and then the deacon invited the congregation to share a sign of peace with one another. The congregants turned to one another and said, "Peace be with you." The **sign of peace**

31. "I Am the Bread of Life," words and music by Steve Angrisano and Tom Booth © 2015. Published by Spirit and Song®, a division of OCP.

32. "Holy," text © 2010, music by Joshua Blakesley and Leland "Grae" McCullough IV © 2012. Published by OCP.

33. "We Proclaim Your Death," text © 2010, music by Joshua Blakesley and Leland "Grae" McCullough IV © 2012. Published by OCP.

34. "Amen," music by Joshua Blakesley and Leland "Grae" McCullough IV © 2012. Published by OCP.

is *a moment in the Mass before the distribution of Communion that gestures reconciliation and unity among the members of the congregation*. Then the congregation rejoined to sing "Lamb of God."[35] Father Matt then led a prayer before we sang Matt Maher and Matt Redman's "Remembrance (Communion Song)."[36] During "Remembrance" the priest broke the consecrated Host, consumed the elements, and began distributing Communion to the congregation. Row by row the congregants came up to receive Communion. Because there were five hundred people present at Mass, the worship team continued playing songs during Communion. They also played "Lord, I Need You"[37] and "How Great Is Our God."[38] After every congregant received Communion, the music stopped and there was a moment of silence. Then Father Matt gave a final blessing to the congregation, asking God to be with them as they went forth from the Mass. The priest then dismissed the congregation with a benediction and a final prayer. The worship team played "This Is Amazing Grace"[39] during the recessional as the priest, deacon, and ministers exited the sanctuary. After the song, the congregants followed suit and exited the church.

---

35. "Lamb of God," music by Joshua Blakesley and Leland "Grae" McCullough IV © 2012. Published by OCP.

36. "Remembrance (The Communion Song)," words and music by Matt Maher and Matt Redman, CCLI #5484616 © 2009 sixsteps Music; spiritandsong.com; Thankyou Music; worshiptogether.com songs (administered by Capitol CMG Publishing).

37. "Lord, I Need You," words and music by Christy Nockels, Daniel Carson, Jesse Reeves, Kristian Stanfill, and Matt Maher, CCLI #5925687 © 2011 sixsteps Music; Sweater Weather Music; Thankyou Music; Valley of Songs Music; worshiptogether.com songs (administered by Capitol CMG Publishing).

38. "How Great Is Our God," words and music by Chris Tomlin, Ed Cash, and Jesse Reeves, CCLI #4348399 © 2004 Rising Springs Music; Vamos Publishing; worshiptogether.com songs; Wondrously Made Songs (administered by Capitol CMG Publishing and Reservoir Media Management, Inc.).

39. "This Is Amazing Grace," words and music by Jeremy Riddle, Josh Farro, and Phil Wickham, CCLI #6333821 © 2012 Phil Wickham Music; Seems Like Music; Sing My Songs; Bethel Music Publishing; WC Music Corp (administered by Bethel Music Publishing, CURB | Word Music Publishing, and Music Services, Inc.).

BIBLICAL, AESTHETIC, THEOLOGICAL, AND PASTORAL JUDGMENTS IN THE DIOCESE'S WORSHIP

Now that we have gained a deeper understanding of the story of the Diocese of Colorado Springs, we can evaluate how its worship aligns with its biblical, aesthetic, theological, and pastoral structures. In this analysis, we will examine the worship tradition of a specific diocese in the context of its Charismatic Renewal values. As we reflect on both the prayer meeting and the Mass, we must remember that Charismatic Catholics do not compete with the Sunday Mass. Instead, the midweek prayer meetings are held in addition to their participation in Mass to enhance the life of the parish. The prayer meetings are centered around seeing what the Spirit wants to do in their broader community. Considering this, we will explore four key points: First, does the Charismatic Renewal worship of the diocese align with biblical principles based on its context? Second, are the worship practices of the prayer meetings aligned with the diocese's broader doxology? Third, what impact do the theological beliefs of the Charismatic Renewal have on the worship practices throughout the diocese? And finally, what role does musical worship play in nurturing and supporting the parishioners?

Biblical Judgment

While the Sunday Mass uses the **Lectionary for Mass**, *the official book containing the specific readings and responsorial psalms assigned to each day of the liturgical year for use during the Mass*, the prayer meetings take a free-flowing approach to Scripture usage. By using the lectionary, Catholic parishes ensure that parishioners engage the whole Bible in a three-year span. What's helpful about this is that Catholics engage the full biblical narrative so long as the parishioners regularly attend Mass. However, if one adheres exclusively to Bible readings from a lectionary, there can be a few potential drawbacks. First, the lectionary readings typically consist of small excerpts from longer passages, which could potentially lead to a loss of contextual understanding. Second, following the structured lectionary could result in utilizing an overly ritualized approach to Bible reading in which the readings are listened to without personal reflection. Perhaps most significantly, relying solely on lectionary readings may hinder personal Bible study as parishioners might rely solely on the clergy's interpretations and homilies. This is why many parishes have Bible studies to augment and deepen the Sunday readings.

In many ways, prayer meetings address the shortcomings of adhering exclusively to readings from the lectionary. First, during the prayer meeting we observed, Barb brought up one of the readings from Mass and offered a devotional reflection. Reflecting personally on passages from the lectionary is very common at prayer meetings. Second, during the prayer meeting many parishioners came up and coupled a Scripture passage with a prophetic word they felt God was giving them. Thus, hearing God entails both being steeped in Scripture and being sensitive to what the Spirit is revealing to parishioners and to the community. Finally, the Scripture readings, prophetic words, and prayers were all seamlessly tied together.

The reason these meetings are called "prayer meetings" is because there is a sense that every act of worship—the music, the prophetic words, and the Scripture readings—are fundamentally all acts of prayer. Parishioners come to prayer meetings with the expectation that God will hear them and respond.[40] Music at a prayer meeting helps facilitate "a conversation that everyone [is] having together with God as a central participant."[41] Perhaps the prayerful and reflective approach to worship and Scripture reading at these prayer meetings is why some of the parishioners said the Charismatic Renewal helped the Bible come alive for them.

40. Kangas, "Worship in the Charismatic Renewal," 94.
41. Kangas, "Worship in the Charismatic Renewal," 95.

Thus, worship at the prayer meetings helps parishioners live a life that is steeped in Scripture.

Aesthetic Judgment

As is the case for biblical judgment, the prayer meetings supplement the Mass in important ways to help parishioners experience holistic encounters with God. Aesthetically, the Mass and prayer meetings function in different but related ways. The Mass is formal and utilizes many silent transitions to encourage a sense of reverence, whereas prayer meetings are participatory and communal. While it might be unusual to find raised hands and bodily movement during the singing of a Mass, it is common and expected to see bodily expressiveness during worship in the prayer meetings. Both, however, follow a similar narrative trajectory for encountering God. Joe Wells, cofounder of One Hope Project, described this narrative trajectory well in an interview I conducted with him:

> [At prayer meetings] we want to serve people and see how we can facilitate a space so people can encounter God. From a Catholic point of view, we're used to the beauty of liturgy. Liturgy has a story arch that takes people on a journey—there's repentance, hearing the Word, and then the Eucharist is the high point. There's a real depth in the liturgy. So when we're leading a prayer service, we're thinking of that arch and how to create that space. At the end of the service, there are moments of silence where people can reflect and encounter God. We're comfortable with silence. We love a big, massive praise song, but we also love quiet moments and silence. From a Charismatic Catholic point of view, we feel blessed to have that full range of dynamics so we can really connect to the liturgy.

For Wells the Mass and the prayer meetings together help foster a full dynamic range of encounter. This was very evident on our visit to Colorado Springs. The way the Charismatic Catholic parishioners talked about their faith, their love of the Mass, and their encounters with God at prayer meetings demonstrated a zealous fervor made possible by regular encounters with the Spirit.

CeCe is cognizant of how the song selection and service flow affects the parishioners' worship at prayer meetings. CeCe said she likes to have structure but leaves a lot of room for spontaneity. For instance, she'll pick a full worship set with her team, but during the prayer meeting, after about the fourth song, the team will typically have a good sense of where the Spirit is leading, so they follow the Spirit's promptings in impromptu ways. They might switch up the order of songs or repeat certain parts of a song. The worship team rehearses prior to the prayer meeting but is ready to go, musically and spiritually, wherever the Spirit is leading. If they sense a special need for healing, they'll stop and stay in that space for however long they need. CeCe also chooses communally oriented songs that are easily learned. Although they strive for musical excellence, decisions on song selection are less about the musicality of the song and more about its singability. All of this was evident at the prayer meeting as the worship team performed ten familiar songs that were interwoven with prayers, prophetic words, and testimonies throughout the night.

Theological Judgment

Considering both the prayer meeting and the Mass together, we can see that Communion at the Sunday Mass was, in a way, the spiritual climax of the week. The Mass is structured so that the Liturgy of the Word creates anticipation for Communion during the Liturgy of the Eucharist. The songs, prayers, Scripture readings, and homily all point toward the Communion where Christ is truly present with the parishioners. Catholics often use the term **Real Presence** to refer to *the belief that Jesus Christ is truly and substantially present in the Eucharist*. Catholics believe that when the priests consecrate the elements of the Eucharist, *the substance* *of the bread and wine is changed into the substance of Christ's body and blood*. This process is called **Transubstantiation**. Hence, the Eucharist, celebrated during Mass, is considered by the *Sacrosanctum Concilium* to be the "source and summit" of the Christian life[42] and is thus the climax of Catholic worship.

Nevertheless, the prayer meeting was essential for the theological development of the parishioners. As discussed in chapter 3, a realized eschatology is operant in Catholic worship, especially as congregants anticipate the future realization of God's kingdom during the Eucharist. However, this theological concept was not only operant but also espoused at the prayer meeting. The parishioners at the prayer meeting emphasized encountering God's kingdom in the present through the power and activity of the Spirit. This was most evident toward the end of the meeting when the group sang "Revelation Song," read Revelation 5, prayed for one another, and raised exuberant shouts of praise. The parishioners were very aware that the Holy Spirit was palpably present in their space. Just as the real presence of Christ marks the high point of worship at the Mass, the manifest presence of the Spirit marked the high point of the prayer meeting. Hence, a Catholic's ability to robustly encounter God corporately through worship happens at both the Mass and the prayer meeting.

Pastoral Judgment

The chosen songs in both the Mass and the prayer meetings minister to the congregants in different but important ways. Singing in the Mass gives congregants the opportunity to participate in the liturgy. It also fosters a sense of communal unity, which marks the Mass as a celebration. Music also accompanies the liturgical actions of the Mass, such as the processional, Scripture readings, the offertory, Communion, and so on. This accompaniment helps underscore the spiritual significance of

---

42. See article 10 of *Sacrosanctum Concilium*.

these actions while helping to establish the flow of the liturgy. As parishioners are drawn into the liturgy through the music, they are drawn into the church's corporate worship.

The prayer meetings consist of praise and worship songs coupled with prayer, Bible meditation, and prophetic words. Thus, music creates a space for worshipers to really tap into what the Holy Spirit is doing in their midst. This approach is far more personal, open, and extemporaneous than the Mass. Worshipers reflect on passages of Scripture to see if the Spirit prompts comments or feelings about the passages via the gift of prophecy. Worshipers also pray for one another and see if anyone wants individual prayer with laying on of hands. The Mass helps parishioners feel like they are part of a deep faith with a long history, whereas the prayer meetings help parishioners feel like they're part of what God is currently doing. Together these worship services help congregants feel like they are both spiritually rooted and freshly commissioned to follow God's leading in the world today.

CONCLUSION

As we consider the worship practices of the Diocese of Colorado Springs between the prayer meeting held at Holy Apostles and the Mass held at Our Lady of the Pines, it's clear that the Charismatic Renewal movement has positively affected the diocese. Under the leadership of Deacon Chuck and Barb, along with the pastoral team, it is clear that these Spirit-filled Catholics are on a mission to bring spiritual renewal to their diocese and to help foster the Spirit's work in the city beyond the walls of the parish.

While some Protestant groups view musical worship as a sacrifice or offering to God, musical worship for both the Mass and the prayer meetings are best understood as prayerful acts of devotion. Music is part of the relational dialogue between God and the people, and as is especially evident in the prayer meeting, worshipers expect to hear from God in worship. Charismatic Catholics are less concerned about the origin of the song (i.e., if the song was written by a Catholic or Protestant). They are more concerned about how the song functions ministerially in a context of prayer. One of the most exciting facets of the Charismatic Renewal movement is its desire for ecumenical work. Beyond using Protestant worship songs at Mass or prayer meetings, Charismatic Catholics often team up with Protestant groups for worship events. The leadership team is working toward increasing ways of coming together with Protestants to worship God in ecumenical settings. Altogether the ministries of Deacon Chuck, Barb, CeCe, and the ministry team have proven to be Spirit-led, gracious, and dynamic.

As in all the other case studies, I would recommend three areas of growth for the Diocese of Colorado Springs: (1) Find new ways to engage the next generation of Charismatic Catholic worshipers. CeCe shared that she sees this as a bit of a challenge—the prayer group has a long history at the diocese but may need some help engaging younger generations. Looking at how groups like One Hope Project are ministering to and discipling young people in the United Kingdom would be a great starting point. (2) Find more pathways for creating ecumenical ministry opportunities with Protestant groups. The diocese is already doing this, but this is such an incredibly fruitful endeavor that it should become a main focus of engagement moving forward. (3) While the prayer meeting is remarkably relational, gracious, and inviting, the closed Communion and formal liturgy of the Mass might be viewed as inhospitable to newcomers. It would be great if the Charismatic Renewal leaders familiar with the open hospitality of the prayer meeting found ways to share these ideas with parish hospitality ministers at Sunday Masses.

This chapter delineated the narrative framework of the Diocese of Colorado Springs to comprehend the ecclesial and social backdrop of its worship music. The analysis took into account various factors, including the church's tradition, historical context, social impact, and aesthetic impressions.

Subsequently, we examined the diocese's worship through biblical, aesthetic, theological, and pastoral lenses. The findings revealed a wonderful movement with the Diocese of Colorado Springs that has and will continue to see God fill the room, the church, and the city with people whose hearts are turned toward the Holy Spirit.

STUDY QUESTIONS

1. In what ways can your church's worship help foster renewal for the whole community?
2. In what ways are both liturgical and contemporary expressions of worship beneficial to the spiritual lives of parishioners in the Diocese of Colorado Springs?
3. How does the Catholic Charismatic Renewal movement foster ecumenical dialogue between traditions?
4. How can your church's worship help foster both a sense of spiritual rootedness and openness to the Spirit's leading?
5. In what ways can you help foster spiritual renewal across your own tradition the way the Charismatic Catholics do for theirs?

KEY TERMS

Charism: a special ability given to Christians by the Holy Spirit to enable them to be a channel of God's love and presence in the world.

Consecration: the moment when the bread and wine are transubstantiated into the real body and blood of Christ.

Covenant community: a form of intentional community where members commit to living out their faith together in a structured, communal way.

Gift of tongues: a spiritual gift that refers to the supernatural ability to speak in an unknown language, often as a response to the Holy Spirit's presence and activity.

Homily: a short sermon or reflection given by the priest during the Mass, following the reading of the Gospel.

Lectionary for Mass: the official book containing the specific readings and responsorial psalms assigned to each day of the liturgical year for use during the Mass.

Life in the Spirit Seminar: a multi-week or weekend program conducted by Catholics to help parishioners grow in their relationship with the Holy Spirit.

Prayer meeting: a communal gathering where participants come together to pray, worship, and experience the presence of the Holy Spirit in a dynamic and often spontaneous way.

Real Presence: the belief that Jesus Christ is truly and substantially present in the Eucharist.

Second Vatican Council: a significant ecumenical council of the Catholic Church that took place from 1962 to 1965.

Sign of peace: a moment in the Mass before the distribution of Communion that gestures reconciliation and unity among the members of the congregation.

Transubstantiation: the process by which the substance of the bread and wine is changed into the substance of Christ's body and blood.

How Worship Can Break Barriers

The intention behind this book is to increase understanding between worshiping communities. When deep understanding is present, we will become more empathetic toward one another, which will help us better carry out the Christian task of bringing about a reality where redemption is full-grown and we, as the new humanity, walk humbly together in the glory of God (Rev. 21:22–27). This is our ultimate condition of unceasing, unrestricted communion with God—a state of eternal worship. Our worship today is a foretaste of this coming reality, and it contributes significantly to our ministry of reconciliation. As we reconcile in worship, walls of prejudice and exclusion are torn down. The greatest potential impact of this project is to bring about reconciliation within the body of Christ so that we can, together, be a great witness in the world. Not only does this nourish a healthy congregational life but also it fosters unity through reconciliation.

To conclude I'd like to explore how worship can transcend barriers and facilitate reconciliation among individuals, communities, and even diverse traditions. As we think about worship in ecumenical dialogue, we can consider how our narrative-hermeneutical method for judging worship can help forge new paths of solidarity. As such, this final chapter reflects on the book as a whole and considers how a narrative-hermeneutical approach for judging worship might unite us as practitioners.

DIFFERENCE, IDENTITY, AND COMMUNITY

Philosopher Scott Bader-Saye writes, "Hospitality requires that a community be capable of receiving difference as gift."[1] Difference is not a problem to be solved but a fact of existence we should appreciate. We are all likely familiar with Paul's body metaphor from Romans 12 and 1 Corinthians 12, where he likens the church to a body with different members. Each member has a different function, yet they are all indispensable and part of the same body. Moreover, we are all likely familiar with the application of these texts that sees different Christian denominations or traditions as distinct from one another but equally important to the global church. Each tradition brings something unique to the table, and when combined they constitute a strong, unified body. Yet in practice it is often more likely to see dissension and judgmentalism between traditions than unity. Our attempts at unity and ecumenical dialogue often get marred by a lack of understanding or a fear of the other. Do we really see difference as gift?

The very fact of identity entails a tension between exclusivity and inclusivity. For a tradition to exist, there must be a certain set of beliefs, practices, and ideologies that adherents ascribe to. If these things were absent, there would be no community, just a group of gathered individuals. Welcoming others into a tradition thus entails a level of conformity into what has already been established. Those who cannot in general conform to the community's identity would thus be excluded. For instance, suppose you held an open gym for basketball. You made it so anyone could join

1. Scott Bader-Saye, *Following Jesus in a Culture of Fear: Choosing Trust over Safety in an Anxious Age* (Grand Rapids: Brazos, 2020), 147.

but expected everybody who showed up to play basketball. If a group of people showed up fully dressed in hockey gear, you would ask them to either conform to minimum requirements of basketball (i.e., wear the appropriate attire and follow the rules of the game), or leave and find another community in which they can play hockey. While anyone is welcome to join and play basketball, you will exclude those who do not conform to the basic tenets of the game. In the same way, a welcoming community of worship will receive others, provided they conform to the basic tenets of their tradition.

Maintaining the integrity of a community's values requires a certain degree of partiality. For instance, during our evaluation of St. John AME Church, we observed the profound significance of the global Black experience in shaping the community's worship practices. The AME Church is rooted in a rich history where Black congregants come together to seek comfort and freedom in a society marked by injustice. When my research assistant and I participated in a service at St. John, we were welcomed with remarkable hospitality as guests. However, it was evident that we were entering a sacred space where congregants depended on one another for solidarity, resilience, and support. While we did not feel unwelcome, we fully recognized that our experience of worship differed from that of those who shared similar backgrounds and confronted the same societal challenges. This distinction is applicable to any worshiping community, but it is particularly pronounced in those that have emerged from specific social contexts. Another example of this is immigrant churches that come together to foster a sense of belonging in an unfamiliar environment. As we contemplate the body of Christ, it is essential to acknowledge that monocultural forms of worship hold significance within the global church, provided they understand that God transcends their unique traditions. A healthy monocultural worship tradition, such as that of St. John, will engage in various outreach ministries, frequently collaborating with churches from diverse traditions to benefit the broader community. Thus, while their worship practices embody the distinct particularities of their own tradition, their outreach efforts remain inclusive and ecumenical.

While tensions surrounding identity sometimes exist, worshiping communities can grow in hospitality. Bader-Saye puts it well: "Being hospitable means welcoming people into something, but if you have fuzzy boundaries, do you have a 'something' to welcome people into? It seems to me that in order to avoid the dangers of being a community defined by exclusion, we have to have an identity that is always being discovered, negotiated, reinterpreted, and through Christ ever again received as gift."[2]

Hospitality is not just about letting people enter into the community but also about allowing them to meaningfully contribute to something that already has a rich history. This point was embodied well by the Charismatic Catholics at the Diocese of Colorado Springs who graciously welcomed us, two Protestant Pentecostals, into everything they were doing in their community. We particularly connected on the workings of the Spirit within both of our faith traditions. Charismatic Catholics regularly welcome Protestants into their prayer meetings and make it a goal to plan special worship services with Protestants to bridge the divide between the two traditions. Indeed, as "Christian unity" is a fundamental aspect of their global mission, CHARIS advocates for ecumenical collaboration among different faith traditions.

Charles Whitehead of the Catholic Charismatic Renewal Service Committee pointed out that one of the challenges of ecumenism might be the loss of identity: "Because we share the experience of the Baptism in the Holy Spirit with Protestant, Pentecostal, and Non-denominational Christians, we have a special part to play in building strong ecumenical friendships. But to do this, we must first be sure of our Catholic identity. We are

2. Bader-Saye, *Following Jesus in a Culture of Fear*, 146.

Catholic first and ecumenical second."[3] Ecumenism should not be understood as the amalgamation of various traditions into a singularly conformed cultural identity; rather, it represents the unification of distinct cultural identities under the banner of Christ. Hence, a hospitable church should maintain a clear identity while remaining open to the new things God is doing in other worshiping communities and traditions.

COMING TOGETHER

Sometime after visiting each of the churches discussed above, I hosted a Zoom meeting with some of the pastors and worship pastors of the churches assessed. It was meant to be a time of communal reflection. Since none of the church leaders had previously met one another, this was also an opportunity for them to gain a better sense of the scope of the project. Prior to the meeting, I sent them the working manuscript of the book so they could read the other chapters. I was curious to see if anything new was revealed to them about their own traditions as they read through the other church assessments. As we discussed the implications of the project, the pastors and worship pastors offered valuable insight and feedback that helped me determine the strengths and shortcomings of the narrative-hermeneutical method.

To start off the conversation, I asked the practitioners if the project helped them better understand their own church's worship tradition. Tim from Life Church said reading the write-up was helpful because it put language to what his church was already doing. He said, "As pastor of a Pentecostal church, I found it good to have some kind of language that felt common and natural. It was helpful having someone from the outside name things that we saw as normal." So while congregants at Life Church already

3. Charles Whitehead, Catholic Charismatic Renewal National Service Committee, September 2003, www.nsc-chariscenter.org/what-is-the-nature-of-the-catholic-charismatic-renewal/.

viewed every element of worship as an opportunity to experience God, the project was able to verbally express what they were doing. Steve from PABC agreed, stating that nothing particularly novel was revealed, but it put into words what a regular churchgoer might have struggled to articulate. Steve also appreciated the honest assessment of PABC's worship that wasn't prejudicial or motivated by ulterior intentions. Braiden from PABC agreed, saying the project's approach was unbiased and accounted for every part of the context. He particularly enjoyed imagining how the different streams of the body of Christ can come together in unity. Jonathan from Pillar Church said the project helped illuminate the "bubble" context in which every church does ministry. He said, "It was refreshing and rare to have someone come in and listen, engage, and analyze in a way that's not carrying what some folks in a bubble would carry around." Jonathan was impressed by the fact that even when things weren't fully expressed through the interviews, we were able to perceive what was going on and talk about them in new ways.

I then asked the practitioners if they found the project's narrative-hermeneutical method for evaluating worship valuable. Before making any judgments, this method seeks to examine the context of the worship service in question. If the full context of something isn't understood, something crucial could be missed. For instance, even as Pillar Church's worship appears pleasant and agreeable to a newcomer, it actually carries an incredible testimony of reconciliation between a once-split denomination and community. Thus, the unity found in Pillar's worship is a testament unto itself. It is only by understanding Pillar's context that we can grasp the deeper meaning of its worship.

Responding to my question, Tim and Sharon both said it was beautiful to hear the stories and perspectives of their own congregants. It allowed them to see how Life's worship has been shaping their community. Similarly, Jonathan said he loved hearing from Pillar's congregants, and he thinks there is incredible value in giving people an opportunity to tell their story. In fact, he received a couple of text messages from focus group participants who said they appreciated the opportunity to share about their church. Steve discussed the importance of having a good evaluative system to foster communal growth, even if the methods can't fully express the story. He said, "Sometimes in the church world we feel that we're breaking our own anointing if we evaluate, but if we don't evaluate, how can we know what the impact is? While we can never fully evaluate what's going on, we can do our very best with our imperfect mode of evaluation here on earth. . . . In evaluating we have a bias toward our traditions, but at the end of the day we must ask, was the presence of the Lord there? Was the Spirit there?"

We can use good assessments to understand our actions' impact, while recognizing that any evaluative system has limitations. By using written evaluations, we can assess our outcomes critically and make sure we are relying on evidence, rather than assumptions, to make decisions. We can see what has been accomplished and what has not.

Jon brought up an important point about the limits of narrative. While we've mentioned Pillar's inspiring story of reconciliation, he wonders how the narrative would be shaped if we also heard from people who left the church during its transition toward dual affiliation. How might Pillar's context be viewed if those excluded from the account spoke into the narrative? We could, perhaps, get a better understanding of the complexities surrounding the split and how different people were affected by it. It would give us a more comprehensive narrative and better insight into the factors that may have led to the split in the first place. By recognizing the limits of our positionality, we can begin to create a more inclusive narrative that takes into account the experiences of everyone around us. This project highlighted the positives of each community's narrative to foster unity between traditions. While this may have been a good first step in ecumenical dialogue between worship traditions, the quest for equity begins with the attempt to honor the full story.

Finally, I asked each of the pastors and worship pastors if, after comparing their own traditions with the other traditions in the book, they felt that they learned anything from the other traditions. Tim pointed out that the recommendations at the end of the chapters were helpful, and other churches demonstrate strength in those areas that Life Church could learn from. Sharon agreed, saying that one of the recommendations led them to look more closely at the cultural contexts of some of their minoritized members, which inspired them to perform some worship songs in their languages. Thus, they learned from other traditions and other cultures.

Jonathan said that evaluating other traditions can help churches expand their local witness. "In our practice as worshiping communities, our witness is the embodiment of our faith. The more we are aware of the broader witness of the church, from the larger US church and even out to the global church, I hope it will help us dig into the specific concerns and relationships people encounter everywhere." In other words, learning about other traditions can help churches better understand and relate to the people in their own communities as they gain insight into how their faith is experienced. While Jon said there's always a lot to learn from the different streams of the faith, he said it's also important to be cognizant of how a particular tradition influences people and how they experience things. Thus, there must be a balance between what makes a particular tradition unique and what can be learned from other traditions. Jon's point addresses the tensions between inclusivity and exclusivity discussed at the start of this chapter. Yet what has been made evident throughout this book is that having a deeper understanding of other traditions' worship practices enhances our own empathy and respect for them. Even as we adhere to the tenets of our own traditions, we grow to love and admire the worship traditions of others.

CONCLUSION

Judgment doesn't necessarily involve moral condemnation. If judgment entails the ability to make sensible decisions, then we continuously judge all sorts of things. We might judge the morality of a situation but could also judge the fit, appropriateness, clarity, or efficacy of an outcome. This project utilized methods from biblical exegesis, art theory, theology, and ministry to determine the parameters of biblical, aesthetic, theological, and pastoral judgments. It also consulted worship practitioners from five different traditions to develop an approach that was distinct but inclusive enough to cover congregational worship from a spectrum of denominations.

This project then put theory to practice by assessing five different churches from around the country. The five churches assessed were all strong and healthy churches with a lot to be commended for. As part of the process, each church was also given recommendations for growth. The point of that was not merely to point out weaknesses or disparage the churches but to demonstrate that if these five healthy churches from varying traditions can still learn and grow, then any church from any tradition can as well. My hope is that these assessments will inspire unity among other churches and encourage them to find ways to work together toward the common goals of social benevolence and evangelism. Also, I hope that through the various critical tools utilized in this project, we all learn to judge worship in a way that fosters understanding and rapprochement between worshiping traditions.

Acknowledgments

This book has been a long time coming! It began as a grant-funded research project, and ended as a comprehensive textbook on evaluating and designing worship. Because of the multifaceted nature of this work, I have many people to thank, perhaps more than for any of my previous books.

First, I'd like to thank the folks at the Calvin Institute of Christian Worship who funded the beginning parts of this project and initially got the ball rolling. In particular I'd like to thank Noel Snyder, John Witvliet, and María Eugenia Cornou. I'd like to thank Monique Ingalls for inviting me to contribute to a Calvin Summer Seminar titled "Power, Participation, and Access: Between Word and Spirit." That seminar proved pivotal to this project. I'd also like to thank the awesome team at Zondervan Academic, especially my fantastic editor David McNutt.

I'd like to thank my home base, Life Pacific University, and the many folks who spoke into this project or allowed me the space to work on it: Daniel Ruarte, Jeff Tolle, Angie Richey, Josh Ortega, Marcus Robinson, Jim W. Adams, Meagan Lord, Deb Baker, and Luci Martinson. I would also like to thank the folks at the Society for Pentecostal Studies and the Summer Institute for Global Charismatic-Pentecostal Studies, especially Leah Payne and Ted Smith.

To get a full sense of the various worship traditions, this project engaged many scholars and practitioners. I'd like to thank the many new and old friends who contributed their wisdom to this project: Tim Vande Griende, Harrison Hollingsworth, Rachel Klompmaker, Asia Lerner-Gay, Andrew Ray Williams, Jenny Donis, Anais Macias, Danielle Cipriano, Dara Delgado, Keith Whitfield, Johnny Knox, Raymond Wise, Nate Myrick, Terry Tripp, Charlin Neal, Andy Wingate, Alastair Emblem, Billy Kangas, Luke Devine, Tony Alonzo, Joe Wells, Jeremy Perigo, Marcell Silva Steuernagel, Steph Budwey, Dulcie Dixon, Alisha Lola Jones, Anna Nekola, Blenda Im, Becca Whitla, and Kyle and Susan Stang. I'd also like to thank those involved in the church visits: Tim and Sharon Lee, Danny Saltzman, Steven Yuke, Braiden Wood, Richie Lord, Billy Durham, Kevin Weaver, Jessica Felix-Jager de Weaver, Dell and Hank Weaver, Wilfredo Felix, Greta Fowler, Edward Menifee, Jonathan Gabhart, Jon Brown, Chris Devos, Chuck and Barb Matzker, and CeCe Beauchamp.

I would like to give an extra special shout out to my dear friend and research assistant Josh Edwards. He traveled with me, took notes, read and commented on chapters, and was a wonderful sounding board and dialogue partner throughout this whole project. Thanks, bro!

I'd like to thank my personal support systems: first, Connie and Mila Felix. Thank you always, I love you. Second, the folks at my church, Pasadena Foursquare Church, especially my pastors Brian and Carolina Majors and Jenn Thigpenn. Third, all my friends and family members not named here who give me life.

And finally, I'd like to thank God, the subject of all my work. May this book serve to glorify you, deepen our worship, and draw hearts closer to your love.

Index